The Dancing Self

Creativity, Modern Dance, Self Psychology and Transformative Education

Perspectives on Creativity
Mark A. Runco, series editor

The Dancing Self

Creativity, Modern Dance, Self Psychology and Transformative Education

Carol M. Press

HAMPTON PRESS, INC.
CRESSKILL, NEW JERSEY

Printed in the United States of America

Library of Congress Cataloging-in-Publication Data

Press, Carol M.
 The dancing self : creativity, modern dance, self psychology
 and transformative education /Carol M. Press
  p. cm. -- (Perspectives on creativity)
 Includes bibliographic references and index.
 ISBN 1-57273-440-X -- ISBN 1-57273-441-8
  1. Modern dance--Study and teaching. 2. Creation
(Literacy, artistic, etc.). 3. Self psychology. I. Title. II. Series.

GV1783 .P72 2002
792.8'071--dc21

                                        2002068789

Photo of Carol Press © Joanne A. Calitri

Hampton Press, Inc.
23 Broadway
Cresskill, NJ 07626

For *Dylan* and *Savannah*, *Savannah* and *Dylan*,
whose creative spirits inspire me everyday

Foreword

Miriam Roskin Berger

This book is unique, a wonderfully original contribution to and for all of us—dancers, teachers, therapists, choreographers, artists—as it integrates concepts we have intuitively understood and that indeed, have diversely informed our disciplines. These ideas first emerged for me when I was a young modern dancer and student. My intent was to ultimately become a psychologist because I thought this field of human study would support the development of these concepts. The writings of Carol Press have helped me to remember that my original motivation to instead become a dance/movement therapist came not so much from an actual desire to practice therapy as from an underlying recognition that this new modality provided the best and, perhaps, the only arena in which I could explore my ideas about dance, the human body, movement, personality, behavior, culture, and creativity. My subsequent trajectory has taken me into dance performance, into psychiatric clinical work, into research in nonverbal behavior, into collaborations with other art disciplines and other nationalities, and into dance education. As the years have passed, I have increasingly realized the connection, the crucial connection, of the topics addressed in this book, as dance therapy practice and research have provided insight into processes that contribute to creation in dance, enhancement of performance, emotional health, and enrichment of dance education. This book has coherently formulated these insights.

Dr. Press focuses on creativity as an experience of the self that supports mental health and provides a broad discussion on how creative involvement, on many levels of subjective experience, connects us to our actions and to our values. The experience of self is closely connected to our relations with others and to culture, and this self-experience can be modified in diverse contexts. Dr. Press brilliantly sees modern dance as an art form that richly illustrates these creative connections. The roots and history of modern dance clearly support this perspective, from its beginning as a way to express feeling through movement to the discovery by dance educators that the study of modern dance produced positive emotional changes in their students. Psychoanalytic self psychology is seen here as an especially useful theoretical lexicon through which to examine these experiences. The focus in self psychology on empathy is directly related to the importance of what I have termed *kinesthetic empathy* in dance therapy, and underscores its role as the core of all dance and all nonverbal communication. And the phenomena of dance as primarily a group experience reflects another core concept of self psychology—the mutability of the self in the arena of new social contexts.

This perspective on the creative process enables us to better understand how it must be nourished, and in Chapter 4 Dr. Press provides an incredibly rich analysis of this process in dance through the lens of self psychology. She delineates the ultimate transformative power of this process to both the creator and the creation. The experience of the great choreographer Paul Taylor is used as an example of this transformative journey, illuminating the steps of this journey through the concepts of creativity in self psychology—compensatory structures, archaic and adult healthy narcissism, transferences of creativity, the multileveled subjective creative process, and the desperation of a fragmented sense of self. Paul Taylor's choreographic masterpieces demonstrate a level of creative achievement that merges feeling and form, an achievement that is reflected in the power of his audiences' response on many levels.

This book culminates in a most inspirational vision. Education can *be* transformed and can *be* transformative by the creative engagement of both educators and students and such education cannot help but nourish and support the health of our society. I think that one of the most important ideas crystallized in this book is the crucial necessity for dance and movement in the education of young children. We are all aware of the role that dance can have in the support of optimum emotional, cognitive, physical, aesthetic, and social development in the growth process of a child. How much more could this development be enhanced through a higher level of creative engagement in the educational process itself!

Dr. Press creatively examines this idea in many dimensions. I was especially taken with her description in Chapter 6 of her gradual letting go of set dance lesson plans and her ultimate reliance on her own creative process moment to moment in the studio. Her description of this creative process is analogous to the process of dance therapy because any therapeutic process is, at its pinnacle, an embodiment of the creative process. Dancers and movers exemplify this analogous relationship most strongly as their therapy work is channeled through the body, the source of creativity. Reliance and trust in creating from what one is given, through created structures, also inflect our educational experience, especially in dance.

This book can be sampled productively at many different points even though the sequential flow of its discourse is crafted with care and meaning. The alchemy of ideas is apparent everywhere in its pages. I feel that this is the book that many of us would have liked to have written! Its ideas will serve to unify the dance community by giving validity to all of us. I say this because I know that dancers and creative artists all intuitively understand that learning occurs intermodally, that movement expresses and creates feeling, that it strengthens cognitive patterns, and that the experience of dance can transform. We all came to dance through many paths and we all comprehend movement on many levels. Dr. Press has merged the paths and synthesized the levels for us, and for the rest of the world as well. Her book is indeed a gift.

Acknowledgments

I have been cultivating the seeds for this book all my life as a dancer. To bring those seeds to some fruition through an interdisciplinary vision has at times felt completely overwhelming. All of the people mentioned here have honored me with the gifts of their encouragement, intelligence, and presence. All of the people mentioned here have supported my own "dancing self." As a result, this book has become more than I imagined. Most especially, I thank my teachers, my students, and the wonderful classroom teachers with whom I work, all who continually remind me that creativity and education are processes of discovering more than what one had imagined before.

From my mother, Bertie Press, I learned early on that a personal aesthetic is deeply enriching. From my father, Jack Press, I learned to tolerate the chaos that often accompanies intense creative work. If nothing else the limitations of time can create such chaos. I could not endure the incredible disarray that has overtaken my surroundings during this process had it not been for my father's creative flexibility.

I originally learned to teach dance to children from my mentor, Lanie Keystone. From watching who Lanie is as a person and a teacher, I began to understand what is most crucial in education. At its best, teaching is an act of love. Every day as I go to teach, I try to remember that.

The roots for this book took hold when I did my doctorate of education in interdisciplinary studies between dance education and clinical psychology at Columbia University Teachers College. I am deeply indebted to my mentor Nancy Schmitz for her constant encouragement and enthusiasm. Additionally, I thank the chair of the Clinical Psychology Department at the time, Rosalea Schonbar, for supporting my explorations in psychology and her obvious belief in my capabilities.

I thank Paul Stepansky for suggesting that I send my work to Mark Runco. Mark brought my work to the attention of Barbara Bernstein, president of Hampton Press. Barbara has offered unwavering support and flexibility. One cannot ask more from a publisher.

My friends and colleagues in dance have been essential. Miriam "Mimi" Roskin Berger honored me by writing the wonderful foreword. Mimi's dedication to dance education kindles our spirits. Angelia Leung and Judy Gantz are inspiring educators and have been steadfast in their encouragement. Judy Alter read an early essay of mine extending clear and concise helpful comments. The works of Penelope Hanstein and Larry Lavender on the teaching of choreography always enliven my thoughts. I thank Tom Hagood for his significant contribution to the dance literature. Tom's intelligent and comprehensive book, *A History of Dance in American Higher Education*, fell into my hands at just the right moment, helping me to make my work better. Additionally, when asked, Tom offers sound good advice on all practical matters and has a great sense of humor.

Paul Taylor has been a witty muse over many years. His choreography and his autobiography *Private Domain* are testaments to the subjective creative processes that enrich our daily lives. And I am deeply grateful to Paul for supporting my examination of his life from a psychoanalytic perspective. He is a true trooper!

Not being a therapist, I entered into the world of self psychology as an outsider. That community has graciously responded. I thank Carol Munschauer for her encouragement and aesthetic sensibility. Anna Ornstein suggested insights and direction that were invaluable to the writing of this book. I thank Allen Siegel and Renée Siegel for their encouragement and Allen for reviewing the chapter on self psychology. George Hagman generously shared his work on creativity and self psychology. His sensitive and brilliant insights into the creative process significantly pushed open the floodgates for my own thoughts. Extending intelligent guidance, George extensively edited the chapters on creativity and Paul Taylor. Needless to say, George's support has been indispensable. Irene Harwood's writings on therapeutic group processes resonate well with educational group dynamics. Irene also has wonderful aesthetic tastes, and is fabulous to shop with for clothes. I thank Carl Rotenberg for sharing his

Contents

Foreword

Miriam Roskin Berger

This book is unique, a wonderfully original contribution to and for all of us—dancers, teachers, therapists, choreographers, artists—as it integrates concepts we have intuitively understood and that indeed, have diversely informed our disciplines. These ideas first emerged for me when I was a young modern dancer and student. My intent was to ultimately become a psychologist because I thought this field of human study would support the development of these concepts. The writings of Carol Press have helped me to remember that my original motivation to instead become a dance/movement therapist came not so much from an actual desire to practice therapy as from an underlying recognition that this new modality provided the best and, perhaps, the only arena in which I could explore my ideas about dance, the human body, movement, personality, behavior, culture, and creativity. My subsequent trajectory has taken me into dance performance, into psychiatric clinical work, into research in nonverbal behavior, into collaborations with other art disciplines and other nationalities, and into dance education. As the years have passed, I have increasingly realized the connection, the crucial connection, of the topics addressed in this book, as dance therapy practice and research have provided insight into processes that contribute to creation in dance, enhancement of performance, emotional health, and enrichment of dance education. This book has coherently formulated these insights.

Dr. Press focuses on creativity as an experience of the self that supports mental health and provides a broad discussion on how creative involvement, on many levels of subjective experience, connects us to our actions and to our values. The experience of self is closely connected to our relations with others and to culture, and this self-experience can be modified in diverse contexts. Dr. Press brilliantly sees modern dance as an art form that richly illustrates these creative connections. The roots and history of modern dance clearly support this perspective, from its beginning as a way to express feeling through movement to the discovery by dance educators that the study of modern dance produced positive emotional changes in their students. Psychoanalytic self psychology is seen here as an especially useful theoretical lexicon through which to examine these experiences. The focus in self psychology on empathy is directly related to the importance of what I have termed *kinesthetic empathy* in dance therapy, and underscores its role as the core of all dance and all nonverbal communication. And the phenomena of dance as primarily a group experience reflects another core concept of self psychology—the mutability of the self in the arena of new social contexts.

This perspective on the creative process enables us to better understand how it must be nourished, and in Chapter 4 Dr. Press provides an incredibly rich analysis of this process in dance through the lens of self psychology. She delineates the ultimate transformative power of this process to both the creator and the creation. The experience of the great choreographer Paul Taylor is used as an example of this transformative journey, illuminating the steps of this journey through the concepts of creativity in self psychology—compensatory structures, archaic and adult healthy narcissism, transferences of creativity, the multileveled subjective creative process, and the desperation of a fragmented sense of self. Paul Taylor's choreographic masterpieces demonstrate a level of creative achievement that merges feeling and form, an achievement that is reflected in the power of his audiences' response on many levels.

This book culminates in a most inspirational vision. Education can *be* transformed and can *be* transformative by the creative engagement of both educators and students and such education cannot help but nourish and support the health of our society. I think that one of the most important ideas crystallized in this book is the crucial necessity for dance and movement in the education of young children. We are all aware of the role that dance can have in the support of optimum emotional, cognitive, physical, aesthetic, and social development in the growth process of a child. How much more could this development be enhanced through a higher level of creative engagement in the educational process itself!

Dr. Press creatively examines this idea in many dimensions. I was especially taken with her description in Chapter 6 of her gradual letting go of set dance lesson plans and her ultimate reliance on her own creative process moment to moment in the studio. Her description of this creative process is analogous to the process of dance therapy because any therapeutic process is, at its pinnacle, an embodiment of the creative process. Dancers and movers exemplify this analogous relationship most strongly as their therapy work is channeled through the body, the source of creativity. Reliance and trust in creating from what one is given, through created structures, also inflect our educational experience, especially in dance.

This book can be sampled productively at many different points even though the sequential flow of its discourse is crafted with care and meaning. The alchemy of ideas is apparent everywhere in its pages. I feel that this is the book that many of us would have liked to have written! Its ideas will serve to unify the dance community by giving validity to all of us. I say this because I know that dancers and creative artists all intuitively understand that learning occurs intermodally, that movement expresses and creates feeling, that it strengthens cognitive patterns, and that the experience of dance can transform. We all came to dance through many paths and we all comprehend movement on many levels. Dr. Press has merged the paths and synthesized the levels for us, and for the rest of the world as well. Her book is indeed a gift.

Acknowledgments

I have been cultivating the seeds for this book all my life as a dancer. To bring those seeds to some fruition through an interdisciplinary vision has at times felt completely overwhelming. All of the people mentioned here have honored me with the gifts of their encouragement, intelligence, and presence. All of the people mentioned here have supported my own "dancing self." As a result, this book has become more than I imagined. Most especially, I thank my teachers, my students, and the wonderful classroom teachers with whom I work, all who continually remind me that creativity and education are processes of discovering more than what one had imagined before.

From my mother, Bertie Press, I learned early on that a personal aesthetic is deeply enriching. From my father, Jack Press, I learned to tolerate the chaos that often accompanies intense creative work. If nothing else the limitations of time can create such chaos. I could not endure the incredible disarray that has overtaken my surroundings during this process had it not been for my father's creative flexibility.

I originally learned to teach dance to children from my mentor, Lanie Keystone. From watching who Lanie is as a person and a teacher, I began to understand what is most crucial in education. At its best, teaching is an act of love. Every day as I go to teach, I try to remember that.

The roots for this book took hold when I did my doctorate of education in interdisciplinary studies between dance education and clinical psychology at Columbia University Teachers College. I am deeply indebted to my mentor Nancy Schmitz for her constant encouragement and enthusiasm. Additionally, I thank the chair of the Clinical Psychology Department at the time, Rosalea Schonbar, for supporting my explorations in psychology and her obvious belief in my capabilities.

I thank Paul Stepansky for suggesting that I send my work to Mark Runco. Mark brought my work to the attention of Barbara Bernstein, president of Hampton Press. Barbara has offered unwavering support and flexibility. One cannot ask more from a publisher.

My friends and colleagues in dance have been essential. Miriam "Mimi" Roskin Berger honored me by writing the wonderful foreword. Mimi's dedication to dance education kindles our spirits. Angelia Leung and Judy Gantz are inspiring educators and have been steadfast in their encouragement. Judy Alter read an early essay of mine extending clear and concise helpful comments. The works of Penelope Hanstein and Larry Lavender on the teaching of choreography always enliven my thoughts. I thank Tom Hagood for his significant contribution to the dance literature. Tom's intelligent and comprehensive book, *A History of Dance in American Higher Education*, fell into my hands at just the right moment, helping me to make my work better. Additionally, when asked, Tom offers sound good advice on all practical matters and has a great sense of humor.

Paul Taylor has been a witty muse over many years. His choreography and his autobiography *Private Domain* are testaments to the subjective creative processes that enrich our daily lives. And I am deeply grateful to Paul for supporting my examination of his life from a psychoanalytic perspective. He is a true trooper!

Not being a therapist, I entered into the world of self psychology as an outsider. That community has graciously responded. I thank Carol Munschauer for her encouragement and aesthetic sensibility. Anna Ornstein suggested insights and direction that were invaluable to the writing of this book. I thank Allen Siegel and Renée Siegel for their encouragement and Allen for reviewing the chapter on self psychology. George Hagman generously shared his work on creativity and self psychology. His sensitive and brilliant insights into the creative process significantly pushed open the floodgates for my own thoughts. Extending intelligent guidance, George extensively edited the chapters on creativity and Paul Taylor. Needless to say, George's support has been indispensable. Irene Harwood's writings on therapeutic group processes resonate well with educational group dynamics. Irene also has wonderful aesthetic tastes, and is fabulous to shop with for clothes. I thank Carl Rotenberg for sharing his

thoughts with me as he read this manuscript, for his inspiring work, for broadening my visual horizons, and for dancing dialogues.

Nancy Colahan is an exquisite dancer, teacher, and choreographer. She lovingly read this book as I wrote it, meeting me for coffee, talking with me about her responses and thoughts. Kathleen Redmond (honorary dancer) permitted me the *incredible* luxury of reading the manuscript out loud to her as it evolved. Kathleen is always encouraging, and most importantly, lets me know when clarity has indeed eluded me. Susan Powell edited the chapter on self psychology with wonderful care. Ilana Morgan's magical gift for teaching dance exhilarates me. Paula Hess constantly smiles at my accomplishments. This book would not have been written without the support and friendship of Ross Godlis.

Over the course of a quarter of a century Olga Naud has taught me more about psychology and life than perhaps anyone. The influence of Nicholas Tingle upon my work, my view of teaching, and my life is beyond words. Nicholas embodies the teacher who sees and acknowledges his students' humanity and responds with his own. His "dancing self" inspires me. This book is dedicated to my niece, Savannah, and nephew, Dylan. Their very presence makes me want to be more than I imagined before.

Ellen Dissanayake's vivid understanding of the intrinsic value of the arts in our lives helped design the foundation upon which my own thoughts stand. Most significantly, *The Dancing Self* would not have been written without the impact of Heinz Kohut's work upon my deliberations. Kohut's writings speak of someone involved in a great creative journey. I believe his theories and thoughts reflect such a journey. As such his legacy leaves us a landscape of life that illuminates the creative and vital elements of our humanity. Modern dance choreographers embody that creativity and vitality to enrich themselves, others, and culture. They teach us about the profound significance of creativity in our everyday lives. I thank them all.

—*Carol M. Press*

Chapter ▪ 1

Introduction

Creativity is a self-experience. Creativity fills life with meaning and dynamic relations, enriching society with significant culture, and, consequently, exemplifying the core of our ideals and our humanity. Creativity's profound effect affirms what binds us together as a species. Creativity contributes immeasurably to the health of humankind; before we understand and accept our differences, we must acknowledge and feel our common bonds.

This commonality is critical to human existence. Our ancestral heritage ensures that we are social animals, born to live in relation with others. Anthropologist Ellen Dissanayake (2000) in her book *ART and Intimacy* asserts that art-making is an intrinsic human capacity that has psychobiological foundations. Through such creative endeavors people experience, express, and elaborate their common interests in finding meaning and competence in their lives. According to Dissanayake, "aesthetic experiences transcend simple short-term self-interest, making us aware of our embeddedness or participation in an expanded frame of reference that is larger than ourselves" (p. 208). Without the intertwining relations between the individual, others, and community, humankind, unable to collaborate to sustain biological life, would have perished.

1

This dynamic relational exchange is quite complex, energized by the felt subjective enterprise on three levels: intrasubjective—experiences of self; intersubjective—experiences of relationships; and metasubjective—experiences of culture (Hagman, 2001). These subjectivities are not felt in isolation from each other; they penetrate and seep through their elusive boundaries, creating a flow of experience that nourishes the foundations of our lives. However, this flow of experience is, of course, intrasubjective. The *individual* experiences self, others and culture, even in societies where shared membership in the group is paramount for psychological stability. Consequently, for ease in writing, when I speak of "subjectivity," I refer to this intrasubjective realm.

Additionally, no intrasubjective experience is formed and felt without the influence of external relations, even when an individual, in the moment, feels compelled only by internal psychological forces. Even a hermit's choice of isolation is in relation to others. Subjective experiences are always within a relational context, always affected by the inter- and metasubjective. Through the articulations of others, and the manifestations of culture, our subjectivity is confirmed, amplified, or affronted. Experiences of culture reflect and expand on the intra- and intersubjective to give form to our knowledge, abilities, hopes, fears, and values. Our desires, frustrations, actions, triumphs, and ideals reverberate through our experiences of the metasubjective. Subjectivity experienced within the context of individuality, relationships, and culture functions like a permeable prism, each face refracting light, receiving light, creating light for the other.

Through these realms of subjectivity, our creative expressions demonstrate a meaningful existence propelled by personal exploration and assertion, which in reciprocity with others, both affects and is affected by culture. This movement toward culture distinguishes our humanity and enables these common bonds to flourish. Today, multiculturalism teaches us the importance not only of acknowledging differences, but, additionally, of valuing and learning from them. Our need to do this is exigent because beneath the differences lies our essential sameness. Dissanayake (2000) asserts the overriding importance of this cultural mutuality:

> The emphasis on cultural diversity has wisely expanded the study of art to include its manifestations in all societies, reminding us of its communal and performative aspects, its multimodal nature in which song, dance, performance, and visual spectacle all combine, its integration with the lives of its practitioners, and its multiformity. This is well and good, but as it stands, not enough.

It is, I believe, more important to learn what we have in common than to show one another what our particular culture does differently or better. If it is recognized that the arts everywhere address the same human concerns that have been part of the human condition for millennia, then we have a means of bringing people together rather than dividing them. (p. 203)

Many aspects of Western modern society do not support this creative destiny. Our lives can feel more concerned with monetary gain than a search for significant meaning. Just because our world has become more "global" does not mean that we are touched by values that bring sustaining intention into our lives, or greater empathic awareness of others. Certainly, our international world no longer carries the distance of a century ago; our technological communication systems potentially bridge gaps in information. The global economy emphasizes our interdependency; what financially affects Australia, Indonesia, Africa, and the United States affects us all. Nothing more demonstrated this interlacing dependency than the Y2K concerns. Indeed, worldwide cooperation will be necessary to deal effectively with the problem of global warming. However, where within all this dependency are our human connections? We leave behind a century marred by two World Wars. We enter a new century marred by terrorism. In the new millennium, how do we continue to relate to ourselves and to each other in vital ways that inspire humankind to actions informed by high ideals?

Creative engagement, on all levels of subjectivity, unites us to our actions and our ideals. As such, creativity is a subject that I feel must be examined again and again to glean and evolve its emotional, psychological, biological, and spiritual contributions. This book is an interdisciplinary investigation of the fortification that creativity brings to a meaningful sense of self, to sustaining relations with others, to a vigorous society and culture, and to the empowering role that education can serve towards these endeavors. To explore these issues, I bridge ideas from contemporary modern dance and psychoanalytic self psychology. Interdisciplinary pursuits can feel overwhelming to researcher and to reader as we attempt to understand the ways of thinking put forth by a field and the vocabulary used. For clarification and easy reference, I supply a glossary of terms related to dance, creativity, and psychoanalysis to assist the reader through the intermingling of these diverse fields.

The *experiences of creativity*, the core of its authentic significance, are deeply felt by the idiosyncratic individual. To allow my thoughts to unfold and evolve, I emphasize the individual's experiences of creativity, which are, however, fundamentally relational. The activation of sense of self into the world, guided by one's values and ideals, permits the individual to discover and express subjective meaning, but, additionally, ensures a vital mutuality of influence between experiences of self, others, and culture. To examine this activation of the subjective sense of self, I connect ideas from modern dance and self psychology to propose and investigate, throughout this book, the following claim: Creativity involves exploration and self-assertion, through a multileveled subjective relationship that serves significant selfobject functions through the construction of an ideal form that embodies and expands self-delineation, self-cohesion, and self-development, and that is ultimately self-transformative.

TRANSFORMATIVE EDUCATION

Psychological transformation is an evolution within one's internal nature, a nature based upon our intrapsychic idiosyncratic patterns of experience, which denote our own specific intrasubjectivity. But we are not isolated human beings. Our lives are not concerned just with our own internal subjective view, no matter how narcissistically compelling, at times, this may feel. We exist within a matrix of surrounding subjectivities. Our lives are intimately connected through dynamic relationships. Consequently, when our internal subjective nature is transformed, this transformation influences not just our sense of self, but our relations and interactions, conscious and unconscious, with others. Additionally, the transformation within others affects our subjectivity and the transformative choices that we make, or don't make. All significance in our lives is, on some level, relational.

Transformation? Is that the ideal destination, the ultimate creation, of education? Education, at its best, engages and enriches our talents, skills, and knowledge, to actively problem solve in a meaningful manner. Transformative education seeks to build these capacities to actively problem solve so that one's inner nature is significantly transformed in relation to self, others, and one's surrounding world. The true gift of education is the transformation of one's sense of self into further development. Transformative education captures the core of the expressive, gratifying, and powerful relations between the individual, others, and culture.

MEANING IN LIFE

From these transformative experiences we acquire a sense of meaning. In Webster's New World Dictionary (1966) meaning is defined as "what is intended to be" (p. 911). To experience meaning in one's life is to feel that one's existence reflects what is intended to be, internally and externally. What we feel is subjective. What we feel is intended to be derives from this intrapsychic realm. But because we are always linked to the inter- and metasubjective, our sense of meaning includes the world as we perceive, experience, influence, and feel its effects upon us. Meaning becomes the propelling force in the multi-leveled subjective exchange.

When we feel in conjunction with others, this reciprocal relation confirms that the interactions between oneself and one's world are fueled by one's subjectivity. Interactive meaning denotes a connection between the subjective and the objective, and the mutual influence between these two arenas. Intention in life can then be experienced, manifested into the world, and actively shared with others. Consequently, a meaningful self-world relation is most fulfilling when experienced on all three levels of subjectivity: self, others, and culture. From here our lives can be experienced with feelings of aliveness, meaningful action, beneficial exchange with others, and values that steer us. In other words, our lives can be nourished by vitality, exploration, self-assertion, reciprocity, and guiding ideals.

MEANING, IDEALS, BEAUTY, AND TRANSCENDENCE

Our ideals, the subjective experience of the values that guide us, inform our perception and comprehension of meaning, of what is intended to be. If we feel disjunctures between our ideals, sense of meaning, and the events in our lives, then we may feel dissatisfied, disillusioned, empty, and without psychological sustenance. For some the resulting action may be angry rebellion or violence, for others depression or withdrawal. Either way a significant aspect of the relations between our sense of self, others, and culture is harmed, and the expression of the ideals that articulate our experiences of being, hindered.

Ellen Dissanayake (2000) and psychoanalyst George Hagman (2000a, 2001, in press) both assert that the arts connect us to our ideals, and consequently to our subjective sense of beauty. We experience beauty because through creative activity we endow the art object with our intrapsychic ideals. This is true for artist and audience. Beauty here does not mean pretty, pleasing in appearance. Purely subjective, "beauty is in the mind of the beholder" (Hagman, in press, p. 16). We engender beauty when we elaborate our subjectivity and felt experiences of meaning, because in order to delineate what feels special and meaningful to us, what defines our sense of being in the world, we need to distinguish these experiences beyond our ordinary existence. We need to experience transcendent beauty.

Hagman (2001) claims: "The form of self-expression contained in artistic creation is best captured in the idea of being, of conveying in the work aspects of how it feels to be the living person who one is" (p. 13). Through this capacity, we experience the expression of the ideals that inform our way of being in the world. By articulating our subjective sense of beauty, elaborating artistically beyond the ordinary, we make sense of the divisions between the subjective and objective, between internal and external, between sense of self and world. We accomplish this by investing the art object with our subjective ideals; hence the artwork itself is experienced as beautiful. Hagman asserts:

> Beauty is an invariant characteristic of anything that is experienced as ideal. . . . Beauty is a special element in the aesthetic experience in which the investment of reality with subjectivity creates an experience of that reality as both ideal and harmonious with our inner life. (p. 16)

Of course, the expression of beauty does not necessarily represent pleasant or peaceful affects. Great art depicting the horrors of war or the pain of isolation often bring about, in the creator and spectator, feelings of completeness. We feel understood. What is essential is for the artwork to capture significant feeling. The meaningful expression of the artist's subjective ideals engenders beauty; beauty articulates a relationship with an ideal. For some artists these ideals are found in the concepts employed. Hagman (2001) presents the example of Duchamp:

> Duchamp's urinal may not be beautiful, but the evocative play of ideas and the exquisite irony captured by the urinal in its context is beautiful. For Duchamp the beauty of appearance (art's retinal aspect) was suspect and highly corruptible, in response he emphasized the aesthetics of ideas and even when he was painting it was the concepts behind the imagery which he found beautiful. (p. 17)

Duchamp's aesthetic idealization of these concepts, expressed through the artwork, creates its transcendent beauty, not its visually pleasing attributes.

The defining quality of beauty captures the subjective and meaningful experiences of life through elaboration. According to Dissanayake (2000) our need for "elaboration is an outgrowth, manifestation, and indication to others of strong feeling or care" (p. 130). In other words, our need for elaboration is relational. Hagman (in press) obviously concurs: "The sense of beauty satisfies a fundamental healthy human need to be in relation to something or someone that is felt to be ideal" (p. 17). The experience of ideal beauty, engendered through the artistic entity, connects our internal significance to the outside world. Art elaborates our ideals, endowed with our subjective sense of beauty, and binds the relations between sense of self, others, and culture.

We transcend beyond the mundane to the core of our shared humanity. The transcendent experience arises "when life interests are touched, experiential depths are sounded, greater possibilities are evoked, and the works that embody these have been constructed and composed with care and commitment" (Dissanayake, 2000, p. 216). Through our creative endeavors we experience and express our ideals, elaborating our sense of beauty, transcending us beyond the common.

Biological survival becomes meaningful when we feel, express, and elaborate our ideals through our subjective sense of beauty, and expand our intrasubjective experience into, and through, the inter- and metasubjective realms. After all, as Hagman (2001) asserts:

> The creative act is intelligible only from within the culture and social milieu out of which it arises.
>
> Culture provides the language of art. . . . This is true of even the most personal aspects of art. The artist who climbs up to the privacy of her garret finds there the tools, maps and measuring instruments of outside culture, and though she might challenge her culture, she cannot escape it. We take our artistic language from culture that becomes the horizon within which aesthetic experience is possible and intelligible. (pp. 9-10)

MEANINGFUL CREATIVITY IN EVERYDAY LIFE AND TRANSFORMATIVE EDUCATION

Fundamentally, creativity transforms something into something new. Creativity, in its elemental nature, is transformative. Creative engagement utilizes our talents, skills, and knowledge to actively problem solve in a meaningful manner. Transformative education is based upon the active engagement of creative processes. Transformative education, based upon creative engagement, impels our lives into vital exchanges between sense of self and others. Indeed, the very comprehension of the divisions between oneself and others is advanced through the creative expression of subjective experiences of self, interacting with one's surrounding world. Through creative exploration and assertion we gain knowledge of who we are, and who we are becoming, all within the multileveled subjective arena. Without this, life can feel drab, without significance, and void of any sustenance from our ideals and sense of transcendent beauty. The importance of creativity in everyday life is to experience and expand authentic meaning and competence, guided by our defining ideals.

Obviously, I do not associate creativity just with those we call "artists." Artists exemplify and magnify the creative engagement that brings nourishing reciprocity. Culturally, artists bring us sustenance that touches deep into the essence of our humanity, extending our subjectivity into the inter- and metasubjective realms. Even though individuals in their daily lives may not create on the same grand scale as artists, the creativity of everyday life is directly related to what artists do and why they do it. The very same core elements that motivate an artist to paint, write, or dance, are the same core elements that push us to decorate our living rooms, to represent externally something of who we are inside, and in so doing to extend transformative meaning into our existence. Psychologist Seymour Sarason (1990) in his book *The Challenge of Art to Psychology*, describes the call to arms for creativity in our daily lives:

> At stake is not art in any conventional sense but the ways in which people can experience satisfaction over their lifetimes from the ordered expression of their imagery, thoughts, and feelings. The satisfaction that comes from making something, and being made and formed by it, is missing in the lives of most people. (p. ix)

Consequently, if we delegate creativity solely to the role of the artist in our societies, a vast source of human potential and fulfillment is lost. Additionally, the foundations that start artists on their creative paths must not be circumvented by an education void of creative significance. The importance of transformative education, based upon creative engagement, sets into motion a way of being in one's life that uses one's talents, skills, and knowledge, to actively problem solve, to find significant and meaningful solutions expressive of our ideals. Ultimately, sustaining and fulfilling relations between the individual, society, and its cultural expressions are established.

Introduction

Unfortunately, the lives of many people
satisfaction and authentic sustenance derived
ment. Sarason (1990), I feel accurately, faults
that do not engage students to use their talen
edge to actively and creatively problem solve
themselves in interaction with their worlds. In
the world are placed upon them. Art education, inclusive of dance,
music, drama, poetry, storytelling, and the visual arts has the power
to support transformative engagement in our educational systems.
By art education I do not mean merely the transferring of information so that students may acquire skills and knowledge. I mean edu-
cating students so that they may use their skills and knowledge to
actively engage art-making processes, and consequently to discover,
explore, and assert their talents. Significantly, art education not only
demonstrates creative activity, but, additionally, demonstrates pedagogical practices useful in other educational domains to further and
develop a creatively engaged sense of self.

Education that is not transformative has dire effects. Outside
of their homes, children spend more time in school than any other
place during their formative years. In some situations, children's
time within the school environment exceeds their time with family.
What takes place at school, how children relate to themselves, to
each other, and to their external worlds, truly has lasting effects for
a lifetime.

The building of this vital, creative, and transformative connection is deeply needed in our times. Only recently in human history have the day to day activities of life not required artistic choices to
be made more directly. We no longer make the bowls used in our
homes; we no longer make them special and personally pleasing
through decoration. Somebody else creates them. Art has been more
and more removed from our daily lives, relegated to the theater and
museums. Dissanayake (2000) asserts the importance of a direct
hands-on aesthetic competency:

> Yet human history reveals that appreciation for beauty, excel-
> lence, and skilled workmanship is inherent, like a taste for
> wholesome food, and needs only direction and reinforcement.
> In all but a few small-scale traditional societies, ritual para-
> phernalia, utensils, textiles, and many other items are inar-
> guably well made and beautiful. (p. 224)

For an active and enriching creative relation to exist between oneself
and one's world, transformative education must encourage individuals to interact subjectively with their environments and to be nourished through this exchange.

MODERN DANCE

Modern dance extends an excellent venue to examine ideas of transformative creative engagement fueled by the multileveled subjective experience. At the turn of the 20th century, several dancers broke away from the traditions of ballet and vaudeville to explore and express artistically the significance between their experiences of self and contemporary life. Since then modern dance has had many incarnations—classic modern dance, postmodern dance, contemporary dance, and dance-theater. I place all these artistic trends under the umbrella of "modern dance" because the philosophical base remains the same. From its inception onward modern dance has blatantly been concerned with the relation between sense of self and one's world. Consequently, to be modern dance, the manifestations of the art form must be historically situated. To be modern dance, the art form must continually change and evolve in response to the intra-, inter-, and metasubjective. What defines the art form is the striving of individual dancers, exploring and expressing through movement the relations of sense of self to self, to others, and to culture, inclusive of the traditions established in modern dance over the last 100 years.

Modern dance choreographers present a window to peer into the creative process, to understand the significance of creativity in everyday life. Choreographer Dan Wagoner's investment of sense of self into his choreography is blatant when he states: "But if someone suggests I change it—well, I can no more do that than change the color of my eyes" (Wagoner, in Kreemer, 1987, p. 32). This profound connection to one's subjective sense of self is apparent throughout the history of the art form. Choreographer Connie Kreemer (1987) articulates this point:

> Since the earliest barefoot steps of Isadora Duncan . . . a distinguishing characteristic of modern dance has been that it allows for a choreographer's individuality. . . . Above all, modern dance has been made by individuals following their own paths. This is what keeps the art vital and fresh. (p. 1)

However, evident within the art form is the deep understanding that these paths are historically situated. According to dance historian Sally Banes (1987), legendary modern choreographer Martha Graham "urged that American choreographers concern themselves with American . . . themes that recognized the serious issues of the day, with modern life and not faraway times or places" (p. 3).

Modern dance choreographers exemplify individuals striving to use their talents, skills, and knowledge, to actively and creatively problem solve, creating meaningful art for themselves and their culture. I use their thoughts, experiences, desires, and musings to look at the multileveled subjective experiences and manifestations of the creative process. I intensify this investigation through an in-depth analysis of choreographer Paul Taylor's (1988) subjective relations to his creative endeavors, vividly illustrated in his autobiography *Private Domain*. Fortunately, modern dance choreographers are often quite eloquent regarding their self-world relations. Consequently, an application of their creative experiences to an understanding of the creativity of everyday life and transformative education is particularly illuminating.

Additionally, my emphasis on modern dance, instead of another art form, reflects my own experience. My subjectivity as a dancer deeply touches my life. I hope my personal connections have guided my explorations and assertions towards greater accuracy. But even more personally, I wanted my creative journey writing this book to be transformative. To do this, to progress and evolve in response to myself, to the ideas of others, and to the creative act, I needed to write from a subjective center. For me, my emotional, psychological, and spiritual core is intimately connected to my body-self, which I desire to express intersubjectively through my relation to the medium of dance, and to words. Indeed, because this initial chapter is actually the last I write, I can attest that the experience has been transformative. My experiences of my body, thoughts, feelings, explorations, assertions, and guiding ideals entering into this multileveled subjective adventure has produced a far greater sense of clarity, expression, and continual investigation than I had previously experienced. To those of you who read this book and have therefore indulged my subjective exchange through you and with you, I am deeply grateful.

PSYCHOANALYSIS AS METAPHOR

In this transformative endeavor, the language of psychoanalysis has been most useful. Language is a complex entity. We represent what is subjectively felt with words, but those very words objectify the experience. To write, to describe, and to stay within the experiential is a difficult feat, one I do not claim to have mastered. I only claim to try. The framework of psychoanalytic self psychology has assisted me in these processes.

Psychoanalysis is a metaphor. No x-ray will ever show the unconscious. One need only examine the many theoretical frameworks within the field to realize we are not dealing with absolutes. Using psychoanalysis does not reduce us to psychic labels, crammed into restrictive psychological boxes, without a sense of control. Through psychoanalytic understanding we extend shape and elaboration to human experience to find greater expression of its significance, and, ultimately, to live life more vigorously. Psychoanalysis, as a metaphor, helps us comprehend and give voice to intangible reality—a creative form, expressing the ideal that life is infinitely complex and meaningful.

In the 1980 book *Advances in Self Psychology*, psychoanalyst Heinz Kohut asserts the mutually beneficial and significant contribution psychoanalysis can make to understanding our humanity:

> I hold that unless psychoanalysis can sooner or later apply the lessons it learns in the laboratory of the clinical setting to the broader arena of human pursuits—to art, religion, philosophy, anthropology, and, above all, to history—it will not have made the contributions that society has a right to expect from it if it is to receive society's support, and it will become a sterile, esoteric enterprise which, in its increasing isolation, will either be an ineffectual enclave in our changing culture or at worst, will altogether cease to exist. I am deeply convinced, however, that . . . psychoanalysis can live up to its potentialities and become an important aid to mankind in its struggle for survival. . . . I am convinced that psychoanalysis, in the hands of some gifted and creative members of our profession, is capable of employing its research tools in the investigations of man's activities in the cultural and social fields, and that it will make contributions of great significance which will assist man in his attempt to gain control over his social and historical destiny. (pp. 536-537)

Psychoanalysis, as a metaphor, helps us subjectively experience and construct transformative meaning, to create more authentically enriching lives for ourselves and others.

FREUD AND CREATIVITY

From the traditional Freudian perspective human beings feel compelled by biological drives, such as sex and hunger, which come into conflict with the need for a smooth-running society (Freud, 1930/1961). Individuals feel guilty and conflicted regarding these drive-wishes. Creativity is an act of sublimation; we unconsciously place these psychic conflicts and their meaning into an external form—the artwork. We find it less threatening to unconsciously integrate our guilt when experienced from a distance through the finished art form. Consequently, sublimation provides an important psychic release for both artist and spectator.

Analyst Hendrick M. Ruitenbeek (1965) describes this presumed role of art within society: "The artistic work sets feelings which rouse guilt and anxiety at such a distance from the person that they can be experienced vividly, yet with minimal pain" (p. 18). Without this important psychological discharge, society would be overrun by our desires for drive-fulfillment and civilization would crumble. Extolling his perspective, Freud (1908/1957), in his paper "Creative Writers and Day-Dreaming," describes the vicarious emancipation of tension experienced by the spectators of art: "Our actual enjoyment of an imaginative work proceeds from a liberation of tensions in our minds" (p. 153). Therefore, from this standpoint, artistic behavior, viewed as sublimation, extends an important function of release that supports the continual existence of civilization by the human race, a species driven by biological needs and desires.

Where does this leave the artist, the creativity of everyday life, and the audience for art? Artists are driven to create to distance themselves from psychic conflict. The creativity of everyday life follows the same path. Gone from this view is a multileveled subjective exchange where artists and spectators attempt to experience and express meaningful significance within their subjectivities and surrounding worlds. Instead, artist and spectator are ruled by drives; art is the psychic container of conflict. However, Freud's most significant and enduring contribution is the role of the unconscious in our lives during our creative, and not so creative, moments.

SELF PSYCHOLOGY AND CREATIVITY

Following Freud's groundbreaking contributions, many psychoanalytic schools built upon the notion of the unconscious. Ego psychology blossomed in America with the work of Heinz Hartmann, and object relations theories emerged in Britain filled with the thoughts of Melanie Klein, Harry Guntrip, W.R.D. Fairbairn, and D.W. Winnicott. Additionally, Freud's contemporary Carl Jung has had an enormous effect upon the field of dance therapy. Self psychology is not the only theoretical paradigm useful to explore self-development and creative transformation. I chose self psychology because its core tenets explore the relations of sense of self to self, to others, and to one's world, and the vital effects these relations have upon the creative endeavors that confront and enrich our daily lives and our society. Additionally, self psychology, a field at one time exclusively identified with the works of Heinz Kohut, continues to grow in vibrant and exciting ways in order not to become rigidly reified.

Self psychology comprehends individuals primarily as relationship seekers. People are still understood at times to feel driven by sexual desire and hunger; however, these biological wishes only become destructive when a fundamental capacity for relationship has been psychologically damaged. According to self psychology, the most emotionally sustaining element of human interaction necessary for growth and development is "empathy," the capacity to imagine, with some degree of accuracy, another's subjective reality. Empathy, therefore, is an act of imagination, to imagine what another is feeling and experiencing. Empathy is not sympathy, compassion, or intuition.

Functioning psychological support systems, enhancing experiences of self-cohesion, are called selfobjects. People, places, things, activities, ideas, can all serve vital selfobject functions. Empathic and responsive caretakers respond to the selfobject needs of children, permitting growth and development. The need for responsiveness and confirmation from functioning selfobjects persists all through life, even though the quality and nature changes with the dynamic evolution of the individual. Adults continue to need the responsiveness of an empathic milieu to reach their full creative potentials. The psychic support of selfobject experience is paramount in the creative and aesthetic domains.

Self psychology, through its understanding of self-repair, extends a view of mental health that demonstrates the importance for an individual to be creatively productive, to have a significantly fulfilling and vital existence. A healthy sense of self is subjectively experienced with feelings of wholeness and cohesiveness. From this foundation the individual enters into a dynamic multileveled subjective exchange with others, experiencing vitality, self-assertion, competency, reciprocity, guiding ideals, fulfillment, and meaning. This productive energy of the individual influences the surrounding society referred to as the group self. The interchanges between human beings become not just the individual components, but the essence of healthy experiences of self, others, and culture. Consequently, from the perspective of self psychology, the psychological health of the individual and the society is embedded in the capacities for creative engagement. Creativity, no longer viewed as the sublimation of hidden conflicts caused by compelling drives, is the means by which a person relates to, and sustains nourishment from, the surrounding world. As such, self psychology provides a very useful vocabulary to examine questions and ideas regarding creativity and transformative education.

Vocabulary assists us to see things in new ways. Einstein postulated the existence of black holes in space before they were discovered. By doing this he expedited their discovery by extending a vocabulary to explore the phenomenon. But if vocabulary itself becomes rigid, it loses its potential to enhance the creative search. I do not present the following book as the only avenue to examine these experiences, but as a perspective to help view possibilities. Heinz Kohut played with ideas that evolved over a relatively brief time span. He strongly encourages the use of vocabulary for the continual creative engagement of ideas, and not the establishment of a rigid system. In *The Restoration of the Self*, Kohut (1977) describes the role of the "playful scientist" (pp. 311-312) and warns against "a worshipful attitude toward established explanatory systems" (p. 312). Perhaps reflecting his own creative journey from a Freudian paradigm to self psychology, Kohut professes: "Ideals are guides, not gods. If they become gods, they stifle man's playful creativeness; they impede the activities of the sector of the human spirit that points most meaningfully into the future" (p. 312).

THE DANCING SELF

The "dancing self" is a metaphor for an individual who feels vitally alive and creatively engaged in the world. The dancing self symbolizes the creative individual, supported by society and its educational enterprises, finding and expressing significant meaning. The reciprocity with culture is evident. Of course, one does not have to be a dancer to elaborate creatively. The avenues individuals use to envelop creative expressions are as varied as there are people. That is what makes creativity so exhilarating and so revealing of who we are. My hope is that by presenting examples of the dancing self, investigating how individuals, through the art of motion, experience the significant enrichment of creative engagement, that others, dancers or not, can find some insight and inspiration for themselves. Symbolically, everyone knows how to "dance"; unfortunately, not everyone knows that she/he knows how to "dance." To live life most meaningfully for our sense of self, others, and culture, each person needs to find the dancing self within. Of the greatest importance, our educational systems must support this intrinsic human need.

The following book is an investigation of the powerful possibilities for the "dancing self" in our lives. To this end, Chapter Two—Modern Dance, Sense of Self, and One's Surrounding World offers the reader an historical perspective on the evolution of the art form. Chapter Three—Self Psychology supplies the reader with the basic vocabulary of self psychology. Chapter Four—Creativity, Self

Psychology, and the Modern Dance Choreographer is the heartbeat of the book, bringing together dance and psychology to exemplify experiences and actions of creativity. Chapter Five—Paul Taylor: A Case Study intensifies the examination of the psychological dimensions of the creative act through the subjective involvement of one choreographer. Chapter Six—Creativity and Transformation: The Heart of Education applies the explorations and assertions of the previous chapters to understanding education geared towards creative fulfillment, enriching experiences of self, others, and culture. Through all this I hope greater possibilities for individuals to creatively engage their worlds with meaning and dynamic reciprocity are seen. My aspirations are grounded on my belief that creativity involves exploration and self-assertion, through a multileveled subjective relationship that serves significant selfobject functions through the construction of an ideal form that embodies and expands self-delineation, self-cohesion, and self-development, and that is ultimately self-transformative.

Chapter ▪ 2

Modern Dance, Sense of Self, and One's Surrounding World

In his letters of 1760, balletmaster Jean George Noverre (1760/1968) decries that "no one has suspected . . . [dance's] power of speaking of the heart" (p. 11). He laments that his fellow choreographers, following patented formulas, have reduced ballet to a "monotonous and dull" state. Almost 150 years later, in 1904, Russian choreographer Michel Fokine argues against ballet's outdated traditions and exclaims: "Above all, the dancing must be interpretative" (Beaumont, 1981, p. 230). Fokine's concerns echoed those that gave birth to modern dance at the turn of the 20th century. These dancers, defying the aesthetics of vaudeville and ballet, threw off the shackles of unnatural movements, confining dance clothes, ballet slippers, and traditional structures to create a new dance—a dance that spoke creatively and imaginatively of their experiences of self, their worlds, and their views of humanity.

EARLY BEGINNINGS

Four women—Isadora Duncan, Ruth St. Denis, Loie Fuller, and Maud Allan—heralded in this new era. All of them performed simple dance routines in the popular theater of the time, designed to entertain. But merely "entertaining" did not satisfy them. Allan's love of music led her to choreograph to Beethoven, Bach, and Schubert, freeing others to use the music of great composers in their dances. Fuller was fascinated with the play of light against cloth. Through her choreography she developed new ways for light, movement, and silk to interact and created beautiful illusions, "becoming fire, opening blossoms, butterflies, water" (Jowitt, 1999, p. 3). Ruth St. Denis choreographed solos illustrating her responses to images of eastern cultures. Duncan's dances freed the upper torso to move expressively; she hoped to find natural movements that would place humanity in greater resonance with the waves, tides, and all the beauty of nature.

These early modern dancers reflected the more liberal women of their era. But, before America would accept them, Europe opened its heart and gave them success. According to dance historian Elizabeth Kendall (1979) in her book *Where She Danced: The Birth of American Art-Dance*:

> Europe recognized what they were doing; without the excitement in Europe about new forms in all the arts, Fuller, Allan, Duncan, and St. Denis would never have lasted. In Europe each was taken up and patronized by artists and poets and intellectuals on a scale undreamed of in America. They were thought to be not just new kinds of artists but new kinds of personalities. Each of the four had brought her mother with her, yet American-style they, the girls, seemed to be in command. (p. 55)

The greatest impact on the emergence of the new dance was the dynamic force of Isadora Duncan. Duncan, feeling that the human spirit must be free to move, hated the confines of ballet and restrictive women's clothing. Dancing barefoot, Duncan sought to find natural expressions for the human body and soul. Believing that ancient Greece was the last civilization to appreciate the natural beauty of the human form, Duncan found her inspiration from the figurines of Grecian vases. According to dance scholar Thomas Hagood (2000), Duncan

> developed a movement technique that was uniquely hers, incorporating the expressive use of the upper body. She "traveled" the stage in movement, developing sequences that were unlike anything anyone had done, or seen, before; running, skipping, leaping with uplifted chest, head thrown back, arms reaching toward heaven. (p. 61)

Duncan's movement emanated from the solar plexus, the lower ribs right above the stomach. Not constricted by a corset, she used the freedom of breath to initiate her dance. Duncan left a legacy through her schools and her writings. But she was not seeking a codified technique, nor did she wish others to imitate her. Duncan's desire was for all to experience, and to express, the essence of their human souls through natural movements:

> I give you something from the heart. I bring you something real. . . . My imitators make caricatures of my dances. They dance with the arms and legs, but not with their souls. . . . Place your hands as I do on your heart, listen to your soul, and all of you will know how to dance as well as I. . . . There is the true revolution. (Duncan, 1903-1927/1981, pp. 53-54)

Duncan's revolution, her "vision and legacy inspired the spirit of dance as it was re-born at the dawn of the 20th century" (Hagood, 2000, p. 62).

Ruth St. Denis originally performed in vaudeville. But her life changed one day when she saw the poster of the Egyptian goddess Isis advertising cigarettes. Intensely drawn to the poster's image, St. Denis embarked on a career performing her imaginative and subjective responses to exotic faraway lands, most especially India. According to Hagood (2000), St. Denis' genuine interest in India coalesced in "her desire to combine the spiritual with the theatrical, and to do so she felt her dance must be grounded in 'high ideas' of philosophy, art, and religion, characteristics that Ruth felt were abundant in Hindu culture" (p. 65).

In 1914, still combining the spiritual with the theatrical, St. Denis met and married her dance partner, former theology student Ted Shawn. Through their company Denishawn they significantly helped spread the gospel of dance released from the constraints of vaudeville and ballet. They toured extensively, opened a school in Los Angeles, and brought a respectability to their world of dance:

> Drawn by the bewitching Denishawn formula of good health and virginal spirituality, significant numbers of middle-class American girls were attracted to the dance for the first time. (Coe, 1985, p. 129)

Those creating these new dance forms had freed themselves from the constrictions of the past. Now, Denishawn inspired three of its company members—Martha Graham, Doris Humphrey, and Charles Weidman—to strike out on their own, to find their own authentic aesthetic, and to create the very base of classic American modern dance.

CLASSIC MODERN DANCE

In 1923, Martha Graham was the first to leave Denishawn. Compelled to discover her own way of dancing, Graham explored the use of her breath to contract and release the muscles of the pelvis and she used this dynamic impulse to initiate movement. The end result was a dance that was powerful, grounded, percussive, and angular, and Graham used this style to develop her own unique choreographic visions, expressive of her sense of self, situated within contemporary life. As evidenced in her relationship to form—the structure of the dance—Graham believed form was useless if it did not evolve from subjective experience. According to Graham (Graham, in Krugman, 1951), modern dance was an art form that had "upset, for all time, form for form's sake. Modern dance turns into the inner self of man, and shows the beauty as well as the ugliness" (p. 89).

Graham (Graham in Sorell, 1963) demonstrated her multileveled subjective relationship to her creative processes and her choreography when she spoke, in 1952, at the Juilliard School of Music. Her 1940 dance, *Letter to the World*, had evolved out of her own idiosyncratic responses to the poetry of Emily Dickinson:

> *Letter to the World* came out of the poems of Emily Dickinson, but also of my family's New England background. The figure of the Ancestress is the figure of my grandmother who, for me as a child, was very beautiful and very unapproachable and very frightening. She was so beautiful because her face was utterly still. She always wore black. She became two things—the mother, the cradler of me, and the figure which is Death. (p. 53)

Graham's choreographic intent was not to objectify Emily Dickinson's poetry, but to express her own subjective relationship to it. Within these responses we see her intrasubjective relation to the qualitative aspects of her medium, her intersubjective familial relations, and her metasubjective relation to the poetry of Emily Dickinson, a cultural icon. Graham's multileveled subjective and feminist contributions to her culture are discussed further in Chapter Four. The elaboration of these relationships, through movement, produced works of art that were unique to Graham. The cornerstone of modern dance has been this subjective exploration, expression, and interaction between sense of self and one's world.

By the late 1920s Charles Weidman and Doris Humphrey had left Denishawn to create their own artwork. For a number of years Humphrey and Weidman shared a school and produced concerts. Weidman developed a comedic mime aesthetic. Humphrey was fascinated with what she called "'the arc between two deaths,' a metaphor for her belief that dance was the play between balance and movement away from balance" (Hagood, 2000, p. 121). In dance terms, she was intrigued with the fall and recovery of the body, the suspension in between, and the effect of one's breath during these phenomena. These ideas were deeply connected to Humphrey's subjective way of being in the world. According to dance historian Selma Jeanne Cohen (1972): "For Doris, the fall and recovery, climaxed by the suspension, spoke the nobility of the human spirit. This was her faith; she would have it no other way" (p. 231). Humphrey's passion produced a movement style that was well grounded, like Graham's, but softer and more rounded, with a strong sense of gravity and rebound. The harder she pushed against gravity the higher she could suspend and soar. From these experiences grew her unique choreographic style. As had Graham, Humphrey codified her technique. Additionally, Humphrey set down her theories on the craft of choreography in her 1959 book, The Art of Making Dances.

Humphrey's protégé José Limón established his own company in the 1950s with Humphrey as artistic director. Limón's style took the sense of rebound from Humphrey and synthesized it to fit his own very masculine sense of self. His original calling to dance came after witnessing a concert in New York by German modern choreographer Harald Kreutzberg:

> There was a terrible power and beauty and eloquence. There was the compelling drama of the modern dance. I saw, with a searing clarity, something a man could do, because dancing like a proud stallion, or an Angel of Death, or a lover out of a Persian miniature was worthy of a man. There was my destiny. (Limón, in Hagood, 2000, p. 212)

Because Limón's choreographic explorations took place under the direction of his mentor, his ability to continue to develop independently of her became paramount, especially as her health declined. With Missa Brevis in 1958, he choreographed his first piece without direct support from Humphrey. Selma Jeanne Cohen (1972) comments on the significance:

> But Missa Brevis he had created alone, and undoubtedly it was a fine, possibly even a great, work. If he could hold on to what he had discovered here for himself, if he could develop this line of creativity that was actually his own, he would be able to survive her. This work was a test for him, a challenge he had to meet with courage and independence. (p. 218)

Limón had been directly drawn to dance through the work of a German choreographer. As modern dance developed in America, Germany simultaneously had a creative evolution with choreographers Harald Kreutzberg, Rudolph Laban, Kurt Joos, and Mary Wigman. Unfortunately, the advent of World War II sharply curtailed the development of German modern dance for many years. Laban, however, has had a tremendous lasting effect by developing the systems of Labanotation and Effort Shape. The former quantitatively records dance; the latter qualitatively records dance. Together they establish not just a comprehensive notation system, but a viable way to examine the very impulses for movement. Wigman studied with Laban. Her protégé Hanya Holm came to America in the early 1930s and established a Wigman school in New York City. Eventually Holm formed her own school and company. For Holm, dance absolutely must be a subjective response indicative of one's sense of self: "Even the simplest movement will be marvelous if it is fulfilled by you, by your real self. When you dance you are naked. . . . Your dances must be built from something within your self" (Holm, in Brown, Mindlin, & Woodford, 1998, pp. 73, 77).

Simultaneously contributing to the modern dance aesthetic were African-American choreographers struggling to be heard and seen. Early African-American choreographers Katherine Dunham and Pearl Primus synthesized their research as anthropologists in the Caribbean and Africa with their personal experiences as African-Americans. African-American modern dance choreographers highlight the intermingling of European and African influences in our culture. Dance scholar Brenda Dixon Gottschild (1998), in her book *Digging the Africanist Presence in American Performance: Dance and Other Contexts*, describes the permeability of these influences: "Africanist presence comes to Americans from home base, from the inside. Like electricity through the wires, we draw from it all the time, but few of us are aware of its source" (p. 23). Gottschild claims that this Africanist presence had a significant and unacknowledged influence on modern dance, such as:

> the torso articulation so essential to modern dance; the legendary pelvic contraction coined as the signature statement in Graham's movement vocabulary; the barefoot dancers reifying contact with the earth, touching it, rolling or lying on it, giving in to it. These particular components of the New Dance had no coordinates in European concert or folk dance traditions. Those traits live in African and African American dance forms, and modern and postmodern dance received this wisdom from the Africanist-inspired American vernacular and pop culture. (p. 49)

A greater expression of the African-American experience through dance clarified a previously hidden aspect of our contemporary culture. According to Gerald E. Myers, editor of *African American Genius in Modern Dance*:

> African-Americans such as Talley Beatty, Donald McKayle, Alvin Ailey, and Eleo Pomare were developing a homegrown, singularly American modern dance that simultaneously delineated their own African-Americanism. Africanizing modern dance in America meant not only a new "look" in the dancing, it also meant a new view of America itself. (p. 31)

African-American choreographer Alvin Ailey began his career in the 1950s, blending his heritage and formal dance training under Lester Horton, creating such masterpieces as *Blues Suite* (1958) and *Revelations* (1960). Lester Horton had broken the race barrier as a choreographer in Los Angeles, and he deeply affected Ailey. Ailey's interracial company was criticized by some African-Americans, but his reply spoke of his belief in the power of movement to communicate our cultural mutuality:

> Japanese dancers understand the blues as well as anybody. When I began using them and some white dancers in *Blues Suite* and *Revelations*, I got flack from some black groups who resented it. They felt anyone not black was out of place. I received many letters in protest. My answer was that their presence universalizes the material. (Ailey, in Brown, Mindlin, & Woodford, 1998, p. 133)

Modern dance choreographers wanted to reflect and respond to contemporary human existence, an existence informed by diverse cultures filtered through the individual subjective relation to culture and society. This multileveled subjective interaction between sense of self and one's world brought several choreographers to use the new dance to support and inform political concerns. The Workers Dance League formed in the early 1930s "gave performances in trade union halls for labor groups and gained the support of the Communist Party" (Brown, Mindlin, & Woodford, 1998, p. 85). Myers, emphasizing the connections between African-American and Caucasian choreographers, claims that a

> legacy of the 1930s was the conviction that the aesthetic and the ethical are interconnected. . . . They danced their con-

cerns about social injustice, the Spanish Civil War, and the
Great Depression, building into the art form's aesthetic the
principle that movement, skillfully deployed, speaks eloquently to moral and social issues. (pp. 31-32)

Modern dance clearly illustrates that experiences of self never develop in a vacuum, but are embedded within and respond to historical
consequences. Modern choreographers' aesthetic endeavors illuminate this multileveled subjective continuum.

To intensify their subjective elaborations through movement
and their search for unique choreographic voices, these early modern dancers invented dance techniques that were idiosyncratically
expressive. Hence, among others, there were Graham, Humphrey,
Holm, and Dunham techniques. In 1948, choreographer Jean
Erdman describes this evolution: "The peculiar qualities of their several techniques emerged in consequence of the various mental-emo-
tional formations of their several personalities" (p. 40). Dance historian Robert Coe (1985), in his book *Dancing in America*, also emphasizes the relevant connection between technique and sense of self:
"But for the choreographer, technique is only a vehicle for self-discovery—and there is nothing more revealing than movement" (p.
135). As expressed by Hanya Holm: "Your body is your language.
Cultivate your language. . . . The responsibility is yours" (Holm, in
Brown, Mindlin, & Woodford, 1998, p. 81). Modern dance technique
had become a vehicle to explore, develop, elaborate, and transform
experiences of self through movement, to seek a subjectively authentic choreographic expression in relation to contemporary life.

At times, the emphasis on individuality caused friction
among these early choreographers. Choreographer Helen Tamiris in
the 1930s tried to unite several choreographers into the Dance
Repertory Theatre, to share concerts and gain more exposure for
their art. According to Hagood (2000):

The Dance Repertory Theatre was designed to be a coopera-
tive effort in producing dance concerts, to attract the greatest
audience, and resolve scheduling conflict. Unfortunately
Dance Repertory Theatre only lasted two seasons before artistic temperament . . . caused it to go under. (p. 111)

There was concern that self-expression not dissolve into self-
indulgence. Jean Erdman (1948) highlights the need to transform
subjective inspiration into an artistic entity, standing separate from
its creator, now experienced by others:

[The choreographer must] turn for inspiration . . . to the great outer and inner world of life, ideas, feelings, and experience. The critical task is to bring this world to focus in moments of realization and then project the realizations into communicative forms. . . . Each new dance is the universe in its own way. It must have the completeness of expression and the ring of authenticity that convince the onlooker that a living world has come to view. (p. 40)

Joining the call for the avoidance of self-indulgence was Louis Horst. Indeed, no discussion of the early beginnings of modern dance is complete without examining the influence of this musician. Horst had been the musical director for Denishawn when Graham, Humphrey, and Weidman were company members. Horst left in 1925, two years after Graham, and eventually became Graham's musical director. But he became much more to the world of modern dance.

Modern dance was a nascent art form based on self-expression. Horst (1954) firmly believed that expression must succumb to form: "The minute you start to preach you are not dancing. Your material must be sublimated to form and stylization or symbolization into a work of art. Until that takes place, it is only self-expressionism" (p. 2). Horst (1939), highlighting artistic forms found in music, used musical elements to define counterparts in dance, such as (1) rhythm = pulse, (2) melody = line and design, and (3) harmony = texture or quality. To educate dancers about music and structure, Horst began in 1928 to teach his classes in preclassic dance (preballet), emphasizing such dances as the Pavane, Gigue, and Minuet. For instance, in his 1937 text *Pre-Classic Dance Forms*, Horst (1937/1972) explains the value he perceives the Pavane can have for the modern dancer:

The pulse and form of the Pavane combine to make an ideal accompaniment for any dance, subjective or objective, in which the mood desired is one of power, slow-moving strength or extreme formality. The slow tempo of the music and the extreme gravity of the steps have also rendered this dance useful as a means of ridiculing eccentricities. (pp. 14, 16)

Horst's influence was immense because he taught composition classes at the Graham school and at summer dance festivals attended by choreographers and dance educators. According to dance critic Marcia Siegel (Siegel in Hagood, 2000): "For years . . . there wasn't a modern dancer who did not know how to make . . . a Pavane as a result of Horst's classes and their many successors in dance departments throughout the country" (p. 121). Additionally, as her long-time musical director, Horst's effect upon Graham was significant. According to dance historian, Don McDonagh (1990):

> Horst . . . encouraged her thematic conceptions of dance and encouraged her to work with music of a suitable nature. His own stated conviction regarding music was that it was a useful frame for dance. He . . . betrayed a mental set that was no more able to conceive of a painting without a frame than of dance without similarly structured limits. (p. 16)

As the art form grew, the restrictions of musical form were perceived as shackles by the younger generation and significant reaction arose against Horst's teachings, as well as the choreographic principles developed by Humphrey. During the 1950s and 1960s, choreographers of the avant-garde rejected his thoughts. Horst should not have been surprised at this, as reflected in his words from November of 1939: "In the field of art one cannot build a rigid wall around this or that growth; the every aim of the sincere modern artist has been to break down established boundaries" (p. 285). Horst was now an "established boundary" and, indeed, the rebellion against these restraints began. The result was an intensification, not of expressionism, but of a more contemporary exploration of the medium of movement and form.

EARLY AVANT-GARDE

Choreographer, Alwin Nikolais' reaction against what he considered self-indulgence is quite clear: "First came the annoyance with the self-expression rampant in the late 40s. . . . Behavior more worthy of clinical study than art was placed on stage in enthusiastic and somewhat orgiastic profusion" (Nikolais, in Brown, Mindlin, & Woodford, 1998, p. 115).

Nikolais had been a musician and a puppeteer; these experiences brought him to an understanding of the medium of movement as expressive motion—the expression was inherent in the motion. Nikolais's subjective and passionate relation to motion is obvious:

> Dancers often get into the pitfall of emotion rather than motion. To me motion is primary—it is the condition of motion which culminates into emotion. In other words it is

our success or failure in action in time and space which culminates in emotion. . . . We do not have to be educated to
understand the abstract language of motion, for motion is the
stuff with which our every moment of life is preciously concerned. (Nikolais, in Brown, Mindlin, & Woodford, 1998, p.
118)

Nikolais extended the human body in motion through the
use of masks and props, and used slide projectors and inventive
lighting to create strange and evocative worlds on stage. The end
result was a new idiosyncratic aesthetic reflective of Nikolais' unique
creative sensibility. His journey evolved from his subjective interaction with his world:

I began to establish my philosophy of man being a fellow trav-
eler within the total universal mechanism rather than the god
from which all things flowed. . . . We might even, then, return
to the vision of self but placed more humbly into the living
landscape, adding grandeur to vision of self . . . enriched by
the resonance of that which surrounds us, a shared energy
interplaying with vital discussions rather than domineering
argument. (Nikolais, in Brown, Mindlin, & Woodford, 1998, p.
117)

Paul Taylor, a dancer for both Merce Cunningham and
Martha Graham, began to show his work. Because his contributions
are discussed at length in Chapter Five, "Paul Taylor: A Case Study,"
I only acknowledge his historical presence during the 1950s as part
of the avant-garde of that time through his first full-length concert in
1957. His mainstream choreographic presence continues today with
what dance critic Deborah Jowitt (1999) calls his "modern dance
world of sunny innocence and midnight depravity" (p. 11).

The most far-reaching effect from this time in modern dance
is the work of choreographer Merce Cunningham. Starting in 1940,
he was a soloist in Graham's company for five years. He began his
own company in 1953. His work, then and now, reveals his intense
fascination with the relationship of movement to time and space. He
treats his dances "more as puzzles than works of art: the pieces are
space and time, shape and rhythm" (Klosty, 1975, p. 24).
Cunningham believes that movement has its own inherent timing,
free from the dictates of music. He choreographs, not to music, but
to the workings of a stopwatch. "Merce worked with the stopwatch
from the belief that rhythm comes out of the nature of the movement
itself and the movement nature of the individual dancer" (Klosty,

1975, p. 24). Again and again, movement phrases are executed to discover their natural timings. By finding the correct timing, Cunningham believes the natural spacing occurs. Carolyn Brown (Brown, in Klosty, 1975) danced in Cunningham's company for 20 years and stresses the importance time and space has for him:

> Merce always appeared to be interested only in the correct timing and spacing, seeming to believe that if these elements were right, any other problems would solve themselves. . . . Viola Farber and I were always amused when after a rehearsal had been a total disaster, Merce's only comment, as he glanced at his stopwatch, would be, "It's two and a half minutes fast." (p. 24)

Cunningham was very influenced by his long-time collaborator and companion, experimental composer John Cage. Out of this partnership, Cunningham began to use methods of chance to choreographic sequences. He isolated the choreography, music, and lighting as independent and equal aspects of theater—isolated, that is, except in their relation to time. In a Cunningham piece, the dancers may not even hear the music until the opening performance, but the amount of time designated for the dance and the music are previously set, down to the second. Cunningham also decentralized the performance space and set up performing Events in large spaces such as gymnasiums. The important aesthetic and cultural significance of Events is discussed in Chapter Four.

Even though some audience members found Cunningham's work exceedingly intellectual and cold, his relationship to his work speaks of the subjective and unique expression of his sense of self through his medium. His choreography illustrates his passionate exploration of time and space, similar to the way Nikolais' work responds to his deep intrigue with motion. All elements of Cunningham's work illuminate his personal tolerance for fragmentation. Indeed, fragmentation permeates his work—from separating music, lights, costumes, and movement, to dividing his pieces up into innumerable different orders, to using chance to put movements and movement sections together, to Cunningham's codified technique. And then there are his dancers. Cunningham dancers exquisitely execute movements that emphasize the independent use of the arms, torso, and legs, from a center that remains stationary. The result is a fragmented body eloquently controlled by the physical center.

All these elements reflect Cunningham's unique vision—a vision that startled and alienated many in the dance world. No one familiar with his work could possibly confuse it with another's. His

choreography today, five decades later, still bears his stamp of individuality. The exact personal meaning for Cunningham is left only to
him, for he wishes the audience to find creatively what they need in
their own observations. According to Carolyn Brown (Brown, in
Klosty, 1975):

> The point I wish to make here is that, like most of Merce's
> dances, I believe, *Second Hand* is deeply meaningful to him.
> Perhaps Merce feels that his dances need have no meaning
> for anyone but himself; certainly he has taken precautions to
> see that little of it is intelligible to an outsider, or for that
> matter to an insider. But he does leave clues. (p. 25)

Cunningham's aesthetic speaks of his humanity within his contemporary existence. His work continues the most basic premise of
modern dance. "Cunningham followed his predecessors in the brief
history of modern dance in perhaps its only tradition: he broke away
to start anew, to start for himself, his way" (Klosty, 1975, p. 20).
Cunningham still carries on this "tradition" and his most recent revolutionary work, combining the latest in computer technology and
dance and its relation to our modern world, is discussed in Chapter
Four.

At times, the avant-garde of the 1950s was accused of dehumanizing the dance. In 1962, Selma Jeanne Cohen addressed this
issue:

> The new choreographers refuse to be literal. . . . They deper-
> sonalize; they do not dehumanize. . . . The dancer's move-
> ment reveals the essence of humanity. . . .The choreographer
> may make a dance about the relation of a straight line and a
> curved one. But as performed by a living body those lines will
> carry connotations. . . .The dancer's movements are connota-
> tive by nature. Meanings should not be superimposed upon
> them. They speak of the human being who performs them.
> (pp. 45, 55-56)

Through the increased exploration of the medium of movement, the
choreographers of the avant-garde created in response to their own
sense of humanity. Their avenues were not the same as their original
mentors, but expressive of their experiences of self, situated within
their own historical times.

Whereas the beginnings of modern dance had mostly sprung
from women, men had become the prominent force in the artistic
revolution in dance during the 1950s. Both were reflective of their

times. The stage was set for the new avant-garde of the 1960s and 1970s, the postmodern rebellion, spurred on by a new sense of freedom and energized by both women and men. This new generation of choreographers emphasized an even greater exploration of the medium and form and its relation to everyday life.

THE POSTMODERN REBELLION

The 1960s were a time of political upheaval and unrest, exacerbated by the Vietnam War. The Civil Rights Movement and the Women's Movement extended a view of democracy that needed to be brought to bear on the actuality of people's lives. A new breed of choreographer emerged. These choreographers wanted not to overlay movement with deep expressive content, but to explore what it meant to "be" in movement. Choreographer Mary Fulkerson (Fulkerson, in Brown, Mindlin, & Woodford, 1998) captures this important difference between more classic modern dance and the postmodern aesthetic: "Modern works seek to *show, to communicate something, to transcend* real life. Post-modern works seek to be, to question the textures and complexities of real life" (pp. 209-210). Democracy and freedom needed to be demonstrated through "art" itself. To accomplish this transition a more contemporary exploration of movement became paramount. Forms that had been used to encapsulate content were questioned further than before. Did a dance have to have a distinct beginning, middle, and end, with an appropriate dramatic epiphany? Weren't basic elements of dance such as time, space, and energy worthy of exploration? Was the division between performer and spectator necessary? And, perhaps most importantly, weren't we all dancers at heart?

For many of these choreographers technical virtuosity was dropped. Nontrained dancers were used, and movements were executed in the casual relaxed mode of everyday life. Choreography was stripped bare to discover natural movement and form. Each generation of modern choreographers seems concerned with natural movement, but the ideas that constitute what is natural are historically situated. According to dance historian Sally Banes (1987), in her book *Terpsichore in Sneakers*, to Duncan and Fuller natural meant to be close to the movements found in nature, in waves, tides, and butterflies. Natural movements captured the essence of these experiences bringing humanity in closer harmony with its own true existence. For Graham and Humphrey natural movements had to be connected to the dynamics of breathing. But for the post-modern choreographers of the 1960s and 1970s, "natural" means something quite different. It means action undistorted for theatrical effectiveness, drained of emotional overlay, literary reference, or manipulated timing. A jump, fall, run, or walk is executed without regard to grace, visual appeal, or technical skill. The action has exactly the amount of abandon and rough edges and takes exactly the length of time it might take outside the theater. (p. 17)

Cunningham, in particular, had opened the way for such experimentation, but Cunningham's dancers always possess great technical proficiency. For this new generation, Cunningham had not gone far enough. But what Cunningham did extend to the choreographers of the early 1960s was a venue for study. John Cage asked musician Robert Ellis Dunn to teach choreography at Cunningham's studio. Dunn did not want to replicate the mistakes he felt prevalent in the teachings of others. According to Dunn (Dunn, in McDonagh, 1990), "I had seen both Doris [Humphrey] and Louis [Horst] give recipes for things, which I thought were very stultifying" (p. 47). Dunn's classes, held from 1960 to 1964, offered a place for the younger generation of choreographers to question and explore their ideas. There were no preconceptions of what dance had to be, no right or wrongs, no judgments. What Dunn asked of his students was that they be clear about their processes.

In 1962, Dunn organized a concert at the Judson Memorial Church showing work by Elaine Summers, John Herbert McDowell, Ruth Emerson, Fred Herko, Steve Paxton, David Gordon, Deborah and Alex Hay, Yvonne Rainer, William Davis, Gretchen McLane, Carol Scothorn, Charles Rotmil, and music by John Cage. Yvonne Rainer (Rainer, in Banes, 1987) describes the thrill felt by the choreographers:

The first concert of dance turned out to be a three-hour marathon for a capacity audience of about 300 sitting from beginning to end in the un-airconditioned 90° heat. . . . We were all wildly ecstatic afterwards, and with good reason. Aside from the enthusiasm of the audience, the church seemed a positive alternative to the once-a-year hire-a-hall mode of operating that had plagued the struggling modern dancer before. Here we could present things more frequently, more informally, and more cheaply, and—most important of all—more cooperatively. (p. 12)

These concerts continued at Judson Church until 1968 with such choreographers as Trisha Brown, Lucinda Childs, Meredith Monk,

Kenneth King, and Phoebe Neville.

The emphasis of these choreographers on "cooperation" resonated with their own historical times. This represents a sharp contrast to the difficulties experienced by choreographers in the Dance Repertory Theatre in the 1930s, when the initial establishing of individuality in a nascent art form was the priority. Reflecting the contemporary spirit of artistic cooperation, visual artists, writers, and composers all participated and choreographed from the very first Judson Church concert. This phenomena affected, not just the art form, but who came as spectator. According to Banes (1987):

> The audiences were also artists, painters, musicians, dancers, writers, film makers, intellectuals, people who lived in the neighborhood of the church, in Greenwich Village. It was an audience acutely aware of the crises in modern art and knowledgeable about the history of alternatives to art traditions, eager to be surprised, shocked, provoked. (p. 13)

Extending the notion of cooperation even further, Yvonne Rainer, Steve Paxton, and Trisha Brown all participated in the improvisational performance group, The Grand Union, that existed between 1970-1976 and that embodied "aspirations to collectivity, equality, and spontaneity" (Banes, 1987, p. 208).

Significantly, during this time Steve Paxton developed "contact improvisation." According to dance and feminist scholar Ann Cooper Albright (1999), his "egalitarian ideology, combined with a growing curiosity about the possible physics of human bodies . . . brought Paxton to the form of duet partnering called contact improvisation" (p. 186). In this art form, two or more dancers, continually touching without the use of their hands, improvise movement through the exchange of bodily weight and energy. In her book *Choreographing Difference: The Body and Identity in Contemporary Dance*, Albright (1997) explains:

> In Contact, the experience of internal sensations and the flow of the movement between two bodies is more important than specific shapes or formal positions. . . . In their place is an improvisational movement form based on the expressive communication involved when two people begin to share their weight and physical support. (pp. 84-85)

Additionally, the communal company Pilobolus was formed in 1971. Significantly, Pilobolus developed in isolation from the rest of the modern and postmodern dance worlds. The founders had never seen dance in New York. But the influence of their historical time was still felt by Moses Pendleton, Jonathan Wolken, and their friend Steve Johnson when they choreographed a dance, *Pilobolus*, titled after a fungus, for their modern dance class at Dartmouth College. Not feeling that they knew how to dance, they at least felt they could move collectively. According to Pendleton (Pendleton, in Brown, Mindlin, & Woodford, 1998):

> When we began, we didn't really feel free, moving in space individually. We literally *had* to hang onto each other. We all figured that we could at least do that much, and it was something larger than any one body could make. It wasn't so difficult if you did create this shape, a thing that moved. We began to play around by combining bodies. (p. 169)

This original collective effort set in motion a method of working that became intrinsic to the Pilobolus creative experience. Dance writer Robert Greskovic (1999) describes this phenomena:

> Central to the post-1960s pedigree of Pilobolus was its very way of working. Instead of following the pervasive single-dancer/choreographer scheme that had dominated American modern dance companies since the birth of the artform in the earlier part of the century, Pilobolus chose a communal angle. Every performer was also directly involved in the creation of choreography. Any work they appeared in they had in some way helped to develop. The fashion for communal living situations during this age was mirrored in the artistic process promoted by Pilobolus. (p. 193)

Out of this communal emphasis, Pilobolus developed an aesthetic of "visual poetry" and athleticism. "Leveraged, counter-balanced weight, acrobatic emphases, anthropomorphic shape modulations and often surreal, pictorial groupings all inter-related to give life and force to Pilobolus creations" (Greskovic, 1999, p. 194). The Pilobolus aesthetic is one intimately and subjectively linked to the communal spirit of their times.

The postmodern choreographers of the 1960s and 1970s, shearing dance away from the trappings of the past, trying to "objectify" what movement could be separate from content, were, nonetheless, continuing the modern dance tradition, the tradition that asks each generation to search themselves for what dance is to them and the culture in which they live. Their subjective experiences of self, drawn to the new experimentation for their own psychological, emotional, and cultural needs, informed their art. For example, in Yvonne Rainer's 1964 work, *Room Service*, two people keep moving a mattress through the space. To the spectator this might appear to be nothing more than the accomplishing of a physical task. But from Rainer's (1965) description, she obviously had a subjective response to the action. This relationship to movement is what makes dance-making a subjective experience, even when the form is pared down to movement for movement's sake without expressive content:

> I was excited by a particular piece of business: 2 of us carry-ing a mattress up an aisle, out the rear exit, around and in again thru [sic] a side exit. Something ludicrous and satisfy-ing about lugging that bulky object around, removing it from scene and re-introducing it. No stylization needed. It seemed to be so self-contained an act as to require no artistic tamper-ing or justification. (p. 168)

Ann Cooper Albright (1997) describes Rainer's desire to objec-tify movement as indicative of "her attempt to resist its scopic objecti-fication within the gendered economy of the male gaze" (p. 20). From this view, Rainer's subjective response through movement resonated with the cultural awareness of the Women's Movement. For a series of performances between 1966 and 1968, Rainer created *Trio A*, in which she attempted to perform movement without dynamic empha-sis or tension, to flatten the phrase so that no moment of movement became more important than another. Here, again, the objectification of pure movement did not remove the dance from subjective experi-ence. According to Albright:

> The irony here is the fact, attested to by so many of her con-temporaries, that watching Rainer do *Trio A* was an incredibly riveting experience. Rather than making her body object-like, or distancing herself from her viewers, Rainer's resistance to the conventions of spectacle in *Trio A* compelled her audience to witness her own movement experience much more fully. (p. 20)

As Rainer herself states: "The body speaks no matter how you try to suppress it" (Rainer in Oliver, 2001, p. 30). Rainer's subjective and feminist contributions to her culture are discussed further in Chapter Four.

George Jackson, in his 1964 review of works choreographed by Yvonne Rainer, Steve Paxton, and James Waring, comments on the relationship of sense of self to the postmodern choreographer:

The participants do not personify attitudes or even assume the role of "being a dancer." . . . These persons are simply being themselves. . . .

Why do these people want to be themselves so badly that they practice doing it in public? . . . Perhaps it is that through practice the self becomes simplified. . . . The metaphysical and psychological traditions of the maxim "know thyself" are suggested by likening the new theatre to Zen psychodrama. (pp. 34, 37)

These choreographers engaged the medium of dance subjectively, not with an emphasis on expressionism, but by exploring movement, time, space, and energy. Judith Dunn (Dunn, in Brown, Mindlin, & Woodford, 1998), a participant in the classes of Robert Ellis Dunn, describes the relationship of sense of self to this experimentation:

In dance . . . the basic unit, the tool is the self. That tool has to be sharpened and tested, permitted to range in an atmosphere which encourages examination and analysis, and is primarily non-judgmental, which focuses on the development of standards rather than having them superimposed as rules which must be first unquestioningly followed and then, only as the grey hairs begin to appear, be discarded. (p. 154)

An eloquent example from this time of postmodern exploration of time and space is Trisha Brown's 1973 dance, *Roof Piece*. On rooftops, literally as far as the eye could see, Brown placed a solitary dancer dressed in orange on each location. The audience was situated on only two roofs. Certainly the connotation of a theatrical space as a proscenium was eliminated. Brown performed a movement sequence while the dancer on the next rooftop watched her. That dancer performed the sequence so that the dancer on the next rooftop could see it, and then repeat it. As in the child's game of telephone, the sequence, of course, became altered as it passed from dancer to dancer. The timing for the movement was the natural timing for each dancer. The timing of the piece was however long it took for the sequence to be passed down the line and then, eventually, to return. The use of the medium in terms of space, time, energy, form, are the basic elements of the piece. There is no specific expressive content to be manifested through the form except for the natural expression of the movement as performed by the individual dancer within the particularities of the spatial settings of rooftops. Yet in its bare bones existence, the piece becomes expressive. Dance writer Don McDonagh (McDonagh, in Livet, 1978) describes his reaction:

I was on a rooftop and I saw it coming as it went around from one dancer to another and then went downtown and vanished. Almost like getting a message from Mars, suddenly it started coming back again as it returned to 420 West Broadway, and that was the piece. It was a gorgeous conception, beautifully executed. I do not know if she has performed it in other places; in Manhattan one of the eerie things was that you were up in a completely different world, totally removed, and there were people going around shopping down below, cars were going past and trucks were making deliveries, and nobody even knew this event was taking place except for the few other people who happened to be on the rooftops that day. (p. 182)

Roof Piece defied all traditional principles of space, time, and form, and exemplified a sequence of pure movement with no direct emotional content. Yet, in my readings of different descriptions of this piece, it feels to me an exquisite expression of fragmentation and isolation in contemporary society, and the efforts that one might go to in isolation to communicate and to accept others. Whether or not this reflects Brown's particular subjective relation to the dance, movement cannot escape being expressive of human existence. The art form is experienced through the intra-, inter-, and metasubjective domains. By paring movement and the medium of dance down to its basics, the postmodern generation of choreographers extended to the next generation a far greater creative palette than earlier dance-makers had used.

CONTEMPORARY MODERN DANCE

The rhythm of tradition, revolution, and rebellion that continually informs modern dance has resulted in an eclecticism in the 1980s and 1990s that has greatly extended the art form. Today there is a greater integration between exploration and development of the medium and the expression of meaningful content. Despite the deep racial injustices still present in America, part of the eclecticism in contemporary dance appears to be a greater mutual, and acknowledged, influence between African-American and Caucasian choreographers. According to dance writer Halifu Osumare:

This is quite a different era than Katherine Dunham's of the '30s and '40s or Alvin Ailey's of the '50s and early '60s. Although our dance masters etched their very strong, individual personas in spite of the stifling social conditions, the

> Black choreographers of the late '70s and '80s have had the
> advantage of an era which supported their individual self-
> conceptions, their iconoclastic artistic explorations and their
> right to say they were human beings first. (p. 27)

African-American choreographer Jowale Willa Jo Zollar established
her company, Urban Bush Women, in 1985, using a foundation of
modern, postmodern, African-American dance and jazz, filtered
through her own subjectivity. Jowale Willa Jo Zollar (Zollar, in
Brown, Mindlin, & Woodford, 1998) comments on the importance of
previous dance traditions and rebellion to her work:

> I feel everything, from Alvin Ailey, Katherine Dunham, Pearl
> Primus, Steve Paxton, all those people laid ground work in
> some way or another, which makes it easier for the next artist
> to work, even if you rebel against what they did—it still
> makes it easier for you to work. (p. 215)

At the same time, there is the work of Jewish and Caucasian choreographer, Doug Elkins. According to Brenda Dixon Gottschild (1998),
Elkins had been a breakdancer with "his African American and
Latino buddies . . . [and] grew up living, loving, and breathing
African American culture. . . . Elkins . . . [acknowledges his] indebt-
edness to African American culture" (p. 146). His work reflects an
integration of breakdancing and hip hop, melded into his own modern idiosyncratic dance, to create an intensely kinetic choreographic
style truly all his own.

Many choreographers have returned to incorporating virtuosity, but, as can be expected, this virtuosity has a distinctly contemporary flavor. Perhaps influenced by the previous work of Pilobolus,
contact improvisation, and the physical fitness craze, virtuosity may
just take the form of a daring athleticism. Before she turned to solo
work in 1988, Molissa Fenley, her work dependent upon speed and
intense athleticism, had her dancers rehearse wearing weights
(Banes, 1987). Through her art, Fenley expresses her subjectivity
and hopes audience members will discover a greater depth to their
own meaningful experiences. When on tour to high schools Fenley
(Fenley, in Brown, Mindlin, & Woodford, 1998) tells the students:

> Look at this work as the bridge between you and me, not
> between you and your friends, not between you and what
> your mother thinks, or anything like that; just you and me.
> Think of that bridge as a direct line into your inner life. Not
> you and me, just you into yourself. (p. 210)

Obviously, this newer emphasis on meaning and virtuosity is not a throwback to the aesthetics of earlier generations but an integration of previously established values in the art form now filtered through contemporary and idiosyncratic perspectives. Meaning and exploration of the medium coalesce. This is true even for the classically informed and technically demanding work of Lar Lubovitch. In his 1985 piece, *A Brahms Symphony*, we are reminded of a bygone era, with music from another century, exquisite traditional partnering, and the serene beauty found in classical ballet. However, this piece clearly speaks of classicism filtered through the modern, and exploratory, Lubovitch. Most significantly, revealed in the work is Lubovitch's love of continual circular motion; positions are not sustained, as in ballet, but moved through expressively. In *A Brahms Symphony* we see the elegance of classicism, digested by Lubovitch, and responded to subjectively through movement. The result is a unique piece of choreography, bearing the subjective and idiosyncratic stamp of Lubovitch expanding on the art form; Lubovitch is present in his redaction of the past.

This contemporary eclecticism comes with the need to intermix a greater sense of "meaning" in dance with the development of the medium. Sally Banes (1987) claims:

> Dance had become so shorn of meaning (other than reflexive) that for a younger generation of choreographers and spectators it was beginning to be regarded as almost meaningless. . . . While the "new dance" choreographers of the eighties still enthusiastically enter into that mediumistic debate, one of the most striking features that sets them off from their post-modern forebears (which sometimes even includes themselves at an earlier time) is the question "What does it mean?" For reasons that have to do with both the history of the avant garde and the temper of our times, the eighties are witnessing an urgent search to reopen the question of content in all the arts, and dance is no exception. (pp. xxiv-xxv)

Narrative, though not necessarily through a linear theatrical progression, has returned to dance. An emphasis on autobiographical material and the introduction of text into what is called dance-theater has become prevalent. The relation of these aspects of dance to contemporary society and the AIDS epidemic is discussed at length in Chapter Four. But the need for a greater experience of direct meaning found in dance appears to coincide with an increase in political and economic stresses. Banes (1987), describing the effect the politics of the 1980s had on dance, asserts:

If in the sixties and seventies we were content to let artworks simply be, rather than mean, and to let criticism describe, rather than interpret, in the eighties we want to find substance and order in an increasingly recalcitrant world. We can no longer afford the permissiveness of the sixties. The modest thriftiness of seventies retrenchment has given way to values in every aspect of American life more suited to the drastic economic cutbacks of Reaganism. Ours is an age of artifice, specialization, conservation, and competition. (p. xxviii)

In the 1980s and 1990s modern dance's eclecticism reflects contemporary life filtered through much of the history of modern dance. Martha Graham's association with her company continued until her death in 1991 at the age of 96. The Martha Graham Company performed until its demise in the year 2000; the future brings hope for its resurrection. Cunningham and Taylor still choreograph and have thriving companies. Years after Limón passed on, his company still exists. After Ailey's death in 1989, Judith Jamison took the helm of his company and they tour extensively throughout the world. Choreographer Garth Fagan has had a modern dance company since 1970 combining his training with Graham, Limón, and Ailey with African and Carribean dance. His Tony Award-winning choreography for "The Lion King" on Broadway has thrust his work into the limelight of American culture. Postmodern choreographers from the 1960s and 1970s still choreograph and evolve. Choreographer Twyla Tharp, whose work defies classification, has bridged her postmodern orientation to choreograph for ballet, musical theater, and ice skaters. And now, at the turn of the 21st century, Tharp has started a brand new company. Additionally, there has been a marked increase in modern dance throughout other countries such as Germany, England, and Japan. Through, most especially, the now international influence of contact improvisation, a proliferation of dance companies using both physically challenged and non-challenged performers has evolved.

In 1991, Russian-born ballet dancer Mikhail "Misha" Baryshnikov, after spending many years dancing in the world of American ballet, joined forces with modern choreographer Mark Morris and began a modern dance company, the White Oak Dance Project. No longer with the troupe, Morris has chosen to concentrate all his energies on his own company. But with Baryshnikov's fame as a flag, the White Oak Dance Project has brought modern dance to thousands of spectators who previously had not seen such work. The contribution is immense. In the autumn of 2000, the White Oak Dance Project's program, "Past Forward," presented works by postmodern choreographers Steve Paxton, Trisha Brown, Yvonne Rainer,

Simone Forti, Deborah Hay, David Gordon, and Lucinda Childs. A whole generation was introduced to the revolutionary experimentation of the Judson Church era.

Exploring the connections between the past and the present, choreographer Connie Kreemer interviewed fifteen modern choreographers in 1987. Gus Solomon, Jr.'s (Solomon, in Kreemer, 1987) response illustrates his multileveled subjective relations between his sense of self, his work, and his contemporary life: "My solutions to the movement problems I set about finding in my dances are the metaphor for the problems of my real life" (p. 181). In many ways, Solomon signifies the variety of traditions in modern dance and the eclecticism of today. He is an African-American choreographer who performs with his company, PARADIGM; he was a member of both the Martha Graham and Merce Cunningham companies; he is identified with the postmodern movement of the 1960s and 1970s; and, today, he teaches at the Tisch School of the Arts at New York University, influencing new and younger choreographers.

After interviewing so many choreographers, Kreemer (1987) sums up her conclusions regarding their place within the history of contemporary modern dance:

> Is there anything that remains true or constant from one generation to the next? Yes—like Isadora Duncan, today's choreographers participate in the art of modern dance. As she searched for her own way, so each artist is seeking a personal path and must be honest to the self in order to find it. (p. 10)

Within the different discoveries, traditions, rebellions, and forms prevalent in the past and today in modern dance lies a single motivating factor—the desire to explore, express, and elaborate, through the medium of movement, a subjective and meaningful connection between sense of self and one's surrounding world—to find the dancing self within. To fully comprehend modern dance's contributions for understanding creativity and transformative education, we must examine the multileveled subjective experiences of self. To begin these endeavors the following chapter outlines the basic vocabulary of self psychology.

Chapter ▪ 3

Self Psychology

A WORLD COHESIVELY DIVIDED

Heinz Kohut (1913-1981) founded psychoanalytic self psychology. Firmly steeped in the Freudian tradition, Kohut served as President of the American Psychoanalytic Association in 1964-1965, and Vice-President of the International Psychoanalytic Association in 1965. According to his biographer, Charles Strozier (1985), "before he was 50, Kohut was labeled—and he bore proudly—the title 'Mr. Psychoanalysis'" (p. 3).

Kohut's work on self psychology reflected a decisive break with the classical Freudian perspective. Given his past, this break from the Freudian tradition meant to lose friends, and, at times, to be ostracized. During the last ten years of his life, when most of his thoughts on self psychology were written, Kohut was terminally ill. He wrote against time and his writings bear the flavor of someone involved in a great creative journey, illustrating not so much an elaboration of a theme, but an evolution of one. Influenced by his initial language, his Germanic sentence structure can be laborious to read. Perhaps, it also reveals the anxiety associated with a creative process that severely broke ties with his past. His final book, *How Does*

Analysis Cure?, published posthumously in 1984, offered a premature finality to his thought, but launched further generations of self psychologists to use and develop what Kohut had begun.

Indeed, since Kohut's death, the field of self psychology has grown and expanded into factions that compliment and, at times, contradict each other. However, these different avenues of self psychology are concerned with self-development. According to analyst James Fisch (1999) "They put the self experience of patient and analyst at the center of their field of observation, and from that vantage point they study developmental derailment and therapeutic repair" (p. 242). These analysts write from the perspective of "therapeutic repair"; however, intrinsic to all their works is a view of mental health that particularly illuminates the development and support of a cohesive sense of self.

Classical self psychologists emphasize the importance of self-object experiences and transferences in the analytic situation and the role of interpretation. They lay the foundation of self psychology, acknowledging the importance of the relations of sense of self to self, to others, and to culture—the multileveled subjectivity of our lives. Analysts Joseph Lichtenberg, Frank Lachmann, and James Fosshage (1992, 1996) emphasize the experiences of self in relation to motivational systems. Lichtenberg (1988) delineates five motivational systems: "the need to fulfill physiological requirements, the need for attachment and affiliation, the need for assertion and exploration, the need to react aversively through antagonism and/or withdrawal, and the need for sensual and sexual satisfaction" (p. 60). Most especially, the needs for exploration, assertion, and sensual motivation play crucial roles in the creative processes of the modern dance choreographer.

The field is further complimented by the theory of intersubjectivity put forth by Robert Stolorow and George Atwood. Stolorow (1998) argues:

> The concept of an intersubjective system brings to focus both the individual's world of inner experience and its embeddedness with other such worlds in a continual flow of reciprocal mutual influence. In this vision, the gap between the intrapsychic and interpersonal realms is closed, and, indeed, the old dichotomy between them is rendered obsolete. (p. 7)

Intersubjectivity expands our understanding of the relational aspects between experiences of self, others, and culture. George Hagman's (1997, 2000a, 2001, in press) work specifically explores creativity through an intersubjective lens. From this perspective, the artist's subjectivity is experienced internally, as well as externally, through the medium and art object. Hence, an intersubjective relation between internal and external aspects of self-experience is established. Additionally, the artist's engagement of an other applies to the interaction with the medium (which in dance includes the dancers), the evolving and finished art object, the anticipated audience, and the artist's field. Of course, intersubjectivity holds many consequences for the educational realm, with the important relations between student and student, student and teacher, and the relation between the individual and subject matter. All these relations are significantly influenced by the metasubjective realm.

Self psychology is additionally enhanced by the contribution of nonlinear developmental systems put forth by Morton Shane, Estelle Shane, and Mary Gales (Shane, 1997). They place emphasis on the development of the new relation between analyst and patient, as the analysand (patient) breaks old patterns of relating. The role of interpretation is questioned, and the increased participation of the analyst through action-oriented provision is explored. In the choreographic process, boundaries exist between choreographer and dancer. In the educational situation boundaries exist between teacher and student. As in any relations, the choreographer and teacher must contemplate what is beneficial and what is detrimental to aid the creative and educational adventure for all participants. The importance of examining what actions, or lack of actions, are used in these processes can be paramount.

With such diversity, how does one begin to understand and use these theories for an interdisciplinary study? I do not examine all the different self-psychological perspectives. Instead, I try to highlight the most relevant ideas for understanding the experiences of self during creativity, the psychological support necessary to undertake aesthetic endeavors, and pedagogical implications for transformative education. Hence, I present a basic outline of the tenets of self psychology to establish a working vocabulary to explore ideas dealing with self-experience, creativity, and education. For clarity and brevity, I refrain from immediately accentuating these connections, but save them to discuss at length in the chapters that follow. For now, I begin, where perhaps all self psychologists do begin, with "empathy."

EMPATHY

Empathy is an experience of imagination. Empathy is the capacity to imagine oneself into the inner life of another with some degree of accuracy, nothing more and nothing less. Empathy is not sympathy or compassion, even though it is hard to envision deep sympathy or compassion that is not sustained by empathy. Additionally, empathy is not intuition, even though intuition, of course, may be unconsciously informed by empathic observations.

Empathy does not mean that one loses one's own psychological boundaries in understanding another—that is psychological merger. Rather, it is the ability to maintain one's own self-awareness and yet imagine another's inner experience; it is "vicarious introspection" (Kohut, 1959/1978, p. 206). Kohut (1987, p. 271) compares this to the artistic experience of watching theater. Audience members open themselves to resonate with the characters portrayed on stage. The result can be deeply moving and engrossing. But the audience never forgets that they are in a theater, that the people on stage are actors. The audience understands and imagines the life displayed on stage, experiences an empathic reverberation with the events, emotions, and psychological states. Empathy requires the capacity to be aware of one's sense of self and other simultaneously and to allow each subjective reality to inform the other through imagination.

The unofficial and unannounced beginning of self psychology is Kohut's 1959 paper, "Introspection, Empathy, and Psychoanalysis: An Examination of the Relationship Between Mode of Observation and Theory." Here Kohut asserts that empathy, used as the mode of observation, defines the field of psychoanalysis, which he describes as the psychology of complex mental states (Kohut, 1984). Kohut believed that analysis had become too educative; analysts had stopped listening to truly hear their patients' subjective experiences and, instead, were placing known theory upon their analysands' realities. Analysts wanted to educate their patients about their drive-related psychic conflicts. Freudian analysts use psychological interpretation to confront the unconscious of the patient, forcing it into consciousness. In so doing, they believe they can alleviate their patients' symptoms of distress and trauma. Instead, Kohut states the foundation of analysis must be empathy, and as such, empathy, as the mode of observation, defines the field of psychoanalysis.

To make appropriate use of empathy, one must understand that empathy itself is not good or bad; the actions taken in response to empathic understanding constitute whether empathy is used for good or ill. In his final public address in 1981, Kohut (1981/1991), choosing to return to the subject of empathy, reiterates this significant point:

> Introspection and empathy should be looked at as informers of appropriate action. . . . [T]hese purposes can be of kindness, and these purposes can be of utter hostility. If you want to hurt somebody, and you want to know where his vulnera-

ble spot is, you have to know him before you can put in the right dig. . . .When the Nazis attached sirens to their dive bombers, they knew with fiendish empathy how people on the ground would react to that with destructive anxiety. This was correct empathy, but not for friendly purposes. Certainly we assume on the whole that when a mother deals with her child, and when an analyst deals with his patient, [and, I add, when a teacher deals with her/his student] correct empathy will inform her appropriate maternal and his appropriate therapeutic analytic action. So (empathy) is an informer of appropriate action, whatever the intentions may be. (pp. 529-530)

Kohut (1977) claims that the infant comes into the world pre-disposed to "expect" an empathic environment similar to the way the respiratory system is predisposed to "expect" oxygen in the air. The infant, as a relationship seeker, needs an empathic milieu to devel-op. This is crucial. Kohut emphasizes that empathy used for even negative purposes is healthier for the individual to experience than an indifferent environment. Such indifference leads to what Kohut (1977, 1984) calls *disintegration anxiety*, when one fears for one's psychological existence.

What constitutes an empathic response is also developmen-tally bound; the infant might need a touch for empathic confirma-tion, whereas a smile from her/his mother from a distance might suffice at times for an older child. In *How Does Analysis Cure?*, Kohut (1984) begins to view such psychological progress in the indi-vidual as following a *developmental line of empathy*. He gives the example of a little boy at the park with his mother watching the pigeons. The child, feeling extra exuberant that day, takes the risk of moving further away from his mother towards the birds. At one point, he looks back at the mother, Kohut determines, not just to calm his anxiety, but to see her pride in his accomplishment, to see her empathic understanding of his adventure. What has taken place? According to Kohut (1981/1991),

a low form of empathy, a body-close form of empathy, expressed in holding and touching and smelling, is now expressed only in facial expressions and perhaps later in words, "I'm proud of you, my boy." (p. 533)

Kohut believes that this natural evolution of empathic con-nection is repeated in the analytic situation. Initially, the analyst extends empathic understanding to the analysand—the understanding phase. As a result, the patient's sense of self eventually becomes more cohesive. The analyst then progresses to interpretations of how and why the analysand came to experience what she/he feels—the explaining phase. This interpretation is based upon empathic immersion by the analyst into the psychological life of the patient, mixed with theory, to offer the patient a higher form of empathic understanding, and to extend the capacity of the analysand to empathically understand her/himself. *Most significantly, the analyst only comes to know if her/his interpretation is accurate and helpful through continued empathic immersion.*

We find in Kohut's thought a multifaceted application of empathy—the capacity to understand what another is feeling. Empathy, describing the basic mode of observation, defines the field of psychoanalysis. Additionally, our empathic imaginations are used to inform our actions for good or ill. Most importantly, empathy is the fundamental psychological element necessary for a responsive environment to foster psychological and emotional growth. All individuals need an empathic milieu that appropriately connects to the developmental line of empathy. This empathic milieu extends beyond the family to one's historical, cultural, and, of course, educational surroundings.

SENSE OF SELF AND GROUP SELF ARE ERA-SPECIFIC AND CULTURALLY BOUND

For Kohut (1975/1978), empathy, as the mode of observation, holds particular import because he claims that psychological difficulties are era-specific, which clearly implies that they are culturally bound. Cultural attitudes construct parental practices that deeply affect the psychological development of children, who will in turn become adults in that society. Additionally, members of a society collectively share the psychological challenges presented by historical consequences, such as war or prosperity. Consequently, Kohut (1976/1978a) postulates the experiences of the group self, analogous to the experiences of the individual self. Kohut examines the formation of societal groups, such as Nazi Germany, and smaller group formations, such as the psychoanalytic community. All basic psychological realities, components, and needs of the individual are understood to exist for the group, or society, as well, just on a much larger scale. Kohut's point may be even more significant today when individuals and nations are becoming more globally aware, and we live with the effects and threats of terrorism. The need to understand multicultural realities is perhaps a greater imperative than ever.

Kohut argues that to be most in tune with the psychological realities of contemporary individuals in American society, analysts must listen anew. Coming from a different historical time, Kohut believes that Freud's patients suffered from different types of trauma than the individuals he saw. Specifically, Kohut (1975/1978) asserts that during Freud's time

> the involvement between the parents and their children was overly intense. The children were emotionally overtaxed by their proximity to adults—be they the parents or nursemaids or others. They were stimulated, touched, cajoled; and they developed all kinds of conflicts as they responded to the stimulation to which the protracted emotional interplay with the adults exposed them. In that sense we might say that the Oedipus complex, while not an artifact, was yet artificially intensified by this overcloseness between adults and children. (pp. 781-782)

Kohut argues, in contrast, that contemporary American families often have both parents working full-time, or are single-parent units, with no extended family available. Children in these cases are much more likely to suffer from understimulation from parents, not overstimulation. Consequently, Kohut (1975/1978) asserts: "There is not enough touching, not enough genuine parental responsiveness; there exists an atmosphere of emotional flatness and sterility" (p. 782). Such a lack of stimulation, instead of producing neurotic conflicts, leads to structural defects in our experiences of self. Authentic mutuality with others is hindered. As analyst Irene Harwood (1998a) claims: "Children who experienced little or no enthusiastic responsiveness from such caretakers, except perhaps by taking on a submissive, compliant false self, can hardly be expected to relate spontaneously and with mature reciprocation" (p. 30). Subjectivity on all levels is impaired. Creativity is stifled. In light of the psychological consequences of the present historical time, Kohut felt the psychoanalytic profession needed to reevaluate its basic theories.

When Kohut empathically listened to his patients, he felt they did not fit the typical Freudian model of neurosis. Kohut (Kohut & Wolf, 1978/1986) saw these patients as suffering from narcissistic personality or behavior disorders that later become known as *disorders of the self*:

> These patients are characterized by a specific vulnerability: their self-esteem is unusually labile and, in particular, they are extremely sensitive to failures, disappointments and

slights. . . . The analysis of the [Freudian] psychic conflicts of these patients did not result in either the expected amelioration of suffering or the hoped-for cessation of undesirable behaviour; . . . it became clear that the essence of the disturbance from which these patients suffered could not be adequately explained within the framework of classical drive-and-defense psychology. (p. 176)

Continuing to explore his work with these patients, Kohut published *The Analysis of the Self: A Systematic Approach to the Psychoanalytic Treatment of Narcissistic Personality Disorders* in 1971, and *The Restoration of the Self* in 1977. With many of his old colleagues abandoning him, Kohut began a study group of younger analysts associated with the Chicago Institute for Psychoanalysis where he taught. Until his death in 1981, Kohut evolved his ideas on narcissism and the development of self-experience in pathology and health. To understand the significance of this we must look at the notion of "narcissism."

FREUD AND NARCISSISM

As the fable goes, Narcissus was a beautiful young boy who, unknowingly, fell in love with his own reflection in a pool of water. The reflection disappeared whenever he tried to reach out and touch it; he died of grief. Obviously, had Narcissus *known* himself, he would not have believed the reflection belonged to another. Narcissus falls obsessively in love with his own reflection exactly because he is without a cohesive sense of self. Consequently, he is in desperate need of mirroring. Nevertheless, from this myth grows our most common notion of *narcissism*, that of one who is selfishly concerned with oneself. Freud incorporates this view of narcissism into his ideas of the human psyche, mechanistically based on biological drives. These drives to satiate hunger and sexual desire are fueled by our libido, our sexual/psychic energy. Freud sees narcissism operating on a continuum from narcissistically cathected (invested) libido—sexual energy preoccupied with one's self—to object love—sexual energy cathected upon another. Here "object" denotes another person, such as when we speak of the "object of our affection."

In this framework the newborn infant begins the continuum in what Freud calls a state of *primary narcissism*; merged with one's surroundings one cannot differentiate between experiences of self and other. Both self and object psychologically merged, all the baby's libido is narcissistically cathected:

The object [mother] . . . is first of all not loved under these circumstances, not cognitively recognized as something separate
from the primitive self. It is either experienced as a part of the
self or used for the maintenance of self-love, self-cathexis,
self-investment—narcissism. (Kohut, 1987, p. 11)

Even for adults, inevitably times arise when individuals
cathect their libido back onto themselves, withdrawing it from others, reminiscent of the primary narcissism of the infant. *Secondary
narcissism*, as Freud (1914/1957) refers to this state, is particularly
visible when a person is in pain:

A person who is tormented by organic pain and discomfort
gives up his interest in the things of the external world, in so
far as they do not concern his sufferings. Closer observation
teaches us that he also withdraws libidinal interest from his
love-objects: so long as he suffers, he ceases to love. (p. 82)

Ultimately, as one progresses on the continuum, the Freudian ideal
is to cathect one's sexual energy upon another in object love. Except
during times of obvious secondary narcissism, too much narcissistic
energy present in the adult is considered "a product of regression or
defense" (Kohut, 1971/1978, p. 619) and pathological.

KOHUT AND NARCISSISM

In contrast, Kohut believes that object love is not a higher ideal than
narcissism. Indeed, Kohut (1971/1978) feels this previous erroneous
notion is based on established values of Western culture, a culture
that "extols altruism and concern for others and disparages egotism
and concern for one's self" (p. 619). He believes this value system
hinders our capacities to look at narcissism with neutrality, as neither inferior nor superior to object love. Kohut (1966/1978) claims
that narcissism does not transform into object love as one matures,
but that narcissism and object love each have their own distinct line
of psychological development, possessing their own continuum from
archaic (early) forms to mature expressions.
     Leaving the theoretical investigation of the developmental
line of object love to others, Kohut concentrates on exploring the
developmental line of narcissism. He no longer views narcissism in
the adult as secondary, regressive, defensive, or pathological. Instead
he sees narcissism evolving in individuals as they develop from

infancy to adulthood. In pathology, psychological trauma causes developmental arrest, not allowing the narcissism to successfully transform. In health, for the individual responded to by an empathic milieu, each stage transforms the previous narcissism into a more mature configuration. Analyst Robert Stolorow (1975/1986) describes well the role of narcissism for the healthy adult: "Mental activity is narcissistic to the degree that its function is to maintain the structural cohesiveness, temporal stability and positive colouring of the self-representation. . . . Narcissism embodies those mental operations whose *function* is to regulate self-esteem" (pp. 198, 205).

Hence, in health, narcissism is no longer the pathological avoidance of others, but the awareness and constructive mainte-nance of sense of self. Kohut (1966/1978) delineates five *transforma-tions of narcissism*: "man's creativity, his ability to be empathic, his capacity to contemplate his own impermanence, his sense of humor, his wisdom" (p. 446). Creativity, no longer viewed as a sublimated form of psychic conflict, is a healthy manifestation of mature narcis-sism, energy used to assert and confirm experiences of self. But what is "self?"

SELF—KOHUT'S PERSPECTIVE

According to Kohut (1977) self,

> as the center of the individual's psychological universe, is, like all reality—physical reality (the data about the world per-ceived by our senses) or psychological reality (the data about the world perceived via introspection and empathy)—not knowable in its essence. (p. 311)

Even though most commonly spoken of as an "entity," *self* is actually an "experience." Our conscious and unconscious experiences of self operate on a continuum between *self-cohesion*, when we feel whole and self-confident, to degrees of *self-fragmentation*, when we feel a drop in self-esteem. In severe cases, self-fragmentation and enfeeble-ment lead to a fear of the disintegration of self often experienced as intense anxiety and/or depression.

Because self is only known through subjective experience and its manifestations, Kohut's (Kohut & Wolf, 1978/1986) defini-tion of self is one of experiencing patterns and actions:

The patterns of ambitions, skills and [idealized] goals; the tensions between them; the programme of action that they create; and the activities that strive towards the realization of this programme are all experienced as continuous in space and time—they are the self, an independent centre of initiative, an independent recipient of impressions. (p. 178)

Kohut organizes these thoughts around a three-part image—a pole of ambitions, a pole of ideals, and one's talents and skills playing the tension arc between the two poles. He refers to this as the *bipolar self*. In Kohut's (1984) last book, *How Does Analysis Cure?*, he gives even stronger emphasis to the development and realm of talents and skills, implying a tripolar self.

This self continues to evolve and develop through an individual's life (Kohut, 1972/1978), but first forms during childhood as the *nuclear self*. With the ideal of a fully responsive empathic environ, *primary structures* of the nuclear self develop. Kohut (1977, 1984) believes that if faulty mechanisms are in place prohibiting full healthy development in one pole of the self, another pole that has constructive mechanisms available for development intensifies in its evolution, creating *compensatory structures*. Kohut (1984) writes:

Disabling disorders of the self come about only when at least two of the three constituents of the self have serious defects because of flawed or insufficient selfobject responses in childhood. . . . [W]e can further ascertain that the selfobjects' inability to respond appropriately to the developmental needs of one of the constituents of the self will bring about an intensified attempt to obtain adequate responses to the developmental needs of the *two others*. (p. 205)

Most importantly, according to Kohut (1977), compensatory structures are not defensive mechanisms whose "sole or predominant function is the covering over of the primary defect in the self" (p. 3). An individual displaying defensive structures has

a pseudovitality. . . [that hides] low self-esteem and depression—a deep sense of uncared-for worthlessness and rejection, an incessant hunger for response, a yearning for reassurance. All in all, the excited hypervitality . . . [is] an attempt to counteract through self-stimulation a feeling of inner deadness and depression. (p. 5)

In contrast, compensatory structure "compensates for this defect. Undergoing a development of its own, it brings about a functional rehabilitation of the self by making up for the weakness in one pole of the self through the strengthening of the other pole" (pp. 3-4). Such a functioning self exhibits authentic vitality and creative productivity in life. In *How Does Analysis Cure?*, Kohut compares the development of compensatory structures to the growth of a tree:

> Just as a tree will, within certain limits, be able to grow around an obstacle so that it can ultimately expose its leaves to the life-sustaining rays of the sun, so will the self in its developmental search abandon the effort to continue in one particular direction and try to move forward in another. (p. 205)

Kohut asserts: "Every self . . . consists to a greater or lesser extent of compensatory structures. There is not one kind of healthy self—there are many kinds. . . . [T]he healthy self will be predominantly composed of either primary or compensatory structures" (p. 44).

The self—this dynamic experience existing over time, consisting of one's ambitions and one's idealized goals and values, activated by one's talents and skills—leads the healthy individual to establish a *program of action*, a blueprint of agency, allowing one to feel one's actions resonate with, and enhance, one's sense of self. According to Kohut (1977) these "ambitions, skills, and ideals form an unbroken continuum that permits joyful creative activity" (p. 63). Through a program of action, the individual's joyful creative activity does not occur in isolation; it is, indeed, an activation into the world, an exchange with the world, that allows the individual to discover and express meaning within a multileveled subjective experience. *This is mature healthy narcissism.* The vitality garnered from lived experience depends upon the ability to respond to one's sense of self through action, to find fulfillment and meaning. Such a self-world relation is most significant when experienced through the intra-, inter-, and metasubjective. In the end, Kohut believes this is imperative for the health of a society. In 1980, he writes:

> A psychologically healthy person, we may say, will live out the particular design that is laid down in the center of his self and achieve his particular nuclear productivity or creativity whatever the attitude of society to his actions may be, whether accepting or rejecting, approving or disapproving. . . . I have become convinced—not as a result of abstract reflec-

tion but on the basis of clinical experience—that the creative-productive efforts brought about by the freeing of the nuclear patterns of a self will lead to socially beneficial results. (p. 498)

A reciprocal relation exists between the health of the individual's sense of self and the health of the group self. The group self also operates on a continuum between cohesion and fragmentation. Kohut believes the rigidity and hatred felt by the Nazis was a symptom of the severe fragmentation of the group self of that society. Understanding the potential destructive nature of such group fragmentation, Kohut strongly emphasizes the need to have a healthy and cohesive group self. According to Kohut (1976/1978a), "a firm group self supports the productivity of the group just as a firm individual self supports the productivity of the individual" (p. 799). A community of individuals needs to be nourished by a shared sense of ambitions, ideals, and the capacities to initiate them further into the world. *Mature healthy narcissism ensures such mutuality.*

To summarize Kohut's view of self: The self, as an experience, operates on a continuum between cohesion and fragmentation. Persisting over time, self is delineated by the patterns of ambitions, ideals, and the talents and skills used to manifest these patterns into a program of action. Within an empathic milieu, primary structures of the self develop. If faulty mechanisms are present for full primary formation in all poles of the self, then compensatory structures must intensify in two of the constituents of self to compensate for the loss of primary structure. A healthy person, experiencing functioning primary and/or compensatory structures, creatively engages the world. Such healthy activity feeds into the health of the group self, and a healthy functioning group self helps ensure the individual health of its members. Reciprocity unfolds.

SELF—FURTHER PERSPECTIVES

Since Kohut, many self psychologists have become concerned with his idea of a bipolar self. It is not that they don't believe that we have strivings that fuel our ambitions, values that energize our goals, and skills and talents to make use of these faculties. But by creating a three-part model of the self, they believe that Kohut creates a self that becomes reified theoretically. Not wanting to succumb to the same pitfalls that Kohut believes Freudian analysis had, self psychology continually reinvents its parts in an attempt to stay empathic and therapeutic instead of educative.

The infant research of developmental psychologist and psychoanalyst Daniel Stern (1985) has made a significant impression on self psychology. Stern does not describe the self as a concept but experientially; consequently, according to Stern, one's subjective sense of self is what is important. "Sense" simply means "(non-self-reflexive) awareness" (p. 7) and Stern strongly believes that this awareness begins before language development. "Of self" means "an invariant pattern of awareness . . . a form of organization" (p. 7). His definition of sense of self is congruous with Kohut's view of the self as being unknowable in its essence:

> Explicitly, [Stern] . . . defines it as the sense of agency, the sense of physical cohesion, the sense of continuity, the sense of affectivity, the sense of a subjective self that can achieve intersubjectivity with another, the sense of creating organization, and the sense of transmitting meaning. (Levin, 1992, p. 198)

This capacity to experience a sense of self evolves during sensitive periods in early childhood, creating domains of experience that continue to develop and reverberate throughout one's lifetime. Stern (1985) describes four different domains of self-experience:

> the sense of an *emergent self*, which forms from birth to age two months, the sense of a *core self*, which forms between the ages of two and six months, the sense of a *subjective self*, which forms between seven to fifteen months, and a sense of a *verbal self*, which forms after that. These senses of self are not viewed as successive phases that replace one another. Once formed, each sense of self remains fully functioning and active throughout life. All continue to grow and coexist. (p. 11)

In the *domain of emergent-relatedness* (0-2 months) the infant begins to create organization out of its myriad of impressions and interactions. Significantly, Stern believes the infant not only becomes aware through organization but is also aware of the process of "organization-coming-into-being" (p. 47). This capacity to experience process as well as product, Stern asserts, is the foundation for all learning and creativity. In the *domain of core-relatedness* (2-6 months) the infant develops a sense of a physical self and is believed to understand that "mother" is separate physically. The infant's sense of self and mother are of "core entities of physical presence, action, affect, and continuity" (p. 27).

The infant enters into the *domain of intersubjective related-ness* (7-9 months) through a sense of a subjective self. The infant becomes aware that separate physical entities have separate minds with "feelings, motives, intentions—that lie behind the physical hap-penings in the domain of core-relatedness" (Stern, 1985, p. 27). In the *domain of verbal relatedness* (15-18 months), a sense of a verbal self allows the infant to convey personal meanings and experience through the symbols of language. The infant begins to have a per-sonal history, and to develop the important capacities for self-reflec-tion and empathy.

Many self psychologists apply the infant research of Stern and others to examine and enhance an understanding of self. As a result, Lichtenberg (1988), through his work on motivational sys-tems, added to the idea of the self as subjective experiences that continue in space and time, serving as the source for initiative and impressions, the manifestations of "organizing and integrating" (p. 61). Beebe and Lachmann (1988) emphasize that self-experience develops in the infant through the "mutual influence" between infant and caretaker:

> Mother and infant generate ways of experiencing each other
> in the early months of life. . . .Our basic proposal is that early
> interaction structures provide one important basis for the
> organization of infant experience. These interaction struc-
> tures are *characteristic patterns of mutual influence*, which the
> infant comes to recognize and expect. . . . [T]he organization
> of behavior and experience is seen primarily as a property of
> the infant-caretaker system at this age [birth to six months],
> rather than primarily the property of the individual. (p. 4)

Clearly gone is the Freudian view of primary narcissism, where the infant experiences itself and mother merged as just one.

In all the definitions of self discussed in this chapter, one thing remains clear: self-experience is undeniably relational. One of the most important aspects of this relation between sense of self and others is the idea of "selfobjects."

SELFOBJECTS

Selfobjects function in our lives as psychological support systems to sustain our intrapsychic experiences of self-cohesion, our sense of our self as whole. Even though in many instances selfobjects are other people, they can also be animals, things, places, ideas, or activities that function to confirm and enhance who we are. For developing children it is imperative that the surrounding individuals function as empathically responsive selfobjects. If not, the psychological development will be thwarted and the individual grown to adulthood will not be able to partake fully of her/his mature healthy narcissism. The person will still be yearning for earlier unfilled psychological needs. These individuals in turn will not be available to function as fully responsive selfobjects for their own children.

In their most basic forms, Kohut describes selfobject experiences using three different terms: mirroring, idealizable, and twinship. Analyst Ernest Wolf (1988) adds the notion of an adversarial selfobject. Kohut's original definitions for selfobjects are in relation to the experiences of childhood. However, the need for selfobject relations is present from birth until death.

Mirroring selfobjects are "those who respond to and confirm the child's innate sense of vigour, greatness and perfection" (Kohut & Wolf, 1978/1986, p. 177). Hence, mirroring does not necessarily mean to duplicate what another does, but to extend psychological sustenance through confirmation of one's subjectivity. The selfobject mirrors back to the child what she/he is feeling. The child, internalizing the confirming experience, begins to feel safe asserting her/himself into the world in response to her/his own subjective feelings. Kohut (1977) refers to this as the "grandiose-exhibitionistic self" (p. 53) of the child and asserts that these early subjective experiences of grandiosity and exhibitionism are "the fountainhead of self-expression" (p. 53). This describes the experience of the young child whose actions, exhibiting her/his self-experience, say "Hey, look at me, I am so wonderful, look what I can do!" The child hopes to experience what Kohut (1966/1978) refers to as "the gleam in the mother's eye" (p. 439). The supportive selfobject responds by expressing delight in the child's age-appropriate grandiosity and exhibitionistic assertions. This prideful confirmation of the child's assertiveness provides the mirroring selfobject function. These experiences help the potential for self-assertion, self-expression, and ambition to develop in the individual.

Idealizable selfobjects are "those to whom the child can look up and with whom he can merge as an image of calmness, infallibility and omnipotence" (Kohut & Wolf, 1978/1986, p. 177). The idealizable selfobject extends to the child a calming and soothing presence that makes her/him feel safe and secure, as when a child feels soothed when picked up by a parent. The child over time internalizes values from this type of selfobject to use as a guide in adulthood to establish goals that authentically resonate with one's ideals.

Grandiosity and idealization are actually two sides of the same coin. The confirmation from mirroring selfobjects works because young children experience the idealization their parents have of them, which reinforces the capacity for children to idealize an other. The confirmation from idealizable selfobjects works because parents experience and accept the grandiosity that their children subjectively experience in them. In other words, rooted in "the gleam in the mother's eye" is the experience of being an "ideal in the object's gaze" (Hagman, in press, pp. 22-23). This duality between grandiosity and the consequential experiences of exhibitionism, self-assertion, and self-expression, and idealization and the consequential experiences of inner peace, awe, and soothing, becomes paramount in understanding the aesthetic experience.

Twinship selfobjects make themselves "available for the reassuring experience of essential alikeness" (Kohut, 1984, p. 193). Kohut illustrates such a need through the example of a female patient. On her bedroom bureau she has a special bottle with a stopper in it to keep the imaginary "genie" inside. This genie in the bottle is

a twin, someone just like herself and yet not herself to whom she could talk, who kept her company and made it possible for her to survive the hours of loneliness when she felt that no one other than her companion in the bottle cared for her. (p. 196)

Kohut originally thinks this patient needs a confirming mirroring selfobject. Eventually he understands she does not want to be mirrored but needs a silent presence, twinship, to sustain her.

The most elemental twinship experience is to know one is in the presence of one's own kind, of other humans, via smell, touch, and shared activities. Through this shared experience, the child develops the self-confidence to explore her/his own skills and talents that ultimately can be used in adulthood to bring forth one's ambitions and ideals into a program of action. Analyst, James Gorney (1998), in his article, "Twinship, Vitality, Pleasure" describes this type of experience:

Twinship is the particular, profound dimension of intersubjectivity in which we experience that large portion of our shared humanity which involves likeness or similarity. No two human beings who have ever lived, or will ever live, have had or can have exactly the same fingerprints. Yet, it is an essential human quality to have fingerprints, and fingerprints are far more similar among humans than they are different. . . . [T]he developing self only gains an accurate estimation of and confidence in its own unique abilities via its vital participation and embeddedness in shared human similarity [italics added]. (pp. 87-88)

Colleagues and peers supply this special type of twinship. Consequently, in teaching I often look upon the experiences of twinship among my students as experiences of peership.

Adversarial selfobjects "sustain the self by providing the experience of being a center of initiative through permitting nondestructive oppositional self-assertiveness" (Wolf, 1988, p. 185). The need for an adversarial selfobject to promote a sense of efficacy and self-agency begins early in life. According to Wolf, the two-year-old who delights in the discovery of the experience of saying "NO!" needs "to experience the [adversarial] selfobject as a benignly opposing force who continues to be supportive and responsive while allowing or even encouraging one to be in active opposition and thus confirming an at least partial autonomy" (p. 55). And, of course, most parents of teenagers must accept this at times highly stressful, adversarial role.

For young children, these selfobjects, experienced as part of themselves, are called *archaic selfobject* experiences. For example, when my niece, Savannah, was three years old, she was a flower girl in a wedding I did not attend. When I asked her about her experiences as a flower girl, she said to me, "You know, you were there, you saw me." When I reminded Savannah that I had not been present, she was temporarily startled. For Savannah, because I apparently functioned as a mirroring archaic selfobject, she assumed I was part of her. Therefore, I must have been present during her big event, when all eyes were upon her, and she displayed, and had confirmed, her young, exuberant, and healthy exhibitionism.

The need for functioning selfobjects in people's lives does not pass with maturity. Instead the nature of the healthy selfobject relation evolves. Kohut (1977) asserts:

> The psychologically healthy adult continues to need the mirroring of the self by self-objects (to be exact: by the self-object aspects of his love objects), and he continues to need targets for his idealization. No implication of immaturity or psychopathology must, therefore, be derived from the fact that another person is used as a self-object—self-object relations occur on all developmental levels and in psychological health as well as in psychological illness. (p. 188n)

As individuals mature so do their relations to selfobjects. For healthy adults, *mature selfobjects* are no longer experienced as just part of themselves, but dynamic self-affirming relationships. The capacity for mutuality is intensified. According to analyst Irene Harwood (1998a): "The mature selfobject . . . is perceived as a separate center of initiative, with needs and wishes of his or her own, with whom one can establish an empathic, reciprocal relationship, based not on demands, but on mutuality, caring, and understanding" (p. 32).

Self-experience is enhanced through such reciprocity. Analyst George Hagman (1997) claims:

> Mature selfobject experience requires the capacity, desire, and ability to expand self-experience so as to include the other. . . . [and] it is through the recognition of otherness within mature selfobject experience that "new" self-experience occurs, adding to the self in often unpredictable and surprising ways. (pp. 85-86)

To have such experiences, Hagman asserts, individuals must be able to experience a sense of relationship, mature confidence, flexibility, personal agency, other recognition, reciprocity, empathy, self-transformation, and altruism. With this arsenal of experience, individuals can enter into mature selfobject relationships, such as friendship, mature love and sexuality, marriage, parenting, and creativity. Most significantly, growth and development for the adult is dependent upon the capacity to engage mature selfobject experiences with a sense of self-agency. "Rather than being the recipient of selfobject ministrations from caretakers (archaic relating), the maturely functioning person acts within the selfobject milieu to 'make it happen'" (p. 93). The individual, in intersubjective relatedness, is a participant and creator of mature selfobject functioning.

The group self also needs *cultural selfobject* experiences, such as the leader who instills a society with a sense of direction and purpose, a religious icon that provides a sense of security and peace, great art that reminds individuals that they share a sense of humanity with others, and a past historical figure who confirms to a society that which they feel adverse to occurring in their own historical times. These cultural selfobjects support a sense of cohesion and heal fragmentation for the group. They are congruent with Kohut's (1984) belief that adults need sustaining selfobjects all through life:

> When the adult experiences the self-sustaining effects of a maturely chosen selfobject, the selfobject experiences of all the preceding stages of life reverberate unconsciously. When we feel uplifted by our admiration for a great cultural ideal, for example, the old uplifting experience of being picked up by our strong and admired mother and having been allowed to merge with her greatness, calmness, and security may be said to form the unconscious undertones of the joy we are experiencing as adults. (pp. 49-50)

The progression from archaic to mature selfobject experience magnifies the capacity for self-experience within the intra-, inter-, and metasubjective realms, strengthening our nourishing exchanges with others and culture.

SELF-STRUCTURES

Self-structures are our subjective ordering of experience into recognizable patterns, conscious and unconscious, which persist over time and are experienced by us as our "self." They are, in essence, our intrapsychic way of being. These intrapsychic formations affect and create the way we manifest our interpersonal world on all levels of subjectivity.

There is probably more debate among self psychologists on how self-structures actually are constructed than any other issue. This concern arises from an important clinical question: Is the way an analysand develops self-repair in analysis congruous with the avenues truly used for self-development in the young child? Certainly, they have something to do with each other, but how far can the analogy be taken? How a self psychologist approaches these questions strongly influences the way she/he conducts an analysis. The implications for clinical work are immense. Self psychologists, as they absolutely should, take what influences their practices very seriously. Individuals come to them vulnerable and in need. What they do in response can enormously affect another's life.

In trying to find the most common ground among self psychologists, I believe, they emphasize the development of self-structures through interaction with an other. No longer are we seen from the Freudian viewpoint, as people conflicted in relationship because our basic nature is fueled by the wish for drive satisfaction. Instead, human beings are seen as relationship seekers. Hence, psychological structures are built through experiences with functioning selfobjects.

To clarify the debate, let's examine the development of an aspect of the psychological structure of a small child before she/he has learned to walk. The empathic mother playing with the child notices when the child wants a toy that is out of reach. She responsively and lovingly reaches for the toy and gives it to her baby. This scenario repeats again and again over time. The self-experiences of both are constructively confirmed through these exchanges. The child develops an expectation of an empathic response from the mother; mother and child establish an empathic bond. With the security created through this continually reinforced bond, the self-confidence of the infant develops, the responsiveness of the mother begins to be internalized by the baby, and self-structure expands.

This illustrates the construction of pattern throu~h the mutual influ-ence of the parent/child dyad. At a time when the mother is distract-ed and the infant wants the toy, the baby, in response to her/his frustration, utilizes the structures so far developed, reaches further than before, and manages to acquire the toy her/himself. A new sense of self-mastery occurs and self-structure develops further.

The baby is expected to need something new from the mother at that moment. Now, rather than needing the mother to reach for the toy, the infant needs a mirroring selfobject response to confirm her/his sense of joy in the accomplishment, to see "the gleam in the mother's eye." In response to the repeated interactions between mother and baby, the baby now can reach for a toy, and the inter-personal realities have slightly altered. Daniel Stern (1985) refers to acquisition of structures in this fashion as RIGs:

> representations of interactions that have been generalized. . . .
> It is important to remember that RIGs are flexible structures
> that average several actual instances and form a prototype to
> represent them all. A RIG is something that has never hap-
> pened before exactly that way, yet it takes into account noth-
> ing that did not actually happen once.
> The experience of being with a self-regulating other [selfob-
> ject] gradually forms RIGs. (p. 110)

Through work such as Stern's the obvious connection between structure formation and learning becomes apparent. *Structure forma-tion is learning regarding one's being in one's environment and inter-acting with that world.*

Self psychologist David Terman (1988) captures this sense of being in this process when he describes the

> system of communication, affective dialogue, in which pattern
> is generated.
> I suggest the phrase "dialogue of construction" to charac-
> terize this process of structure. *The doing is the making* [ital-
> ics added]. The dialogue is the structure. The repetition—not
> the absence or interruption—creates the enduring pattern.
> This is the essential stuff of which we are made—and
> remade. (p. 125)

The arguments among self psychologists stem from empha-sis. Which part of the interaction between child and mother creates the most significant self-structures? Essentially, two types of inter-action occur that enable structure to develop: (1) the mother and child establish an empathic bond through the mother's responsiveness; and (2) the mother causes a minimal empathic break with her baby and the baby's frustrated want and desire for the toy compels her/him to reach further than before to acquire the toy. From the standpoint of mental health, these two aspects of relationship easily work hand in hand as extensions of a dialogue of construction.

But from the point of view of self-repair, the question of whether the experience of frustration is necessary for structure building to occur is in the forefront of discussion in self psychology. Kohut is very clear on his feelings that some level of nonintentional frustration is necessary for self-repair to take place. He believes that even though an empathic bond between analyst and analysand and between parent and child is established, that analysts and parents, (and, I add, teachers) are not perfect. Without trying to frustrate the other, parents, analysts, and teachers have empathic failures. If a secure empathic bond is in place, children, patients, and students internalize the selfobject function of the parent, analyst, or teacher and begin to take over the selfobject function for themselves in response to experiences of frustration. Hence, an experience of self-mastery and structure forms.

Kohut calls this process *transmuting internalization*. For Kohut, this is the process that transforms archaic narcissism into more mature expressions and lends greater cohesion to self-structure. He believes that such transmuting only occurs as a result of *optimal frustration*. Such frustration can only be optimal when it exists in an environment that is not chronically nonempathic. Most significantly for analysis, the analyst *never* deliberately frustrates the analysand. But because we are all limited human beings, breaks in our empathy just naturally occur. Additionally, there can be inherent frustrations in life. For instance, within the analytic situation patients may experience the time restrictions that are a natural aspect of the analytic process as frustrating.

Some self psychologists have taken exception to the idea that frustration must be present for structure to form. During analysis, is it the frustrating break over the weekend or the reconnecting to the empathic analyst on Monday that secures structure for the patient? The argument partly stems from the break with the Freudian tradition. Freudian analysts did not wish to gratify the unconscious drive wishes of analysands; therefore, they felt required to remain distant from offering any gratification to their patients. Such a strong emphasis on frustration resonates too much for some with the idea of being nongratifying.

Kohut, himself, seems to have pointed towards the possibility of structure formation in the absence of optimal frustration that resonates more directly with Terman's dialogue of construction and Stern's RIGs. Analyst Allen Siegel (1999) argues:

Although Kohut did not have the time to work this issue through, it seems that his idea of empathy as "a broad therapeutic action" pointed to another route through which internalizations could occur. In this route of internalizations, the compassionate, understanding, validating, and supportive aspects of the empathic selfobjects are taken in and eventually become structures of the self. These structures create an internal attitude toward the self that is similar to the compassionate attitude of the caring selfobjects. This is a route of structure building that does not depend upon frustrations of any sort. I surmise that Kohut labored with this idea for a while but had to disavow its importance because of his overriding tie to the idea of transmuting internalization via optimal frustrations. . . . Kohut's tenacious insistence on transmuting internalization as the sole route for the accrual of psychological structure reflects his enduring tie to Freud and to classical analysis. (pp. 60, 58)

To understand the significant theoretical, clinical, and educational implications, we must look at the self-psychological perspectives on transference, countertransference, interpretation, and provisions.

TRANSFERENCE, COUNTERTRANSFERENCE, INTERPRETATION, AND PROVISION

Transference originally meant the crossing of information from the unconscious barrier into the preconscious realm (Siegel, 1996). From this Freudian perspective, slips of the tongue are transferences. Over time transference has taken on a different meaning. Transference is the way we create, the way we empower another, with what we psychologically need to find in the other. Important to emphasize here is that transference is created in the same way that selfobject experience is created and engaged. "No one can actively be a selfobject" (Siegel, 1999, p. 77). Our transferences are based upon our past and the way our self-structures have developed through relational interactions. If healthy development has taken place, we create flexible transferences that are close to reality; the kind, loving friend is, indeed, a kind and loving friend. As the relationship develops, more information, gathered through interaction, is acquired regarding the psychology of the friend. This information is mixed with our selfobject and transference needs to create relations that gain depth through knowledge of the other. The ability to establish relations with people who resonate with the transferences we have of them is a sign of mental health. Indeed, establishing mature selfobject relations rests upon this ability.

With unhealthy self-development, the transference illustrates the relational patterns with faulty selfobjects. The individual finds in relation, through transference, what she/he psychologically expects. For example, the individual who experienced unresponsive selfobjects when young, may, as an adult, easily experience others as unresponsive, whether they are or not. Or the individual establishes transferences that may be unrealistic, but signify the hope that the individual has to try to find fulfillment for unmet needs. In this scenario, Kohut believes we seek selfobject transferences that pick up where self-development has gone awry. Selfobject transferences have the flavor of our selfobject needs for mirroring, idealization, twinship/peership, or an adversary.

For instance, if the young child has not received adequate mirroring, as an adult that individual continues to seek out mirroring selfobjects through transference; however, because the individual's self development is not intact, the transferences have an archaic stance to them. The individual, instead of being able to establish mature selfobject relations, looks for more archaic selfobject experiences. Unfortunately, the mirroring of adults cannot make up for the lack of mirroring received from the archaic selfobject. This leaves the adult vulnerable. An extreme example is the performer who, experiencing untransformed archaic narcissism, feels devastated because she/he only received ten curtain calls instead of twenty. No matter how responsive the audience is, the transference needs of the performer for mirroring selfobjects is overwhelming.

Kohut believes that in analysis the patient establishes a selfobject transference with the analyst that signifies where the self-defect (hole) or the more severe self-deficit (lacking) first developed. Beyond taking an empathic stance, the analyst must not do anything to make such a transference take place. Only by permitting the selfobject transference to unfold naturally can the analyst begin to empathically understand the patient. The patient finds her/himself in a responsive empathic milieu and establishes an empathic bond with the therapist. When an optimal frustration occurs in this setting, the analysand, now having a constructive selfobject relation, begins to internalize the function of the analyst through transmuting internalization. The analyst aids this process by remaining as empathic as possible and by offering psychological interpretations that tie an understanding of the current situation to the trauma of the past.

For example, an analysand experiencing an archaic mirroring transference towards the therapist may crave attention from the relationship. As a result the patient may feel angry with the analyst after the weekend break. The analyst expresses understanding of what the patient feels, exemplifying the understanding phase of analysis. Additionally, if the empathic bond between patient and analyst has been sufficiently repaired by the analysand feeling understood, the therapist extends that understanding to an interpretation, exemplifying the explaining phase of analysis. The purpose of the interpretation is to empathically tie the past to the present, thus bringing the empathic bond to a higher level of cognitive understanding. This represents communication further along on the developmental line of empathy. Such an interpretation might be that, indeed, the experience of the lack of availability of the analyst resonates for the patient with specific abandonment issues related to mirroring selfobjects from childhood. Such an experience then enables the patient to connect to her/his own personal narrative and to understand it within the life she/he now leads. This new level of understanding is internalized and self-development continues where before it was thwarted. This is the purpose of interpretation. This example illustrates Kohut's belief that in analysis "new structures are not formed de novo but that enfeebled structures of the self are strengthened and rehabilitated during the course of analysis" (Siegel, 1999, p. 62).

Some self psychologists appear to believe that new structures can be formed during therapy (Siegel, 1999). From this perspective what needs emphasis is the establishment of a new selfobject relation with the therapist that provides a corrective selfobject experience. Hence, it is not necessarily just the empathic milieu and interpretation that is necessary, but what the analyst does for the patient that needs particular attention. Analyst Howard Bacal (1985) adopts the term

> optimal responsiveness, defined as the responsivity of the analyst that is therapeutically most relevant at any particular moment in the context of a particular patient and his illness. Empathy or vicarious introspection is the process by which the therapist comes to understand the patient by tuning in to his inner world. Optimal responsiveness, on the other hand, refers to the therapist's acts of communicating his understanding to his patient. (p. 202)

Illustrating the importance of response to a dialogue of construction, David Terman (1988) describes optimal responsiveness as

> the appropriate ways the analyst can respond in accordance with the patient's phase-appropriate and individually specific requirements for growth or repair. This felicitous term emphasizes the necessity for participation and response in

the formation of pattern, and helps us look beyond the nar-
row confines of the concept of frustration to consider a much
richer and broader spectrum of experience—both in development and the therapeutic process.
   The emphasis on participation in the formation of pattern
is not to deny that frustration also creates pattern. It does. (p.
124)

   In acknowledging the participation of the analyst in the formation of psychic patterns, the analyst's awareness of her/his own
transferences in the analytic situation becomes particularly highlighted. Sometimes these transferences are understood to be *countertransferences*, even though not all transferences of the analyst are
countertransferences. Countertransference directly implies a reaction to the transference of the analysand. Let's say you are an analyst and your patient, through transference, perceives you as uncar-
ing and repeatedly loses her/his temper at you for what the patient
experiences as your "cold responses." The patient empowers you, the
analyst, with these traits because she/he unconsciously continues a
pattern of relational interaction from childhood when the archaic
selfobject functions were faulty. Through transference the patient is
signaling you where the self-defect lies. If you have a psychological
investment in perceiving yourself as a caring person, you might, after
a prolonged time, find yourself experiencing anger at your patient, a
countertransference in reaction to her/his transference. If you experience an impasse with your patient as a result, then you might seek
consultation with another analyst to understand more fully the way
your own subjectivity is interfering in the analytic process.
   Kohut (1968/1978) describes the case of an analyst coming
to him for consultation regarding his nonproductive work with a particular patient. Eventually it becomes clear that the patient has initially mobilized an idealizing selfobject transference, trying to pick up
where the selfobject needs of childhood were not met. A specific
expression of this transference is the recurring presence of "an
inspired, idealistic priest" (p. 499) in the dreams of this Catholic
patient. When repeatedly told about these dreams, aspects in the
therapist of unresolved archaic narcissistic grandiosity cannot tolerate the intense idealization from the patient. Because archaic strivings cannot find appropriate manifestations in healthy adult interaction, the analyst represses the countertransference by rebuffing the
patient's idealization. He informs the patient that HE, the analyst, is
not Catholic. He rejects the patient's attempt to form an idealizing
transference with him that permits the patient to pick up where self-
derailment developed. By coming to terms in consultation with his
own countertransference, the analyst alleviates the harm done, and

the selfobject transference is once again allowed to evolve in the patient. Kohut (1984) emphasizes the tremendous importance of the analyst's self-awareness:

> If we want to see clearly, we must keep the lenses of our magnifying glasses clean; we must, in particular, recognize our countertransferences and thus minimize the influence of factors that distort our perception of the analysand's communications and of his personality. (p. 37)

Not all transferences are countertransference reactions. There are always in a therapeutic alliance two subjectivities in the room. Those subjectivities automatically are responding to each other and experiencing transferences. In this intersubjective dyad the analyst's awareness of what transference influences she/he brings to the therapeutic situation is paramount. Such transferences are not necessarily detrimental to the analytic process, but part of the dialogue of construction. Indeed, the analyst's transferences and countertransferences often help the analyst to better understand the subjectivity of the patient. Who an analyst is in terms of her/his own intrapsychic being affects the process.

Looking at child development Kohut (1976/1978b) argues "it is less important to determine what the parents *do* than what they *are*" (p. 850). In other words, from Kohut's (1977) perspective:

> The *nuclear* self . . . is not formed via conscious encouragement and praise and via conscious discouragement and rebuke, but by the deeply anchored responsiveness of the self-objects, which, in the last analysis, is a function of the self-objects' own nuclear selves. (p. 100)

In the analytic situation, analyst and patient each bring their selves to the arena. The analyst's optimal responsiveness, her/his acts of communicating understanding to the patient, is partly dependent upon her/his own deeply embedded psychic structures.

Important questions arise. First, with optimal responsiveness what adequate guidelines does a therapist follow in terms of establishing therapeutic boundaries on her/his acts of communicating understanding? A specific action that a therapist takes beyond empathic immersion and interpretation is called a *provision*. The Shanes (1996) introduce the idea of "optimal restraint" to indicate "a response within the therapeutic dyad that is neither in excess of what is needed or desired by the patient, nor so withholding or so unspontaneous that it serves to derail the process" (p. 43). This implies the need for a very finely tuned balance. Second, can provision take the place of interpretation in the analytic situation? Empathic interpretation, itself, provides an act, a provision, that can be therapeutically helpful. Some self psychologists (Siegel, 1999) express concern that with the rise of an emphasis on provision, the basic analytic tool of interpretation is being tossed to the wayside too often. Additionally, what a patient experiences as an empathic interpretation and as a responsive provision is idiosyncratic to that particular individual. Analysts Doris Brothers and Ellen Lewinberg (1999) emphasize this important point:

> Just as an analyst's response is empathic only to the extent that the patient perceives it as such, so the analyst's actions constitute selfobject experiences only to the extent that they result in positive changes in the patient's self-experience. (p. 266)

What is most important in this debate, and ultimately most relevant to understanding artistic and educational processes, is the obvious necessity for analysts (as well as parents and educators) to be self-aware and self-reflective so they do not psychologically exploit their patients (children and students) for their own unresolved narcissistic needs. To accomplish this analysts must be aware of the mutual influence between therapist and patient, and both must place trust in each other. If analysts can acknowledge this subjective and affective dialogue of construction taking place in analysis then "the psychological well-being of both analyst and patient is enhanced during its course" (Brothers & Lewinberg, 1999, p. 260). After all, most therapists (and teachers) enter their professions with the hope of aiding others; to accomplish this provides a selfobject function for the therapist and establishes a sense of well-being. Brothers and Lewinberg sensitively point out that analysands who intrapsychically sense that they are trusted to provide this selfobject function for their analysts, probably experience, in the end, an increase in self-esteem.

SUMMARY

Self psychology, in all its current pathways, is most significantly a psychology of experience. The tool used to understand subjective experience is the empathic imagination. Empathy is a universal human need. There is not an infant born anywhere in the world who is not in need of empathic response. Self psychologists use this elemental human need to understand their patients' intrapsychic ways of being, their experiences of self, and their intersubjective relations, to best inform their responses and actions. The intent is to bring about self-repair so that one's sense of self may be experienced as whole and cohesive, extending an experience of fulfillment and vitality through one's actions in life.

The importance of empathy used as the mode of observation in psychoanalysis is highlighted by the ideas that self and group self are era-specific. One cannot significantly separate self-experience from culture. To do so is to assume that we live in isolation. In the end, the human condition is relational. To understand how sense of self and group self function within a culture, one must be empathically sensitive to the subjectivity of the individual and the community within which that individual lives. Subjectivity is a multileveled experience.

Narcissism is the way we attempt to maintain the structural cohesiveness of self. In pathology, narcissism seeks archaic fulfillment in situations that cannot support these needs. In health, narcissism seeks mature fulfillment through actions that enhance our experiences of self and our surroundings. The healthy development of narcissism from archaic to mature expressions culminates in the abilities to be creative, empathic, accepting of one's impermanence, humorous, and wise. Creative activity supports vitality. Through such vital action we experience self, others, and culture; we are engaged on the intra-, inter-, and metasubjective levels.

Sense of self exists on a continuum between cohesion and fragmentation. In fragmentation, without confirming experiences and actions, one can feel in pieces. In cohesion, one feels whole and can take actions that resonate with one's ambitions, ideals, and talents, establishing a sense of self-agency, providing a vital and significant way of being. Self does not exist in isolation, but is most fully experienced and nourished through interaction with the surrounding world. In the end, the cohesion of the group self is dependent upon the health of the individual members.

Our experiences of self are supported in these endeavors through the selfobject functioning of others, whether they are people, animals, things, places, ideas, or activities that confirm and enhance our sense of self. The most basic forms of these psychological support systems, selfobjects, are described as mirroring, idealizable, twinship/peership, and adversarial. These selfobject experiences are also developmental from archaic to mature functions. Our need for them never dissipates, but changes and evolves. The group self of a society needs cultural selfobject functions to maintain cohesiveness; this is perhaps the most significant purpose of culture.

Through interactions with functioning selfobjects, our sense of self evolves as our subjective patterns and organizing of our experience creates self-structures—our intrapsychic ways of being in the world and interacting with it. These structures develop through patterns of mutual influence between child and caretaker. Hence, our sense of self develops through empathic and responsive relations. We either internalize the constructive behavior, or, when confronted with optimal frustration, experience transmuting internalization. Our sense of self-mastery and being expands.

Daniel Stern has emphasized four domains of relatedness that develop through mutual influence: emergent—a sense of bringing organization into being; core—a sense of having a body-self; intersubjective—a sense of having a separate mind from others; and verbal—a sense of being able to symbolize internal experience. These domains continue to grow and develop throughout our lives.

Several self psychologists have been influenced by the work of Stern and other researchers, extending these ideas into a system of motivations. These motivational systems consist of the need for physiological requirements, attachment/affiliation, assertion/exploration, aversion through antagonism and/or withdrawal, and sensual/sexual pleasure. These systems develop during early childhood but continue to inform our intrapsychic ways of being and our relations all through life.

There is debate among self psychologists concerning the role, if any, of optimal frustration for self-repair during analysis. Most agree that self-structure is secured for the analysand through constructive interactions and through recovery from empathic failures. But theoretical emphasis has great implications for clinical practice. The role of interpretation and the role of provision are argued. What I believe is most important to acknowledge, and to use for interdisciplinary application, is the utmost necessity for self-awareness and self-reflection on the part of a practitioner to examine transferences and one's abilities to be responsive in any given situation. This organizes a sense of trust for oneself and one's relations with others. With that orientation, the intersubjective realities always present between individuals can be experienced, explored, and developed to create exchanges that propel health, vitality, and meaningful interaction and existence.

Analyst Judith Guss Teicholz (2000) in her article "The Analyst's Empathy, Subjectivity, and Authenticity: Affect as the Common Denominator," compares "this psychic agility in the analyst . . . to . . . the movements of a dancer" (p. 45). Teicholz cites a program note from a modern dance festival held at Jacob's Pillow to illustrate her point:

> It's the establishment of a clear center that enables the great dancer to move. Freely and fully, she explores the range out-

side of her metaphoric centerline. Reaching in multiple directions, she leaps and lifts with an absolute commitment to that center. It is being grounded in her own center that allows the dancer to take flight. (p. 45)

In the following chapter, the modern dancer's subjectivity and creativity, her/his capacity to experience being "centered" is explored using the vocabulary of self psychology. An investigation of creativity involving exploration and self-assertion, through a multileveled subjective relation that serves significant selfobject functions through the construction of an ideal form that embodies and expands self-delineation, self-cohesion, and self-development, and that is ultimately self-transformative will be extended. Ultimately, in order to enhance experiences of self, others, and culture, modern dancers search for the dancing self within.

Chapter ▪ 4

Creativity, Self Psychology and the Modern Dance Choreographer

A healthy person engages the world with exploration, assertion, vitality, and reciprocity to creatively and productively nourish self, other, and community. The relation between the experiences of exploration, assertion, vitality, and reciprocity, and the ability to be productive, holds many keys to understanding creativity, why it mystifies us, and why it is valued by society. One's vitality is nourished and sustained by exploration and self-assertion, for to be vital is not just to be authentic, but to feel a connection between one's subjective sense of self and one's actions in the world. Through action one feels the exhilaration of being alive, of finding competence and meaning, and feeling that one's intersection with the world sustains and develops one's nature. At the same time, this intersection is dynamic and one's vitality is reinforced and expanded by the environment. Productivity demonstrates this reciprocal exchange between sense of self and the surrounding field. Creativity involves exploration and self-assertion, through a multileveled subjective relationship that serves significant selfobject functions through the construction of an ideal form that embodies and expands self-delineation, self-cohesion, and self-development, and that is ultimately self-transformative.

These psychological events hold true for the artist as for the rest of us; however, the intensification of the relation between artist and creativity produces a magnification of the subjective realities of these processes. Therefore, this chapter emphasizes the conscious and unconscious experiences of the artist, with the belief that such an unveiling expands our understanding of creativity in general, and its enhancement of our sense of fulfillment, vitality, meaning, and mutuality.

VULNERABILITY, OPENNESS, AND SUBJECTIVITY

Kohut's (1960/1978) first published comments on creativity are his 1957 remarks, "Childhood Experience and Creative Imagination— Contribution to Panel on the Psychology of Imagination." Writing from the Freudian psychoeconomic perspective of affects, with its emphasis on the psychological dynamics of trauma and repression, Kohut speaks of the capacity of the creative artist to feel with intensity and to be open to experience:

> The great in art and the truly pioneeringly creative in science seem to have preserved the capacity to experience reality, at least temporarily, with less of the buffering structures that protect the average adult: from traumatization—but also from creativeness and discovery. (p. 273)

While teaching a seminar at the University of Chicago in the late 1960s, Kohut expands on this idea. Kohut (1987) attributes this special ability of the artist to a permeable or shallow "sieve." Kohut uses the visual metaphor of a sieve to describe psychological structure: "Psychological structure is gradually acquired through various experiential interactions with the environment, so that layer after layer of a yet sieve-like substance is built up. . . . Structure is a sieve in depth" (p. 160). The permeability of the artist's sieve permits access to the inner layers of her/his psychological structure; hence, the artist's ability to capture feelings in depth, to access structures from childhood with intensity, and to experience vulnerability. Others in society have stronger buffering systems that protect them from these levels of intensity, decreasing their vulnerabilities, especially to traumatization, but rendering them more removed from their deeper wells of affect. Kohut (1960/1978), emphasizing the openness and vulnerability of the artist, and the consequential and beneficial psychological effect on others, writes:

In order to safeguard his psychoeconomic balance, the creative personality is compelled to employ creative activity to a greater extent than the person who is more successful in absorbing immediate impressions and their inner elaborations through reliable neutralizing and buffering structures. . . . Individuals with noncreative personality structures . . . may obtain a fleeting return to the freshness and intensity of childhood experience from which they are usually barred by participating—as readers, listeners, beholders—in the creations of the artist. It is this return to an old, exhilarating mode of experience which accounts at least in part, for our intense enjoyment of art. And our admiration for the artist rests on our grateful recognition that he has returned to us, at least temporarily, a piece of our own childhood. (pp. 273-274)

Martha Graham's (Graham, in Brown, Mindlin, & Woodford, 1998) philosophical approach to modern dance describes such experience:

To understand dance for what it is, it is necessary we know from whence it comes and where it goes. It comes from the depths of man's inner nature, the unconscious, where memory dwells. As such it inhabits the dancer. It goes into the experience of man, the spectator, awakening similar memories. (p. 50)

By repeated involvement in the act of creation, the artist fends off fragmentation that such accessibility to depth of structure may cause. To insure her/his stability Kohut (1966/1978) believes the artist is "compelled" to create, causing the artist's relation to creativity to resemble, at times, an addiction. Through their "addiction" artists extend to society an accessibility to feeling, lost to many. Indeed, here in Kohut's early thoughts we see the precursors to the notion of creativity and creative products as functioning selfobjects for both the artist and society. The words of choreographer Charles Weidman (Weidman, in Brown, Mindlin, & Woodford, 1998) capture this dynamic between artist and audience:

The world of illusion which the audience expects from the artist is, in fact, the world of their real selves, the image of their own world, the translation of their hopes and fears, their joys and sufferings into the magic of the stage. (p. 67)

Of course, as his career progresses Kohut ceases to write in psychoeconomic terms; however, infant research confirms Kohut's

thoughts on the permeable sieve, the accessibility to depth of structure. In *The Interpersonal World of the Infant*, Daniel Stern (1985)
describes the "emergent self" of the infant from birth to two months
of age. He proposes that the infant, across all modalities, experiences
life in terms of "shapes, intensities, and temporal patterns—the more
'global' qualities of experience" (p. 51). These qualitative experiences
are congruous with the basic elements of exploration in modern
dance—space, energy, and time. Stern notes the experience of "vitality affects." These are "elusive qualities . . . captured by dynamic,
kinetic terms, such as 'surging,' 'fading away,' 'fleeting,' 'explosive,'
'crescendo,' 'decrescendo,' 'bursting,' 'drawn out,' and so on" (p. 54),
which, at times, have the sensation of a "rush" (p. 56). Identifying
the potentials of the relation between vitality affects and dance,
Stern states:

> Abstract dance and music are examples par excellence of the
> expressiveness of vitality affects. . . . The choreographer is
> most often trying to express a way of feeling, not a specific
> content of feeling. . . . Like dance for the adult, the social
> world experienced by the infant is primarily one of vitality
> affects before it is a world of formal acts. It is also analogous
> to the physical world of amodal perception, which is primarily
> one of abstractable qualities of shape, number, intensity level
> not a world of things seen, heard, or touched. (pp. 56-57)

Stern also identifies "categorical affects," which refer to emotions that are named such as "angry" and "sad"; "activation," which
refers to the "intensity or urgency of the feeling quality"; and "hedonic tone," which refers to "the degree to which the feeling quality is
pleasurable or unpleasurable" (p. 55). Including categorical affects,
activation, hedonic tone, and vitality affects, along with the qualities
of perception of shape, intensities, and time that cross modalities,
Stern writes:

> These are the basic elements of early subjective experience. . . .
> Infants are not lost at sea in a wash of abstractable qualities of
> experience. They are gradually and systematically ordering
> these elements of experience to identify self-invariant and
> other-invariant constellations. . . .
> *This global subjective world of emerging organization is and
> remains the fundamental domain of human subjectivity. . . . [I]t
> is the ultimate reservoir that can be dipped into for all creative
> experience. . . . That domain alone is concerned with the com-
> ing-into-being of organization that is at the heart of creating
> and learning* [italics added]. (p. 67)

Consequently, the essential ability to engage the creative process of the coming-into-being of organization, the process of creating a form out of experience, is directly connected to the ability to access the depths of one's subjective sense of self. Learning and creativity are based upon this essential ability.

Ellen Dissanayake (2000), in *ART and Intimacy*, also believes the capacities for creative engagement and intimate mutuality are rooted in the early mother/infant dyad. Within this relation, Dissanayake highlights not just the global qualities of perception outlined by Stern, but the dynamic exchange between mother and infant using amodal communication—"baby talk." She writes:

> From the first weeks, in all cultures, human mothers (and even other adults) behave differently with infants than with adults or even older children. In most cases a mother's vocalizations to the baby and her facial expressions, gestures, and head and body movements are exaggerated—made clear and rhythmic. Babies in turn respond with corresponding sounds, expressions, and movements of their own, and over the first months a mutual multimedia ritual performance emerges and develops. Exquisitely satisfying to both participants, it inundates both mother and baby with a special pleasure that is all the more powerful because it is not just felt alone (like the interest, excitement, or joy felt while privately thinking about or watching one's baby) but is mirrored or shared. (p. 29)

The sharing, confirming, and mirroring mutuality of these early amodal experiences develops the potential for artistically expressing, through modalities, our sense of meaning and ideals. Our aesthetic activities reinforce our intrinsic relational nature, grounded in the mother/infant dyad. Mutuality and creative engagement are intimately connected. Dissanayake (2000) asserts the need to recognize these significant bonds created through amodal perceptions:

> What is not widely appreciated is that infants recognize the positive intentions and feelings of another person through rhythmically patterned cyclical movements (of face, body, and voice) that are coordinated (in timing and intensity—that is, rhythm and mode) to their own expressive movements. (p. 42)

Dissanayake describes the "sense of intermingled movement and sensory overlapping that characterizes infant experiences" (p. 6), as rhythms and modes. "Rhythm has to with an *unfolding in time*, the patterned course of an experience; modes are *qualities* of that experience" (p. 6). Our creative endeavors, expressive of these subjective experiences of rhythm and modes, secure our sense of reciprocity. Dissanayake believes that confirmation of mutuality is a fundamental biological need:

> As humans, we evolved to be the kind of creature who *needs* the signs of mutuality—praise, recognition, encouragement, comfort, affectionate touching, and fond smiles—just as we evolved to need food, water, and light. Otherwise, we are incomplete and can even perish. Lacking mutuality, we lack humanity. (p. 42)

George Hagman (in press), in his article, "A Sense of Beauty," also finds within the mother/infant dyad the seeds for our need to create ideal artistic forms:

> My thesis is that the psychological foundation of the sense of beauty is the archaic experience of the infant joyously caught up in interaction with the responsive mother's face. The combined qualities of both symmetry and unique expressiveness in the mother's face are progressively elaborated over the course of development with other experiences. The reciprocal nature of pleasurable, satisfying and secure interactions is linked to all later experiences of beauty and the search for and cultivation of the sense of beauty becomes a lifelong human motivation. From a self-psychological perspective the sense of beauty can be understood as a selfobject experience which optimally combines the experience of being in the presence of an idealized other and the sense of having one's perfection mirrored. (pp. 18-19)

Beauty is not concerned with surface qualities. The capacity to create beauty refers to the ability to demonstrate in an external form the significance of the experiences of idealization and through this activity to feel nourished by a meaningful expression of subjective reality, transcendent of the mundane. In other words, through the creation of beauty we engender aesthetic selfobject experiences. Internal and external are experienced harmoniously, even if the depiction of subjective reality confronts ugliness and pain. The early intersubjective sources of beauty are expanded and developed throughout our lifetimes, bringing about mature selfobject experiences, connecting us to the metasubjective. Hence, we are not compelled to create in order to fulfill psychologically immature needs to once again be infants with our mothers; our quest is for the meaningful integration and expansion of our life experiences, for self-transformation. Hagman (in press) writes:

Although the deepest unconscious sources of the sense of beauty may in fact lie in the experience of the mother's face, it is the way in which new experiences both possess and also move beyond these archaic sources which defines the beautiful. (p. 20)

Kohut, Stern, Dissanayake, and Hagman all assert the vital and compelling connections between the expression of subjective experience and the making of art. Many modern choreographers extend, as a global explanation for the desires and needs to create, access to the depth of their experiences of subjectivity. Ann Halprin (1955) feels that the choreographer must "be awed by the very act of living" (p. 10). Rosalind Newman (Newman, in Kreemer, 1987) describes this subjective connection:

You cannot get away from the fact of your own humanness, and when I go into the studio to make those steps, I'm dealing with my arms, legs, and torso which are connected and part of my vulnerability, my backlog of feelings and thoughts and memories of the world, of other people, of night, day, food, money, sex.
Aliveness is what I deal with. (p. 205)

In Nancy Meehan's words:

The dances are a way of penetrating the veil, eliminating the clutter that gets into the mind and stops one from experiencing deeper aspects of one's own psyche. . . . Art is a means of entrance to areas of the psyche not otherwise available. (Meehan, in Kreemer, 1987, pp. 141, 144)

And the words of Martha Graham clearly highlight the connections between sense of subjective self, vulnerability, openness, and vitality:

You have only one thing—I am not speaking of your skill. That you can get. You have yourself. You stand or fail on that, on the vulnerability of that self to life. . . . [I]n order to work, in order to be excited, you have to be re-born on the instant and you have to permit yourself to feel. You have to permit yourself to be vulnerable. . . . You must be touched by it, and your body must be alive. (Graham, in Sorell, 1963, p. 54)

The question arises here: What enables the artist to be vulnerable and open, to have a permeable sieve and the capacity to access the depths of structure? I approach the idea of vulnerability solely from the perspective of the openness to experience; the essential quality of vulnerability is the capacity to be open. Whether vulnerability leaves someone open to attack or open to a dynamic flow of experience is circumstantial. Kohut believes this vulnerability and openness stems from the capacity to access deep psychological subjective structure. Stern believes the infant creates organization through qualities of perception such as shapes, intensity, and temporal patterns, and modalities such as visual, auditory, and kinesthetic, thus establishing a subjective reservoir to draw upon for later creative experience. Dissanayake and Hagman assert this subjective reservoir derives from the mother/infant dyad. If all these views are correct, then possibly part of the vulnerability of the artist is *an increased sensitivity to qualitative experience and modality*, which then establishes an avenue, *an entryway*, for the artist to access the depths of structure and to be open to experience.

For instance, in modern dance the basic tools of exploration are the body's relationship to space, energy, and time. Space refers not just to an area for dancing, but to the fact that the body exists in space and therefore has shape and design; energy (at times called effort or force) refers to the qualitative attitude towards the movement's execution, such as sustained or percussive; time, of course, refers to duration, pulse, rhythms of movement. Space, energy, and time, viewed from the perspective of the dancer, are sophisticated levels of shape, intensity, and temporal patterns.

Modern dancers widely use improvisation to explore these qualities of perception. In this mode, the choreographer tries to connect to her/his subjectivity spontaneously to evolve an idiosyncratic relation to space, time, and energy through movement. In their book, *The Intimate Act of Choreography*, Blom and Chaplin (1982) describe this experience:

> Improvisation is a way of tapping the stream of the subconscious without intellectual censorship, allowing spontaneous and simultaneous exploring, creating, and performing. Improvisation emerges as an inner-directed movement response to an image, an idea, or a sensory stimulus. (p. 6)

What allows this inner-directed movement response to emerge? The modern dancer's sensitivity to and exploration of these qualitative experiences of perception is through the modality of proprioception, the awareness of the sensation of one's movements, as if dominated by a sensual motivational system. For the choreographer/dancer sensation is never far from reach.

THE SENSUAL MOTIVATIONAL SYSTEM
AND THE MODERN DANCER

In *Psychoanalysis and Motivation*, analyst Joseph Lichtenberg (1989) outlines five motivational systems: the need for regulation of physiological requirements, the need for attachment/affiliation, the need for exploration/assertion, the need for antagonism/withdrawal, and the need for sensual/sexual response. Similar to Stern's claim that the domains established during infancy do not cancel each other out, as in phases, but continue to develop and affect subjective experience throughout life, motivational systems develop in infancy and contribute to our existence on a daily basis. What is significant is the subjective way that the particular motivational systems dominate the foreground or recede into the background, depending upon the individual's psychic structure and development.

Lichtenberg (1989) clearly distinguishes between the sensual and the sexual as developed in the infant, while acknowledging the obvious connections:

> By sensual enjoyment, I refer to a particular feeling of pleasure that is triggered by many of the activities caregivers employ to soothe and express affection to infants and that infants employ to soothe themselves. When the affect state of sensual enjoyment dominates experience, it may serve as a "switch"—the outcome may be a diminution of tension leading to relaxation or a heightening of sensation leading to sexual excitement. By sexual excitement, I refer to a particular feeling of heightened stimulation that progresses upward to orgastic levels. Sexual excitement, like sensual enjoyment, is triggered by many of the same activities that caregivers employ to soothe and express affection and that children employ to soothe themselves.
>
> Sensual enjoyment is, I believe, the outcome of an innate program of neonates and becomes a regular occurrence of normal daily lived experience. . . . The evidence suggests that sensual enjoyment is a more powerful motive force throughout the life cycle than has been previously recognized, whereas sexual excitement seeking is more periodic and episodic. (pp. 217, 219)

The significance of separating sensual from sexual is to emphasize an important aspect of human life—the ability to be sensitive to sensation in such a way that one's experience of self is confirmed. Asserting the potential of self psychology to contribute to understanding the cohesion derived from sensuality, Lichtenberg (1989) writes:

The tendency of self psychology has been to use rather broad concepts, such as "empathic responsiveness leading to a self-object experience." I believe that often embedded in the general terms that self psychology uses for normal development are references to the experiences I consider as triggering sensual enjoyment: touching, stroking, rocking, soothing, rhythmic vocalizing. Put another way, I suggest that often the affect state described as a selfobject experience includes sensual enjoyment and that the soothing aspect of sensual enjoyment is cohesion restoring. (pp. 233-234)

This sense of sensuality appears closely related to Stern's notion of vitality affects, described earlier in kinetic terms, which connects qualitative experiences to the dynamics of movement. Both emphasize the bodily-felt experience. Modern dance choreographers Loie Fuller and Alwin Nikolais assert that dance captures the essence of the relations between motion and sensation. At the turn of the 20th century, Fuller (Fuller, in Brown, Mindlin, & Woodford, 1998) asserts:

What is the dance? It is motion.
What is motion? The expression of sensation.
What is sensation? The reaction in the human body produced by an impression or an idea perceived by the mind. (p. 17)

Half a century later, Nikolais (Nikolais, in Brown, Mindlin, & Woodford, 1998) defines the modern dancer through one's sensory relation to motion:

So in the final analysis the dancer is a specialist in the sensitivity to, the perception and the skilled execution of motion. Not movement but rather the qualified itinerary en route. The difference may be made even clearer by giving the example of two men walking from Hunter College to 42nd and Broadway. One man may accomplish it totally unaware of and imperceptive to the trip, having his mind solely on the arrival. He has simply moved from one location to another. The other may, bright-eyed and bright-brained, observe and sense all thru [sic] which he passes. He has more than moved—he is in motion. (p. 118)

To summarize so far: For both Kohut and Stern, individuals, while creatively involved, are vulnerable and open to experience through the capacity to access the inner depths of psychological structure—our intrapsychic ways of being—that define our sense of a subjective self. According to Stern, the infant begins to develop a subjective sense of self by experiencing qualities of perception—shape, intensity, time—that cross over separate modalities—visual, auditory, kinesthetic. These qualities of perception contribute to the experience of vitality affects that kinetically convey a way of feeling instead of content of feeling. So before the baby cognitively understands she/he is being diapered, the infant cues into the qualitative way the caregiver performs the act. The baby may even come to prefer the way one caregiver qualitatively performs the act compared to another caregiver. Using one's connection to qualities of perception through different modalities, one's experiences of vitality affects, categorical affects such as "happy" and "sad," activation that indicates level of urgency, and hedonic tone that registers levels of pleasure, the infant develops the beginnings of subjective experience. The process of one's coming-into-being is begun. This ability to be involved in process while product is emerging, Stern claims is our very foundation for creativity and learning. Hagman and Dissanayake highlight that these foundations are relational, firmly grounded in the early interactions between caregivers and infants.

I suggest that modern dancers enter into this subjective and open foundation of creativity and learning with a relatively dominant sensual motivational system. Indeed, I suggest connections to sensation enable the dancer to access and experience the depths of subjectivity. Through this heightened awareness of kinesthetic and sensory experience, the choreographer connects to qualities of perception and vitality affects to inform a sense of subjective self through motion. Additionally, Lichtenberg claims that the sensual is an important affect component of selfobject experience. These essential connections to sensuality, qualities of perception, vitality affects, subjectivity, are what enable the choreographer to establish a subjective relation with motion and to have the most fundamental selfobject experience necessary to choreograph—the experience of movement to serve as a selfobject.

THE SELFOBJECT FUNCTION OF MOVEMENT

Choreographer Kenneth King captures the essence of a relationship to vitality affects, subjectivity, and the selfobject experience of movement when he asserts:

> There are many formidable challenges to making dances.
> First and foremost it's the action of dancing that completes
> my own sense of being. . . .

I'm a tall, lean, slim person and I like that feeling, the
body being light and unimpeded. I like to move full out, very
expansively and rapidly. I've devised a lot of arm and spine
movements that are all my own, so the body coils, twists,
bounds, spins, spirals, gyrates, dips, bounces, curves. . . .
But the most important thing is to find out how one dances
for one's self. (King, in Kreemer, 1987, pp. 154, 157)

Dan Wagoner, through his interactive relation with movement, clearly illustrates movement's capacity to serve a selfobject function:

I am absolutely absorbed with movement. I love movement.
And I trust movement. So all of my dances begin with movement, and the basic problem or idea is always a movement
problem. As I make movement choices, I dance them over and
over, turn them around, add on—explore in as many directions as possible and then trust the movement will lead me
somewhere interesting. (Wagoner, in Kreemer, 1987, p. 31)

Twyla Tharp (Tharp, in Perron, 2001) describes her motivation to discover "honest" movement, illustrating the relation between
idiosyncratic subjectivity and the selfobject function of movement for
the choreographer:

When I started working, I wanted to go to a place where I felt I
had a right to be, where I wasn't taking somebody else's
material . . . I was getting to something that was so pure and
nonderivative . . . that I could call it my own and start from
there. In terms of the invention of movement, it's a matter of
honesty. It may have been an illusion, but nonetheless it
drove me to do a lot of work in the studio. (p. 48)

Additionally, the capacity for movement to serve a selfobject
function is intensified because modern dancers technically train
their bodies, the instruments of their art, not to accomplish the ethe-
real, effortless facade of ballet, but to discover the relationship
between the weight of their bodies and gravity. Embodied through
motion, this relation to gravity enables the dancer to be off balance
and to recover, to suspend through space, and to push off the
ground with force. This force is not meant, necessarily, to appear
effortless, as is the case in ballet, but is used dynamically to propel
the body through space. Dance critic Joan Acocella (1993) compares
the work of modern choreographer Mark Morris to ballet:

He is far less concerned with beauty of line, with the visual design of the body, than ballet dancers, and more concerned with the *actual, muscular enactment of the dance phrase* [italics added]. . . . In a sense, this is just an extension of an old argument about gravity. "Ballet dancers are antigravity," Morris says. "That's the big difference; it's not political anymore, it's about gravity." "Gravity is our friend. . . . At least, we modern dancers like it." (pp. 201, 76)

The pelvis is the center of gravity for the human body. Modern dancers work hard to build strength in the muscles, most specifically the lower one-third of the abdominals, used to activate and control this center of gravity—the weight of the pelvis. Dancers refer to the feeling derived from such an accomplishment as being "centered." By having control from one's center of gravity, the dancer can relinquish the type of control, such as excess tension held in other parts of the body, that inhibit the fullest range of movement potential. Shelley Washington (Washington, in Perron, 2001), dancer with Twyla Tharp from 1975-1990, describes the increased potential for quick speed when centered: "Plié, getting into the ground, earth, dropping their weight, total abandon. They need to have a strong center to release the extremities. And the speed. No one can quite believe the amount of steps per second" (p. 102). For the modern dancer, the motivation to be "centered" is to have the greatest accessibility to the freedom and power of movement to discover and express one's deep felt experiences. This reminds me of Kohut's (1987) description of a good analysis:

The success of analysis is not to create people who cannot have strong feelings, who cannot be passionate, who cannot fly off in a rage or be violent, but to enable them to choose when, where and how to express their strong feelings. (p. 165)

In order to gain this centered visceral connection, dancers must train not in a mode of imitation, but by sensing through motion the awareness of one's center of gravity. The emphasis is on sensation—the bodily-felt experience. Additionally, such an emphasis demands that dancers become aware of how they, at times, in minute and almost indiscernible ways, initiate movement. Such movement patterns have a tremendous effect on the way one moves through space. A very simple illustration from everyday experience is to become aware of what parts of your body you use to pick up the telephone. The action needs a simple movement of the arm, but many people develop the pattern of lifting the shoulder as well. Not only is this unnecessary to accomplish the action efficiently, but such a movement pattern causes stress because raising the shoulder causes one to breath less deeply. For dancers to initiate movement centered and efficiently, they must become aware, through sensation, of their whole bodies and their idiosyncratic and subjective movement patterns. To accomplish this often promotes profound psychological and emotional experiences of self-awareness and self-discovery, and to work to change such a pattern brings alteration, growth, a sense of self-agency and self-transformation.

"Somatics," exemplified in the methods of Alexander (1971), Bartenieff Fundamentals (1996), Feldenkrais (1975), Kinetic Awareness (Saltonstall, 1988), and Laban Movement Analysis (Laban, 1948/1963, 1950/1960; Thornton, 1971) is a mode of technical training used in modern dance that emphasizes and values this direct sensory connection to one's body as the most elemental tool of learning to dance. According to choreographer and teacher Sylvie Fortin (1998), somatic training asserts "the primacy of the subjective experience as a reliable source of knowledge and the acknowledgment of a bodily level of meaning" (p. 61). Choreographer Mark Dendy (Open Rehearsal, July 25, 2000, Santa Barbara, CA) simply calls this "inner space knowledge." A subjective connection to one's sense of body-self supports experiences of self-cohesion. The capacities to communicate through movement and to interact with one's world are enhanced. Fortin asserts: "Embedded in both the notion of empowerment and somatics is the development of a better understanding of one's own experience in order to recognize one's own power as a knower and a creator of the world" (p. 55). Indeed, meaning is embodied in life through such a multileveled subjective reciprocity between sense of self and one's world in a mature selfobject experience.

By engaging dance training/technique through the empowerment of one's sensory awareness of one's center of gravity and movement patterns, the dancer discovers the greatest amount of freedom to move through space dynamically, to change shape and levels of energy, and to vary time. Through such freedom the choreographer explores the significant and subjective connections between sense of self, vitality affects, qualities of perception, and sensuality—if successful, expressive and meaningful choreography evolves. By the coming-into-being of movement that reflects and expands on one's subjectivity, the sensory experience of dance supplies an essential selfobject function.

Analyst George Hagman (2000a) describes the selfobject experience as "transcendent" (p. 284). I believe that for the modern dancer this experience of transcendence captures the affect state associated with the cohesion derived from sensual soothing and enjoyment described earlier by Lichtenberg as part of the selfobject experience. The modern dancer's ability to conjure up movements, derived from a sensual connection to one's physical center and developed in response to one's subjective sense of self, I believe gives the mature selfobject function of movement a powerful and transcendent quality. Consequently, a dancer's sense of idealization and aesthetic beauty is most probably compelled by the sustaining qualities of sensation. Through dance-making, the elaboration of this confirming idealization expresses meaning, competence, vitality, and the need for reciprocity.

The question arises: What draws an individual to train with an emphasis on sensory awareness? The answer can only be sought through the idiosyncratic psychology of each person. To suggest the generality that modern dancers connect to their deep subjective structures through a sensual motivational system is one thing, but how each dancer came to be dominated by such motivation is individual. I do believe that the modern dancer's heightened sensitivity to qualities of perception, through sensory awareness, is at the core of her/his ability to capture the depths of her/his subjectivity. This is the wellspring of vulnerability, of openness, for the dancer. However, it is the exploration and assertion of this subjectivity through action/motion/movement into the world that enables the transcendent selfobject function and the vitalizing experiences of meaning, competence, ideals, and beauty. Without it, one cannot begin the choreographic process.

EXPLORATION, SELF-ASSERTION, AND VITALITY

Joseph Lichtenberg (1989) delineates the idea of an exploratory-assertive motivational system claiming that "exploration . . . [is] closer to the 'Aha!' of insight and assertion . . . [is] closer to power and mastery" (p. 129). Put another way, exploration is closer to the process of discovery and assertion to the process of action. Lichtenberg believes that infants derive pleasure from the realization that their actions have brought about a specific result. He goes further, arguing that the found efficacy for the infant produces a subjective sense of "realness" and "ownness." This cohesive experience for the infant, derived from the mastery of efficacy, produces the pleasure. Lichtenberg claims: "Problem solving by exploration and assertion together triggers the pleasure that comes from a sense of efficacy and competence" (p. 126). Lichtenberg argues that this capacity for competence initiates feelings of aliveness, in other words, vitality:

> Looked at in this way, the exploratory and assertive activity of infants would not be to seek stimuli as such, but to experience the particular affective sense of aliveness of the aroused exploratory state. Competence would then be a measure of infants' ability to organize and regulate their activity to produce a new version of the desired state. (p. 136)

Such competence, propelled by the pleasure of efficacy, assures the experience of authentic aliveness through exploration and assertion of one's actions—vitality.

Ellen Dissanayake (2000) reminds us that our biological heritage is based upon our "hands-on" competence:

> Human brains and minds evolved to enable the learning of manual skills from others and the devising of practical solutions for the requirements of ancestral environments—to cope, "hands-on," with the demands of life. Simply by doing what we were born to do evokes a sense—subliminal or fully felt—of competence, of being at home in the world. (p. 100)

The pleasure and vitality felt through competency is fortified by the making of art. "First and foremost . . . the arts are things that people *do with their bodies*" (p. 178).

Analyst Charles Kligerman (1980), in his article "Art and the Self of the Artist," claims that part of the motivation to create is "an innate intrinsic joy in creating, related to what has been termed 'functional' pleasure. This is perhaps the most important factor, but the one we know least about" (p. 387). I suggest that part of this intrinsic joy in creating is derived from the efficacy pleasure associated with exploration and self-assertion, and the competence to create and recreate this scenario. *For the modern dance choreographer, the basic motivational joy in creating may stem from the capacity not just to experience sensual pleasure, but to explore sensory awareness, and through this exploration to assert through action one's idiosyncratic subjective relation to sensation.* This elemental joy is enhanced further by increased competence through the dynamic interplay between sense of self and the surrounding subjective fields. This will be examined later in discussing the dancer's subjective relation to the medium and the creation of an ideal form—the dance.

Additionally, the connections between joy, exploration, self-assertion, vitality, competence, reciprocity, and creativity are significant not just for the artist, but also for the spectator. The spectator actively engages the artwork to find efficacy in the pleasure of partaking of art. This pleasure brings forth the subjective feelings of idealization and beauty as experienced by the spectator. George Hagman (in press), in his article "The Sense of Beauty," claims: "Beauty is always an act of creation for the viewer and the creator" (p. 22). From Hagman's perspective an appreciation of art is interactive, and this process produces "a vital feeling of engagement with the object" (p. 22). Hence, through exploration, self-assertion, and efficacy audience participants find and experience their own joyful vitality and competence in relation to art. They are dynamically engaged on the intra-, inter-, and metasubjective planes.

For Kohut the ability for exploratory self-assertion develops into one's ambitions. Kohut (1977) claims the pole of ambitions of the bipolar self harbors "the fountainhead of self-expression" (p. 53). Using these ambitions in conjunction with one's ideals, talents and skills, the individual engages a program of action. This program of action allows one to assert one's subjectivity into an exchange with the world. Kohut sees this healthy narcissism as the foundation for joyful creative activity.

Analyst Prudence Leib (1990), in her article "The Origins of Ambition," outlines two types of healthy needs met by the activation of ambitions—self-healing and self-expressive. "Self-healing functions include various means of directly or vicariously meeting needs that were unmet or defectively met during childhood and mastering childhood traumata" (p. 121). This indicates a need and desire for self-repair through one's assertions. Self-expressive functions arise from the psychological need (I suggest, derived from an exploratory-assertive motivational system) "to use innate talent and strengths" (p. 117). Within this realm, Leib includes:

the need to think, to create, perform or write music, to create visual images or structures, to perform mechanical functions, to organize, to build, to design, to use arithmetic ability, to understand the natural or interpersonal world, to ·ise words, to communicate, to influence people, to exercise interpersonal power, to nurture, to use innate physical strengths or grace, to help others. (p. 121)

Clearly these innate strengths and talents can be used to create self-healing; however, when used solely for the efficacy of expression they go beyond self-healing into the self-expressive function. Even though helpful to examine these ideas in a clear black-and-white division, I suspect that many creative actions actually entail elements of both self-healing and self-expressive needs.

Analyst Carl Rotenberg (1992) notes that it is not uncommon during analysis for analysands, as they progress towards self-repair, to pursue creative activities. This most likely is aligned with the self-healing function of self-assertion. Rotenberg (1988) also claims "that creativity is a major transformational force in the life of everyone" (p. 196). This more universal life force may include aspects of self-healing, but, obviously, goes beyond self-repair into the realm of expression that brings its own idiosyncratic and subjective rewards. With the trials and tribulations of the processes of creativity, one hopes in the end that these rewards are based on a sense of efficacy pleasure.

These actions of authentically felt exploration and self-assertion, whether to serve self-healing or self-expressive functions, provide a sense of vitality when entered into the intersubjective realm of exchange with an "other"—an experience of reciprocity. This awareness of other extends the capacity to experience the mature selfobject function. George Hagman (1997), in his article "Mature Selfobject Experience," points out that "the most skilled, refined, and accomplished creative efforts are made possible through the artist's engagement with the object of their creative efforts in a mature selfobject experience" (p. 101). In the creation of art, the object/other includes the artist's medium, the emerging artwork, collection of works, the anticipated audience, and the art field in general.

The experience of the other denotes an intersubjective relation. Hagman (2000a), in his article "The Creative Process," acknowledges the significant intersubjective relations between creator and product and highlights two views of this intersubjective experience. One is the dialectic between the subjectivity of the artist inside and the subjectivity of the artist outside as it is presented through the medium of the art. Additionally, the medium itself takes on subjectivity for the artist, and it is the intersubjective reciprocal exchange with the medium/other that permits the mature selfobject experience to take place. Hagman (2001), in his article "A New Aesthetics for Psychoanalysis," further explains this dual dialectic:

> Once an action is taken altering the object in some way, it can be said that subjectivity is externalized and the artist enters into a relationship with an object which is now invested with qualities of the artist's own subjective experience. . . . [T]he qualities of the external object are essential (as in the maternal infant dialogue). In fact the action taken upon the object must include the qualities of the object (its color, plasticity, etc.) as well as the changing relationship between internal and external aspects of subjectivity. (pp. 11-12)

Applying this to the modern dancer, I believe that the psychological attachment to proprioception and qualitative perceptions, specifically through a sensual relation to vitality affects, is what enables the dancer to endow the body-based medium of dance with subjectivity. The ability to do this, the sensitivity and openness to such experience, I believe is what we refer to as "talent," with its probable integration of hereditary and environmental factors. To understand the journey, navigated with exploration, assertion, vitality, and reciprocity that the artist travels through this multifaceted intersubjective relation, we must examine the psychological processes of the creative act.

CREATIVITY AS A THREE-PHASE PROCESS

Analysts frequently write about creativity examining the issues surrounding the self-repair of a patient, particularly as it manifests in a blockage to creative activity (Hagman, 2000a; Kohut, 1977; Tuch, 1995). Additionally, analysts are concerned with understanding the psychological and cultural significance of a piece of art, such as Freud's (1914/1953) examination of the statue of Moses created by Michelangelo, or Muslin's (1991) interpretation of Hamlet. Even though self psychology, from my perspective, is a psychology about a vital and creative connection to life, only two self psychologists, Heinz Kohut (1976/1978a) and George Hagman (2000a), articulate the psychological processes, conscious and unconscious, associated with creative engagement.

Kohut (1976/1978a) and Hagman (2000a) each outline a three-phase creative encounter. These phases may be cyclical, and even mesh together for the artist, but it is helpful theoretically to examine them as a linear progression. Even though Kohut and Hagman's descriptions are closely related, they clearly vary in emphasis. Kohut uses his understanding of creativity to expand on his ideas on narcissism (or perhaps it is the other way around, and he uses his understanding of narcissism to expand on his ideas on creativity). Highlighting the transformation of mature healthy narcissism, Kohut's phases track the relation of sense of self to one's narcissistic energies as they engage the process and artistic medium. According to Kohut (1966/1978), "the transformation of narcissism, however, is a feature of the creator's *relation* [italics added] to his work" (p. 446). Because one's narcissistic energies interact with the medium and the emerging artwork, Kohut's view certainly implies relationship; however, Hagman, illustrating the progression in self psychology since Kohut, makes this relation explicit and extensively highlights the intersubjective interaction. Emphasizing mature self-object experience, he strongly acknowledges the presence of the other in the creative process. Both views offer vivid imagery that illuminates the felt experiences of creativity.

Kohut (1976/1978a) refers to the initial phase as the "precreative" time, when an artist experiences "precreative narcissistic tension . . . the narcissistic energies . . . remain in uncommitted suspension, waiting to be absorbed by the creative activity" (pp. 816-817). Because one's narcissistic energies are already invested toward the yet to exist artistic work, they are not completely available to sustain the artist's sense of self. The artist may experience fragmentation and a lack of self-cohesion. Hagman (2000a), immediately emphasizing the intersubjective relation between creator and product, describes the initial phase as one of "inspiration and self-crisis" when "the *artwork* [italics added] remains fragmentary and incomplete" (p. 285).

The availability of the medium and artwork to serve as functional selfobjects for the artist is curtailed. Kohut's vision of the uncommitted suspension of one's narcissistic energies and Hagman's understanding of the desire to engage the artistic medium, both signify that these are vulnerable times for artists, when they are trying to access the deeper levels of affects described earlier by Kohut, Stern, Dissanayake, and Hagman. These times require courage, and the selfobject needs of artists are usually heightened. Artists may feel the anxiety, depression, and hypochondria associated with a more fragmented sense of self. But if the artist does not possess some experience of self-stability, fragmentation becomes overwhelming and creativity cannot proceed.

According to Paul Taylor (1988), in his autobiography *Private Domain*, Merce Cunningham's original choice to use chance grew out of dealing with what appears to be the anxieties of the initial stage of the creative process. Taylor reports that Merce

> once told me that before using chance he had been going through a reclusive period and had found it difficult to work or even leave his loft much, and that John [Cage] had come to the rescue by encouraging him to use chance methods, thereby relieving him of the strain of decision making and enabling him to return to his creative work. (p. 47)

By alleviating his anxiety, chance methods freed Cunningham to reengage his creative processes, to move beyond the conscious manipulations of the mind to explore time and space, and, ultimately, derive an aesthetic that was uniquely his.

Many modern choreographers vividly confirm experiences of a precreative, inspirational time associated with self-crisis. Rosalind Newman states: "Beginnings have always been difficult for me. Before I begin, I feel sick. . . . It's that sense of vagueness of making something out of nothing when you just don't know what the hell you're doing, or what it is you want" (Newman, in Kreemer, 1987, p. 197). Dan Wagoner poignantly describes these experiences as

> times so frightening and depressing that it's only a thread by which I hold on to the idea that I am a choreographer. . . . [It] is the metaphysical problem of aesthetically jumping off a cliff—or at least spinning dangerously along the rim. It's this adventure that terrifies and at the same time exhilarates. (Wagoner, in Kreemer, 1987, pp. 26, 28)

Choreographer Betty Lind's (1960) description highlights the tenuous intersubjective experience:

> [A choreographer] begins the tension—the deep struggle between the need to pour forth the ideas and emotions . . . and the need to keep them in check in order to give them coherence, shape, form, meaning. And now is the time when all the frustrations come welling up, the sense of inadequacy, the insuperable obstacles that seem to confront him on every side. It is not an easy thing to look deep within one's self and to try to create something that will be alive—that will stand forth in its wholeness, in its own kind of truth. (p. 101)

In this initial and psychologically risky phase, the stirrings for creative activity begin as artists play with ideas and let go of preconceived conceptions in order to create something new derivative of their subjective experiences. At this point, choreographers often make use of improvisation as a form of exploratory and assertive play. These experiences of play help bring forth movement that is spontaneous and fresh. To choreographer Murray Louis (1980), the significance of playful improvisation is undeniable: "Improvisation is the practice of creativity" (p. 124). Choreographer Arnie Zane, working in collaboration with Bill T. Jones, describes the importance of improvisation to their initial processes:

> We'll have ideas, a title maybe, or some hooks to latch onto, but then, ultimately, the movement always comes first. We go into the studio with our latest and most welcomed addition, the JVC portable video system, and we improvise to our hearts delight, then sit and scrutinize our improvisation and try to find new directions. (Zane, in Kreemer, 1987, p. 115)

Kohut (1976/1978a) describes the second phase as one of "original thought" and "frantic creativity." Here the narcissistic energies of the artist are transferred, invested into the emerging artwork and, hence, as in the previous phase, are not at the complete disposal of the artist for the regulation of self-esteem. Kohut believes the transformation of narcissism from the artist to the emerging artwork is so intense that in hindsight the artist does not necessarily fully remember being the initiator of the work; the work has, indeed, taken on a life of its own. Choreographer Mel Wong succinctly speaks of this process: "Many times special things just happen and I accept them and they take me into another direction. Often when I'm choreographing it seems as if I'm not even doing it, somebody else is" (Wong, in Kreemer, 1987, p. 75).

Hagman (2000a) refers to the second phase as a time of "aesthetic resonance" to highlight "the intensification of feeling which the artist experiences both internally and externally because of the conjunction between self and work" (p. 287). Certainly other aspects of one's life can supply selfobject functions during the creative process, but the idea of aesthetic resonance captures the relationship between the artist and the coming-into-organization of the work. Without this experience of aesthetic resonance, the psychological and artistic challenges of the creative process are overwhelming and the emerging artwork cannot function as a selfobject for the artist.

Choreographer Rhoda Winter (1955) describes this second phase of creativity, integrating both Kohut's and Hagman's views:

> The creative impulse initiating the artistic effort itself, is in turn reinforced and re-stimulated by the organized form of the effort as it develops. There is the initial desire which sets off the art effort. Then the medium itself seems to "take over" and guide what happens, as the subject begins to develop. A closer examination reveals that what is happening is that the artist is attending closely to the sensorial stimuli the unfinished form is giving back to him as he works on it. The form is not directing the artist's action in some mysterious manner. It is the artist himself who is the directing force, as he experiences or perceives the nuances of change taking place in the form. (p. 3)

Winter's description illustrates her intersubjective aesthetic resonance with the form, initiated by her explorations and assertions, creating a mature selfobject experience. Hagman (1997) describes such activity:

> The self-experience of the artist is enhanced and vitalized when her self-expressive interests converge with the expressive potential of the medium. . . . In this light the "object" of the artist's creative efforts . . . can be understood to possess its own subjectivity, and the creative selfobject experience to be a dialectic in which the self of the artist and the independent subjective nature of the art form are engaged through the artist's effort and skill. (pp. 101-102)

And what psychologically happens to artists when in the exploration of their mediums they encounter dead ends, false starts, or as choreographers say, "when it is not working?" Hagman (1997) argues that these selfobject failures of the emerging art form contribute to the torment experienced by some artists: "In fact the torment of many creative personalities can be explained by their repeated encounters with selfobject failure (followed hopefully by restoration) as they pursue increasingly elusive and complex aesthetic challenges" (p. 102). The psychological risk and necessity for courage exemplified in these creative acts must be sustained by the subjective aesthetic resonance the artist feels with her/his medium and artwork.

During the final phase of quiet work, Kohut (1976/1978a) asserts that "the original ideas of the preceding phase are checked, ordered, and put into a communicative form" (p. 816). The artist's narcissistic energies are now more evenly distributed between one's sense of self and the product. However, the work is still a narcissistic extension of self, establishing a selfobject relation between artist and product. But, according to Kohut, embedded in this selfobject relation is the need for an ideal self-image. Indeed, Kohut (1987) claims: "The self is now in the work. . . . This is an extension of the self that is being perfected" (p. 277).

Hagman (2000a) refers to the final phase as the time of "transmuting externalization . . . when the artist's feeling of certainty gives way to sober reflection and reassessment" (p. 288). The artist, with a more objective eye, stands further back from the form to discover what is needed to finish the work, to connect it more directly to the aesthetic ideals the artist subjectively experiences. At this time, the artist may experience selfobject failure, not with another person, but with the artwork. Hagman, in agreement with Kohut, claims that the artist, in a final attempt to create an ideal image of her/his subjectivity through the form, works diligently

> to restore the selfobject tie, not through the accrual of self-structure [as in transmuting internalization], but through alteration of the artwork. . . . [T]he artist approaches the work

more synthetically with an eye toward the total organization of the work and the relationship between its formal components. (p. 289)

In order to accomplish this feat, the choreographer examines the work, not just from the kinetic viewpoint, but from the visual. Bill T. Jones proclaims the importance for the choreographer to create work that visually stands on its own, "to make works that deeply affect people and yet are cool and distant enough so that they can be observed like a sculpture, as a presence is observed. 'Food for the eye,' as [dance critic] Tobi Tobias once wrote" (Jones, in Kreemer, 1987, p. 121).

Significantly, as the artist attempts to deal with a subjective and critical evaluation of the artwork as it draws near to completion, she/he must muster a sense of courage and efficacy to cross over to the final step. In this way, according to Hagman (2000a), "the artist experiences his own power in bringing about the restoration of self-experience" (p. 290). Exploration, self-assertion, and efficacy combine in the intersubjective field to finalize an ideal form in order to bring about meaningful restoration. Hagman claims the artist is driven to

seek our the wonder of the aesthetic selfobject experience . . . to articulate and perfect a formally organized and ideal representation of lived experience. The skillful and talented artist can feel the potential for this experience in artistic activity; this is perhaps the source of the feeling of joy, which Kligerman described. (p. 290)

Consequently, this is, I believe, an extension of the basic motivational joy in creating derived from the efficacy pleasure associated with exploration and self-assertion. But now the efficacy is used to design an ideal representation through an intersubjective relation creating a more sophisticated, elaborated, and empowering experience of competence and transcendent joy.

Therefore, the artist must finally experience the transmuting externalization of an ideal image of meaningful subjectivity to have the art object function fully as a mature selfobject. Hagman (2000a) asserts the significance of this act:

Through art what is temporary and ineffable is expressed in terms that are permanent (even eternal), vivid, and beautiful. What is common becomes sublime. What is incomplete becomes whole. This is crucial to our understanding of creativity: the artist does not simply express feeling; rather, feel-

ing must be expressed in an ideal form. It is the accomplishment of an idealized formal organization that gives the cohesion, vitality, and continuity to the aesthetic experience and
thus the self-experience of the artist, and, by extension, the
experience of his or her audience. . . .

Although the artist seeks to express self-experience in ideal
form through his artwork, the idealization must authentically
reflect the artist's inner life. . . . The great work of art must be
idealized but true, expressing in objective form the depth and
breadth of the artist's inner life. (pp. 283-284)

Without the necessary idealization to supply a significant
and transcendent selfobject function genuinely reflecting the intersubjective relation between artist and medium, the work will remain
hollow. When successful, the artist has illuminated a meaningful
sense of being in the world and "beauty" is created. Choreographer
Leslie Satin (2000/01), in her essay "The Legs of the Theorist,"
describes choreographer Jimmy Waring's subjective relation to beauty and delight:

One thing about dancing with Jimmy Waring is that I learned
to take beauty seriously. Jimmy cared deeply about beauty
and its place in art, but he wasn't caught up in its conven-
tions; whatever else beauty meant in his work, it never meant
mere decoration. Acutely attuned to the details of a pose or
action, he hammered at a dancer until the shape was right,
but he created such utterly odd, absurd, *beautiful* shapes and
actions to perfect. One part of his legacy is the delight in finding beauty unexpectedly. (p. 122)

Indeed, Hagman (in press), in his article "A Sense of Beauty," claims
that our experience of beauty may be so powerful that our fears of
mortality are calmed. Within this idea of mortality Hagman includes:

the general vulnerability of a person to abandonment, self-crisis and loss. . . . [B]eauty is such a transcendent and ideal
experience that for a moment death and loss are overcome. . . .
[T]he pure and exquisite expression of the subjective, the
intangible and fragile, is given substance, formal perfection
and perhaps even immortality. (pp. 35, 21)

Hagman (in press) extends another way to examine transmuting externalization. He separates the affects connected to the
content—"non-aesthetic emotions"—from the affects connected to

the medium and the form—"aesthetic emotions" (p. 17). Content may reflect anything that incites a significant encounter for the artist, and consequently connects to her/his inner life. Hagman emphasizes that even emotions such as anger, murderous rage, and lust that embody the content, can be transformed by a great artist into an ideal form that is experienced as beautiful. For example, Paul Taylor's dance *Last Look* (1985) captures the depravity of society, but expresses the content through an ideal of motion that simultaneously seizes the potential destructive nature of humanity and transcends the audience to an aesthetic experience. But in striking contrast to the nonaesthetic emotions expressed in *Last Look*, Taylor's piece *Roses* (1985) contains content based on an appreciation of beauty itself, expressed through a transcendent form.

Even though for theoretical reasons it is helpful to examine the affects related to content and form separately, Hagman (in press) asserts that the aesthetic experience is actually "an amalgamation of aesthetic and non-aesthetic emotions" (p. 17). This is particularly easy to understand in dance, because content may be directly related to the bodily-felt experience of the medium. For example, content could be the subjective perception of the sensation and motion associated with weight. So the content itself may be a direct experience of the body, which is part of the medium. The medium, of course, is the foundation of the form. Consequently, in modern dance, because the medium is the body—the basic root of subjectivity for the dancer—the blending of the emotions concerned with content and form is often easily perceived.

From this perspective, the early postmodern choreographers, discussed at length in Chapter Two, wanted to get away from content that was not directly related to the medium as experienced in everyday life. For example, Steve Paxton's use of walking exemplifies "a shared experience that allows for personal idiosyncrasies and individual styles. There is no single correct way of walking" (Banes, 1987, p. 60). Paxton created several pieces that had, as the most basic aspect of content, the experience of walking. In *Satisfyin Lover* (1967) the crux of the piece is a large group of people who walk across the stage. There is certainly none of the intense direct content of, for instance, José Limón's masterpiece *The Moor's Pavane* (1949) based on Shakespeare's *Othello*. The result of Paxton's piece is a form that captures the content, which is the *experience of walking in everyday life*, and walking is a major element of the body-based medium and the form. Dance critic Jill Johnston (Johnston, in Banes, 1987) describes the effect on her as spectator:

> the incredible assortment of bodies, the any old bodies of our any old lives. . . . walking one after the other across the gym-

nasium in their any old clothes. The fat, the skinny, the medium, the slouched and slumped, the straight and tall, the bowlegged and knock-kneed, the awkward, the elegant, the coarse, the delicate, the pregnant, the virginal, the you name it, by implication every postural possibility in the postural spectrum, that's you and me in all our ordinary everyday who cares postural splendor. (p. 60)

What makes art special, during any era, is the relationship between the subjective content and the ideal formalization of this subjectivity. Hagman (in press) claims: "Primarily the restorative function of beauty is tied to the relationship between expressive content [nonaesthetic emotions] . . . and the perfection of form [aesthetic emotions] (by which the content is given organization, balance and most importantly wholeness)" (p. 20). For Hagman, the result of this integration is the capacity to find meaning in the work. This is the fundamental motivation for the experience of transmuting externalization, when the content and form have blended in a meaningful and significantly expressive ideal, bringing about an experience of transcendence. This is what makes art "beautiful."

These processes, of course, are not necessarily conscious to the creator. For example, I find the creation of an ideal of formal perfection as part of the creative process daunting; I prefer to let it lie as an unconscious motivation, deeply hidden. If I thought I was trying to create perfection, *I would never begin!* Perfection and ideal, objectively, mean the same things. Idiosyncratically, they do not *feel* the same to me. Perfection feels to me finite; even if I was capable of achieving it, I feel I would have no place to go beyond it. My journey would end. In contrast, my sense of an ideal inspires me. An ideal feels to me fluid, capable of alteration as I evolve—which, of course, it is, because an ideal is only an elaboration of my own idealization!

In my idiosyncratic response to the word "perfection," I am missing the important point that artists do not actually try to *produce* perfection, but to *pursue* it. Artists attempt to give form to what is most meaningful, most significant, most vital to their inner lives. Expressing and elaborating what is beyond the ordinary mundane aspects of life extends an experience of a transcendent ideal and perfection. Hagman (2001), in his article "A New Aesthetics for Psychoanalysis," illuminates this point:

A characteristic of all successful artistic efforts is that the result evokes the experience of beauty which transcends the artists intention. . . . [B]eauty can never be produced (except by imitation) but only evoked as a result of the pursuit of perfection. (p. 17)

The seeds for our aesthetic endeavors are the amodal experiences of the early relations between infant and caregiver described by Hagman, the global qualities of perception described by Stern, and the rhythm and modes described by Dissanayake. These relations, unless damaged, carry the ideal bliss of the pleasure humans intrinsically find in their offspring. Our biological survival is dependent upon this deeply rewarding and transcendent bond. The beginnings of intimacy and aesthetic pleasure are planted through the healthy idealization inherent in these relations.

In our creative endeavors we elaborate on these initial experiences, giving them texture, weaving them into new configurations now touched and expanded by the lived experiences of our lives. We are connected to our past, integrated with our present, propelled with hope for our future. If successful, we feel whole. We partake of, and are nourished by, the functioning aesthetic selfobject. Hagman (2001) continues:

> We all value and seek beauty as an opportunity for selfobject experience. When we are in the presence of something beautiful we are enlivened, we feel whole and happy. . . . [T]he artist does not make or produce a selfobject experience, he or she through the creative process engenders selfobject experience, and thus beauty; whether beauty is found in the external attributes of the object or in the interrelationship among the ideas that are concretized in the work. (pp. 16-17)

Consequently, the artist does not attempt to produce perfection, or an ideal for that matter, but to extend an external existence to subjective reality, and in the process to be enriched and transformed. Our creative responses, outgrowths from our early intimate and aesthetic ways of being, intermingled now with the present, elaborate the ideals that makes life meaningful. This is the pursuit of the artist, even when subjective experience, elaborated through art, is filled with angst and pain, expressive of turmoil and grief. Whatever the nonaesthetic emotional content, the expression through an aesthetic medium, resonating with our subjective rhythm and modes, brings about the mature selfobject experience in the creating and engaging of art.

What makes this profoundly meaningful is the journey, composed of hard work, discipline, exploration, self-assertion, and competence, expressive of what feels significant in life. Without a compelling connection to deeply felt action, words like "beauty," "perfection," and "ideal," are empty (G. Hagman, personal communication, January 3, 2001). For the choreographer/dancer this sense of action can be particularly powerful because the action is felt so directly through the body-self. By the end of the performance one is covered with sweat and feeling the rush of endorphins. But these actions are also empty without a sense of guiding ideals, of what makes life feel special beyond the ordinary.

I think of my work existing on a continuum. To the far left would stand forms/dances/writings of mine that are so bad I wouldn't want to claim ownership. To the far right would stand forms that are my ideals of formal perfection. I really, really want anything I create to stand to the right of the center of this continuum. Additionally, each time I create a form, I hope it is further to the right than my last creation. I am obviously in pursuit of my aesthetic ideals. Through such progression I experience a long-term process, a forward-moving journey, that convinces me that what I have done, to borrow a phrase from analyst D. W. Winnicott (1971/1986), is "good-enough" for the moment. I can progress further toward my ideal of perfection later.

But what is important to understand here is that my experience of a continuum only works because there is an ideal of perfection at one end (G. Hagman, personal communication, November 11, 2000). The capturing of unique action and idealization together makes art and art-making significant. The idiosyncratic integration of action, idealization, elaboration, and meaning provides a psychological grounding to partake of the aesthetic selfobject experience most completely, on all levels of subjectivity. Through this integration we find our experiences of beauty, ideals, perfection, reflected and expanded, illustrating what we take seriously in our lives, shared now with others. This is the significance of transmuting externalization; this is the significance of art-making.

But we all find ways to navigate through these processes, so demanding of psychic risk. My psychological use of a continuum reflects my idiosyncratic and subjective way of handling the anxieties of the creative process. My idealization, I believe, is clouded over by my sheer relief that when I have reached the final creative experience I can say, "Carol, it is 'good-enough'!" Just feeling it is good-enough thrills me—the thrill of good-enough may be my own tolerable level of idealization. Feeling that I might reach the goal of "good-enough" by the end keeps me going and functions as a container for my anxieties; the idea of creating an ideal image of perfection might just push me over the edge.

So, even though the thought of striving towards perfection would instigate creative paralysis in my life, I am aware of guiding ideals that bring meaning to my life and propel me towards mutuality, towards sharing artistically who I am and seeking nourishment from the creation of others. In the end, words like perfection, ideal, beauty, transcendence, meaning, creativity are all just avenues we use to comprehend what subjectively makes life worth living, individually and collectively. Each of us, with vitality and reciprocity, translates these words into subjective experience to express significance. Other than that, they are just words.

Even with the perfecting of an ideal image functioning as an aesthetic selfobject, both Hagman (2000a) and Kohut (1964/1978) believe that when the work is finally done, there is a decrease in the artist's psychological investment in the work. Kohut particularly emphasizes this as a result of the work having been communicated. Hagman articulates that this experience reinforces the creative process to being again: "In most cases the aesthetic resonance with the completed artwork will fade, and although the work may always hold some positive meaning for the artist, the search for transcendence and renewal must be reengaged" (p. 290).

Surely choreographers disengage the concentration of their energies from one finished piece as they encounter the next. I have always been amazed, though, that a visual artist paints a picture, sells it, and never sees it again. Perhaps if I had a greater power to connect to my work as an ideal form, this might not feel so foreign to me. I might internalize the experiences of transmuting externalization more fully and find letting go easier. But I do not believe that my response is solely idiosyncratic—just partly.

In dance, for an artwork to exist it needs the dancer. Many choreographers perform their own works. Each performance can feel different. For those dances set on others, the choreographer not only deals with her/his own subjective relation to motion, but the performers idiosyncratic movement preferences. In the documentary film *Paul Taylor: Dancemaker* (Scheuer, Kupfer, & Diamond, 1998), Taylor states he is fortunate if he gets 60 percent of what he really wants from his dancers. Additionally, with every cast change the piece can feel different to choreographer and audience. For instance, when Taylor (1988) first choreographs *Little Circus* (1955), David Vaughan dances the role of ringmaster. "When the part is later danced more menacingly by Jimmy Waring, it osmoses from what was intended as comedy into something more macabre" (p. 61). British choreographer Richard Alston

> revealed that one of the reasons why he decided to join the [Rambert Dance] company was his interest in seeing how a work evolves with repeated performance. As a repertory company, Rambert provided opportunities for him to revise his choreography, either during the early performances of a work or when re-casting it, sometimes years later. (Kane, 1999, pp. 14-15)

In dance, the artwork is "alive" based on the sheer immediacy of the dancer's presence. Without the action of dancing, no dance exists. Except for the elusive memory, the ephemeral nature of dance is paramount. Merce Cunningham (Cunningham, in Brown, Mindlin, & Woodford, 1998) captures the passion and vitality necessary to be sustained by an artform that vanishes:

> you have to love dancing to stick to it. it gives you nothing back, no manuscripts to store away, no paintings to show on walls and maybe hang in museums, no poems to be printed and sold, nothing but that single fleeting moment when you feel alive. it is not for unsteady souls. (p. 90)

Over time, the intensity of the relation of the choreographer to the dance usually decreases; however, the sheer immediacy of the "lived experience" that creates the very existence of choreography may cause a greater sense of resonance for the choreographer. Hence, the selfobject function of the artwork may carry greater significance than for those artists not involved in a performing art form. Additionally, and as a choreographer I find this a most soothing thought, when done with a dance, because its existence is a lived experience, I can always change it down the road, should I discover a perhaps more ideal movement expression. As a writer, I truly lament that this is not true when it comes to the published word.

But, in the end, I cannot reiterate enough that all creative activity carries the idiosyncratic patterning of the creator. Choreographer Tere O'Connor (Open Discussion with the Artist, July 13, 2000, Santa Barbara, CA) makes dance-theater pieces intermingling movement with text. He writes the text in solitude, then works with his dancers to clarify and develop the characterizations further and to incorporate movement. His work is not meant to be recast and is not for sale for other companies to put in their repertories. Once done with a piece, O'Connor is completely prepared to move on to creating the next one. He doesn't resurrect his work. O'Connor also paints; when done with creating the painting, he tosses it out.

Hagman (2000a) makes a final and significant point regarding the ending stage of creativity. The culminating experience of transmuting externalization is when "the artist's inner experience changes in response to the artwork" (p. 289). This implies that the artist, if successful, ultimately experiences not just self-delineation and self-cohesion, but self-development and self-transformation. I elaborate more on this idea when discussing the selfobject function of form.

To summarize: Kohut and Hagman each describe three phases of creativity. Kohut's phases track the journey of one's narcissistic energies from the precreative time when one's narcissistic energies are in suspension, to the time of frantic creativity and original thought when there is an outpouring of narcissistic energy, to the final time of quiet work when the external object has enough coherence that the artist can finish her/his subjective and ideal molding of it. Hagman's phases track the intersubjective relation that the artist creates with the medium and the artwork. Phase one is inspiration and self-crisis, when the relation is obscure and the capacity for selfobject functioning limited. Phase two is aesthetic resonance, when the artist feels a dynamic conjuncture with the emerging artwork and there is a reciprocal relation between evolving object and artist. Phase three is transmuting externalization, when the artist reflects upon what has been created to refine it into an ideal image. Consequently, the artwork, demonstrating the artist's subjective meaningful expression of beauty, has the capacity to extend a mature and transcendent selfobject function through intersubjective relating. The creator may even feel transcendent of the vulnerability of mortality. The ultimate result of transmuting externalization is self-development and self-transformation. One's dynamic exchange with culture expands.

THE SELFOBJECT FUNCTION OF FORM

Dan Wagoner, illustrating his intersubjective relation to his art form and its deeply felt effect upon his life, appears to have experienced transcendent transmuting externalization:

> I'm really trying to get something across to myself. Choosing a problem that's to be solved by movement, exploring the problem as deeply as I can, and from this making movement choices that are finally put together as a dance, gives me a structure within which to dance and live. . . .
> As this chain of activity fills the years, it becomes a history or record of a life. . . . This is the only way I can judge if a dance works. If it becomes a strong part of my life, then I feel it works. (Wagoner, in Kreemer, 1987, pp. 28, 31, 32)

Wagoner's relation to his individual dances extends further to include his repertory functioning as a history of his life. The building of such a repertory intensifies the capacity for the choreographer's inner experience to be altered. Indeed, as choreographers develop their collections of work, consistencies occur, styles of movement evolve, aesthetic signatures that profoundly speak of their individual selves become strikingly apparent. This is true even for a choreographer like Tere O'Connor (Open Discussion with the Artist, July 13, 2000, Santa Barbara, CA) who does not feel the same type of direct connection to past pieces as Wagoner. O'Connor's work began as purely kinetic, before developing into dance-theater. His choreographic evolution signifies his path to unearth, clarify, and refine his own personal voice and vision.

More direct examples are Belgium choreographer Anne Teresa De Keersmaeker's "familiar vocabulary of spiral air turns into the floor and energetic rebounds" (Genter, 1999, p. 87) and choreographer Laura Dean's early vibrant and intense connection to spinning. Dean is

> adamant about having discovered and developed her style of spinning on her own. This style was characterized by an even distribution of weight across both feet, with the body and arms free to take a variety of positions as the dancer spins. (Matheson, 1999, p. 89)

Wendy Perron (2001) identifies Twyla Tharp's aesthetic signatures in her two pieces, *Mozart Clarinet Quintet K. 581* (2000) and *Surfer at the River Styx* (2000):

> *Like all her work* [italics added], these two pieces demand the dancers to be fully alive every nanosecond and to merge ballet and modern dance seamlessly. From ballet, Tharp uses the strength and suppleness of the legs as well as the expansiveness of the upper body; from modern, the stirrings in the core of the body. Tharp herself brings the ability to create flow, no matter how disjunctive the movements are. (p. 46)

Dance critic Lewis Segal's (2001) review of the same two dances also highlights the continuity of Tharp's idiosyncratic presence in her work: "Twyla Tharp still packs more movement into less time with a greater sense of flow—indeed, a kind of throwaway ease—than anybody in dance" (p. F1).

Dance critic Joan Acocella (1993), in her biography of choreographer Mark Morris, describes his psychological and subjective tie to one of his prominent aesthetic signatures:

What Morris is interested in is exposure, and this helps to
explain another curiosity of his choreography, his love of the
buttocks. . . . Morris is constantly showing the buttocks. . . .
   "I love to see their butts," says Morris. That love is not erot-
ic, or not mostly. If it were, the butts would look sexier. . . .
No, what he is after is the thing that is *underneath*, both literally and metaphorically. The buttocks are an innocent, hard-
working part of the body—soft and round, the seat of humili-
ty, the place that gets kicked. To Morris they seem to represent something modest and tender and unacknowledged, the
body's vulnerability. At the same time, what they represent in
dance terms is the body's dignity, for they are the motor of
action: they contain the pelvis, from which the movement
originates. So in both senses the buttocks harbor a fundamental truth, and one that in Morris's eyes is validated by the
fact that it requires exposure. (pp. 76-79)

Such a specific and personal aesthetic of a choreographer further
enhances the selfobject function of the form, because now form is not
composed of an individual dance, but a collection of dances that exemplify the artist's subjectivity through idiosyncratic artistic choices.
   Choreographer Moses Pendleton comments: "The dance does
reflect the life" (Pendleton, in Smith, 1985, p. 52). Dance critic
Amanda Smith (1985) supports these inferences in her review of
Pendleton's choreographic television piece, *Moses Pendleton Presents
Moses Pendleton*:

   Zany and extravagant as it is, *Moses Pendleton Presents
   Moses Pendleton* is nonetheless a portrait of an artist coming
   to terms with his demons, channeling the life force into
   dance. It is a work about dance as a life-sustaining activity,
   and it implies that dance is a metaphor for life itself. (p. 53)

   I believe the cohesion and development experienced through
such choreographic processes, through the process of transmuting
externalization, resonates with the role interpretation plays in analysis. Analysts Peter Buirski and Pamela Haglund (1999) in their article "The Selfobject Function of Interpretation" discuss the way interpretation in analysis, extended within the context of an empathic
therapeutic relationship, serves a selfobject function:

   That is, new cognitive understanding not only satisfies the
   longing to be understood, but the function of *making sense of
   the totality of one's life experience* [italics added] also pro-

motes self-understanding, self-delineation, self-continuity and self-cohesion. Furthermore, new self-understanding contributes to the construction of new organizations of experience. (p. 33)

Essentially, Haglund and Buirski argue that the giving of form, in this case verbal shape, to experience serves a vital selfobject function. "What we are trying to emphasize is that putting into words the patient's developmental dynamics has the selfobject function of promoting self-understanding—the understanding of one's organization of experience in the context of one's personal development" (p. 36).

I am not at all suggesting that choreographing should or could take the place of an analysis. Nor am I suggesting that analysis can take the place of creative engagement in life, even though a successful analysis should clearly enhance one's capacities to be creatively productive. I am suggesting that choreographers find the creation of the form—the dance—its ability to stand separate from them, and the unfolding of a collection of works, as fulfilling significant mature selfobject needs, and ultimately extending self-understanding. In this way, the act of choreographing and the existence of the choreography/repertory articulate the creator's sense of self. Choreographer Louis Falco blatantly states that choreographing "translates my daily life into some order and seems to define it" (Falco in Dunning, 1978, p. 16). I argue that when choreographing can fulfill such a function through exploration and self-assertion, the unfolding processes, and the idealized final form, creative engagement can supply self-definition, self-cohesiveness, and self-development, and is ultimately self-transformative.

Hagman (1997), describing further the mature selfobject experience, asserts: "My claim will be that it is through the recognition of otherness within mature selfobject experience that 'new' self-experience occurs, adding to the self in often unpredictable and surprising ways" (p. 86). In the case of choreographing, the "otherness" is the medium, the emerging and finished artwork, repertory, the anticipated audience, and the art field, all of which the dancer endows with her/his own subjectivity. This intersubjective connection between the choreographer's internal subjectivity and the external subjectivity of the "other" propels the mature selfobject function and leads to new discoveries of self. Consequently, if successful, the choreographer, by giving form to her/his subjectivity, experiences self-stabilization, self-delineation, self-development, and self-transformation. Defining both Kohut's views on creativity and narcissism and Hagman's views on creativity and mature selfobject experience, choreographer Betty Lind (1960) states: "The artist has lost part of himself in giving life to his vision but in the process he has become immeasurably enriched" (p. 101). Indeed, "over time . . . the choreographer and dancer become the dance as well. They are danced by the dance" (G. Hagman, personal communication, January 20, 2001).

Certainly, the psychological gains for the artist from the experiences of creativity—exploratory self-assertion, vitality, competency, reciprocity with an other, confirmation, self-cohesion, self-transformation—are immense, but there is always psychological risk. The artist must possess enough psychological strength to destabilize, without overwhelming fragmentation, in order to venture into new realms and discoveries. The need for functioning selfobjects is paramount. The ability to find sustaining selfobjects is a sign of health. Artists must have the capacity to shore up their selves and find fulfillment for their selfobject needs as they progress through the significant and challenging phases of creativity.

COMPENSATORY STRUCTURES, CREATIVITY, AND THE CASE OF MR. M.

Does this mean that if a person develops defects in a primary structure of the nuclear self there is no capacity to eventually sustain the psychological commitment to the creative process? No, in this situation compensatory structures may become significant. Compensatory structures, as previously described, develop when one avenue of growth is faulty or curtailed, and another pathway supplements. "Kohut defines a compensatory structure as a talent, skill or even a relationship that is reliable and may function . . . as a source of healthy self-esteem" (Siegel, 1996, p. 108). For Kohut (1984), the intrapsychic patterning of a healthy individual, capable of creativity, does not necessarily employ equal divisions between ambitions, ideals, and talents, or primary and compensatory structures.

Indeed, Kohut (1984) specifically believes that people who achieve the highest levels of creative accomplishment have high levels of compensatory structures: "It is my impression that the most productive and creative lives are lived by those who, despite high degrees of traumatization in childhood, are able to acquire new structures by finding new routes toward inner completeness" (p. 44). Such people during childhood are able to employ creative psychological solutions to experiences of trauma and as a result continue healthier development. In Kohut's words:

> I believe we can state with assurance that it is not a measure
> of pathology but a sign of resourcefulness and health when a
> self—nondefensively—demonstrates in the transference that it

had, already during its early development, turned away from hopeless frustrations and found new paths or at least made partially successful moves in the new direction. (p. 45)

To demonstrate the importance that compensatory structures can play in creative productivity, Kohut (1977) supplies the case study of Mr. M., a writer blocked in his creative endeavors by elements of his archaic untransformed narcissism. Mr. M.'s writer's block is in response to a defective sense of self. When Mr. M. was a child, his mother was not capable of providing a sufficient mirroring selfobject function; therefore, Mr. M. developed a defect in a primary structure of his nuclear self. Attempting to establish compensatory structures for this primary defect, Mr. M. turned more intensely to his father, searching for an idealizable selfobject to strengthen the second constituent of the self, the pole of ideals. Unfortunately, his father, because of his own defective sense of self, was not able to fully accept Mr. M.'s idealization; however, his father's responses are less traumatic than his mother's. Kohut, emphasizing Mr. M.'s attempt to acquire structures, through his relation with his father and his father's talents, to compensate for the chronic empathic failures of his mother, writes:

Mr. M. must have tried, during his childhood, first to idealize and then to acquire (i.e., to integrate into his own self) certain of his father's abilities—abilities which seem to have played an important role in the father's personality and which the father seemed to have valued highly—especially his father's skill in the use of language, of words. (p. 11)

Consequently, it is not just the idealization of his father that is significant, but additionally, the idealization that Mr. M. associates with the ability to use language proficiently. Important to remember here, *self is not an entity, but a pattern of experience*. In Mr. M.'s experience of self, his relation to the capacity to use words becomes a compensatory structure. Therefore, compensatory structures are sought in the pole of ideals and the realm of talents and skills. As an adult, Mr. M. works as a writer; we assume he has some talent with words, giving some cohesion to the constituent of self that supports his talents and skills.

But, because of the lack of sustaining mirroring from his mother and the faulty responsiveness on the part of his father, the compensatory structure is fragmented and Mr. M. experiences destabilizing archaic narcissism when he writes. To keep from feeling overwhelmed he must inhibit the full potential of his aesthetic imagination. He is not capable of fully using his talents to find the greatest vitality possible in connection to them. In order for these talents to come to fruition he needs greater self-cohesion.

By initially entering into a mirroring transference with the analyst, Mr. M. succeeds in strengthening some aspects of the primary structure in the pole of ambitions and self-expression. But Kohut feels this work remains incomplete. No matter, because the significant increase in psychic stability for Mr. M. comes in response to the strengthening of the compensatory structures. After the initial mirroring transference, Mr. M. establishes an idealizing selfobject transference with the analyst. Through this therapeutic dyad and transmuting internalization, the compensatory structures gain in sustenance and Mr. M. is capable of experiencing transformed mature healthy narcissism and enacting a program of action. These actions, most specifically, entail Mr. M. establishing a school of writing for others.

Kohut (1977) summarizes Mr. M.'s understanding of the connections between his now healthier sense of self and his ability to be creatively productive:

> We have been able to strengthen my compensatory psychological structures sufficiently so that I can now be active and creative. . . . The devotion to meaningful goals and the very act of creating solidify my self, give me a feeling of being alive, real, and worthwhile. . . . I have . . . found a psychological equilibrium between *the product* (an extension of myself)—my absorbing devotion to it, my joy in perfecting it—and *the self* (a center of productive initiative)—the exhilarating experience that I am producing the work, that I have produced it. Although I am thus joyfully aware of myself, I no longer become hypomanically overstimulated while creating, nor do I fear, as I used to, that my self will be drained away into the product of my creativeness. The self as a joyfully experienced center of initiative and the product of which I am proud are in an unbroken psychological connection now. (pp. 17-18)

Mr. M. no longer is overwhelmed by archaic untransformed narcissism; his transformed mature healthy narcissism permits him to maintain enough self-stability to withstand the psychological stresses and strains naturally brought about by the creative processes as described earlier by Kohut and Hagman. He establishes aesthetic resonance with his work and seeks to perfect the product of his labors to experience transmuting externalization—"The devotion to meaningful goals and the very act of creating solidify my self, give me a feeling of being alive, real, and worthwhile." Most significantly, the case of Mr. M. illustrates the necessity for the artist to work from a healthy aspect of self, whether primary or compensatory, to transverse the psychologically risky and subjectively enriching path of creativity.

Chapter Five, "Paul Taylor: A Case Study," provides an example of compensatory structures connected to the self-expression of artistic talents—the poles of ambitions and skills. For many modern dance choreographers we can surmise the possibility that self-cohesion may be experienced through compensatory structures. Additionally, a healthy connection to a sensual motivational system, which provides reliable primary and/or compensatory structures, may be paramount. As with the development of the dominance of a motivational system, the significance of the possibility that sensory awareness may supply compensatory structure to self-experience can only be examined through the idiosyncratic subjectivity of each individual choreographer. When sensuality does extend compensatory structure, reinforcement of this structure, for instance through somatic experience, surely lends cohesion to the choreographer as she/he undergoes the creative process.

TRANSFERENCES OF CREATIVITY

Even for the psychologically healthy artist, the psychological courage necessary to be creative may require sustenance—selfobject experience—to ensure self-cohesion. To illustrate avenues artists may take to acquire cohesion, Kohut (1976/1978a) describes "transferences of creativity" in which individuals engaged in intense creative activity, in order to fulfill their intensified needs for selfobjects seek out selfobject transferences to buttress their self-esteem. Some artists are fortunate enough to align themselves with transferences of creativity that continually function as sustaining selfobjects; for others the relationships wane and new transferences of creativity are required for the beginning of a new creative endeavor. To approach these transferences simply, they supply temporary compensatory sustaining experiences, or if lucky, more continual support, during creative periods when one's sense of self is involved in risk-taking.

For Kohut (1976/1978a), the most poignant example is Freud's relationship with Wilheim Fliess during Freud's self-analysis. Kohut feels that Freud's intense idealization of Fliess at this time is directly related to Freud's writing "his decisive scientific contribution and greatest work, *The Interpretation of Dreams*" (p. 804). Kohut asserts that after the work is done, Freud's need for Fliess as an idealized selfobject dissolves:

In other words, for Freud during his most important creative spell, Fliess was the embodiment of idealized power; and Freud was able to dispense with the illusory sense of Fliess's greatness and thus with the narcissistic relationship [the transference of creativity] . . . after he had completed his great creative task. (pp. 822-823)

Kohut cites other artists as examples. For each artist, the nature of the transference of creativity—mirroring, idealizing, or twinship—is based on where the individual psychological structure of that particular artist is most fragile. For Nietzsche, the transference of creativity is fulfilled by an idealizing transference. Kohut (1980) claims: "There is Nietzsche's attachment to the idealized Wagner during the time when he prepared himself for the great outpouring of his most original works" (p. 493). Kohut sees Eugene O'Neill fulfilling this need with a mirroring transference:

There is O'Neill's lifelong, desperate search for the selfobject that would satisfy his need for perfect "mirroring," for that "gleam in the mother's eye" which his drug-addicted mother had not provided for him. When he finally found it in his third wife, he was able to create his best works. (pp. 493-494)

Kohut (1976/1978a) believes that Picasso established a transference of creativity of twinship (alter-ego) with the painter Georges Braque:

The presence of an alter ego and the narcissistic relationship to it [transference of creativity], one might speculate, protected the self of the artist [Picasso] from the danger of irreversible fragmentation to which it felt exposed while it was drained of narcissistic energies during periods when the genius-artist allowed the visual universe to break into meaningless pieces before he reassembled them and, in so doing, gave Western man a new perception of the visible world. (p. 820)

In modern dance there have been many obvious transferences of creativity: the relationship between Martha Graham and her musical director, Louis Horst; Doris Humphrey and her dance partner, Charles Weidman, and her protégé, José Limón; Merce Cunningham and his musical director, composer John Cage; Judith Dunn and her work with musician Bill Dixon; the collaborative experience for those participating in the Judson Dance Theater during the 1960s, and in general, choreographers' relationships to their dancers and to other choreographers.

Twyla Tharp's (Tharp, in Perron, 2001) relationship to her company members embodies transferences of creativity. She describes her dancers as "great"; her sustaining idealization is clear. Most revealing, her definition of greatness does not include their technical virtuosity, but highlights their subjective relations to movement and to their way of "being":

> Greatness; how do I see greatness? Ambition, sweetness, personableness . . . I mean there's something absolutely connected, a commitment that goes beyond sincerity. English does not supply the right descriptions for greatness—you just feel it. (p. 46)

Tharp's appreciation of her dancers' subjectivities signifies her subjective relations to them. Without them, her creative elaborations have no existence:

> Roslyne Stern, *Dance Magazine* president, remembers that when Tharp was presented with the Dance Magazine Award in 1981, she surrounded herself with her dancers, saying that they deserved the award as much as she did. (p. 48)

Sustenance comes not only from people functioning as selfobjects, but also from representations of others that have been internalized. For instance, Martha Graham acknowledges the influence of her father—the person who initially informed Graham, when she was young, that movement never lies. His insistence to her that "that which you are comes out in your movement. . . . Movement is like a barometer, a barometer of the soul's weather" (Graham, in Sorell, 1963, p. 53) encapsulates the guiding compass of Martha Graham's life as an artist—the belief that movement reveals all. Molissa Fenley gains self-sustenance from her idealized view of Martha Graham: "Choreographically, the person I've learned the most from is Martha Graham. She is my hero" (Fenley, in Kreemer, 1987, p. 215). Dan Wagoner has a strong internalized idealistic image of his father as a man having "more insight and wisdom than anyone I have ever known" (Wagoner, in Kreemer, 1987, p. 27). One can empathically imagine the reassurance that such an internalized image must offer during psychologically perilous and vulnerable times.

Of course, as emphasized earlier, functioning selfobjects do not have to be people, but can be places, things, activities, ideas, pets, and so forth. Kohut (1976/1978a) writes that because of the inherent vulnerability during creativity, artists need to "attempt to protect their creative activity by surrounding it with superstitions

and rituals" (p. 819). I see this as an extension of the idea of transferences of creativity, and I believe that choreographers use such rituals as functioning selfobjects to sustain self-cohesion. In my own
experiences as a choreographer, the daily ritualistic ascension into a
familiar studio, a space that reminds me that indeed the day before I
was able to create some sense from movement, provides me with a
deep reassurance.

I believe one is never too young in life, while undertaking the
creative process, to pay attention to the transferences of creativity
and rituals that arise. When my nephew Dylan was nine, he com-
plained to me that the dance class I taught his third grade class was
held weekly instead of daily. With such a long break, he found it difficult to remember the choreography that he and his friend were working on. When I suggested that they work on the piece outside of class,
Dylan looked at me aghast, as if, I, of all people, should understand
better. He emphatically exclaimed to me: "I need the dance room! I
need the atmosphere!" Obviously, I had not been sensitive enough to
his need for his own daily ascension into a familiar studio space.

THE SENSE OF GROUP SELF, GROUP COHESION, AND CULTURAL SELFOBJECTS

Ellen Dissanayake (1988), in her book *What is Art For?*, claims that
rituals and ceremonies worldwide, in addition to reinforcing self-
cohesion, are paramount for group cohesion. Such events yield
stronger impressions on members of society when they are "made
special" by artistic expression. Therefore, from her perspective, the
development of artistic behavior was, first, and foremost, to enrich
the psychological and emotional strength of the group. Dissanayake
asserts that the arts produce "an embodiment and reinforcement of
socially shared significances" (p. 200). Because they function as selfobjects to support group cohesion, Kohut (1984) refers to these art
products and shared experiences as cultural selfobjects.

These claims do not begin to fully answer the question: How
is it that art makes something special, not just for the individual,
but for the group? Especially, as I repeatedly argue in this book, the
creation of art connects so directly to the subjectivity of the individual. A further understanding of the commonality between group
members that enables the arts to function as cultural selfobjects is
needed.

Both Hagman (in press) and Dissanayake (2000) claim that
the roots for art-making are found in the mother/infant dyad and
the healthy human experiences of idealization that permeate this
relation. Dissanayake, in agreement with Stern, emphasizes rhythms

and modes, the amodal perceptions key to the young infant's interactions with her/his environment and the people who inhabit it. Our
unconscious patterns of these early interactions are then elaborated
later in life, to acknowledge the significance and meaning they carry.
Through these creative activities we contextualize our primal experiences of rhythms and modes with new life experiences, dynamically
engaging the intra-, inter-, and metasubjective. Ultimately, these
aesthetic elaborations are transformative for the individual and the
group. Dissanayake asserts:

> It is important not to lose sight of the fact that ceremonies
> work by *producing changes in and structuring feelings*. . . . As
> rhythmic-modal sensitivities and capacities evolved to enable
> the emotional dispositions by which mothers and infants
> engaged in mutuality, so could elaborations of these sensitivi-
> ties and capacities become vehicles for social coordination and
> concord, instilling belonging, meaning, and competence, which
> are feelings that comprise psychological well-being. (p. 140)

Creative endeavors, whether elaborated by the group in ceremony,
by the artist, or by the individual decorating her/his kitchen, resonate with these early experiences of rhythms and modes. Through
aesthetic elaboration, these deeply felt aspects of our humanity are
brought beyond the mundane, to meaningful experiences of subjective beauty and transcendence.

Consequently, early idealization, rhythms and modes, and
qualities of perception—foundations of subjectivity and mutuality—
continue to nourish us through the arts. Kohut (1960/1978) argues
that the arts link participants to primal aspects of themselves that
have become dulled or buried, providing an avenue for experiences of
greater authenticity. Significantly, Daniel Stern (1985) extends an
understanding of how these essential early human experiences have
become dulled and buried.

Stern perceives these aesthetic yearnings, of the individual
and the group, to be ignited by the disjuncture that occurs when the
young child crosses the threshold from preverbal experience to symbolic language. Before language development during the second year
of life, infants mainly experience across modalities through qualities
of perception and vitality affects. Even though the different senses—
touch, sight, hearing—are used Stern still believes the global gestalt
of experience is primary. Stern uses the example of an infant gazing
at a patch of yellow sunlight on the wall. Before language development "the infant will experience the intensity, warmth, shape, bright-
ness, pleasure, and other amodal aspects of the patch. The fact that
it is yellow light is not primary" (p. 176).

Language changes this. With symbolic representation comes a greater emphasis on modality, in this case visual perception, and a greater separation from more global qualities. According to Stern (1985):

> Someone will enter the room and say, "Oh, *look* at the *yellow* sun*light!*" Words in this case separate out precisely those properties that anchor the experience to a single modality of sensation. By binding it to words, they isolate the experience from the amodal flux [qualities of perception] in which it was originally experienced. Language can thus fracture amodal global experience. A discontinuity in experience is introduced.
> What probably happens in development is that the language version "yellow sunlight" of such perceptual experiences becomes the official version, and the amodal version goes underground and can only resurface when conditions suppress or outweigh the dominance of the linguistic version. Such conditions might include certain contemplative states, certain emotional states, and the perception of certain works of art that are designed to evoke experiences defying verbal categorization. (p. 176)

The individuals that comprise the group have all experienced this developmental wedge between the qualitative experience and the symbolic representation. "Language forces a space between interpersonal experience as lived and as represented" (Stern, 1985, p. 182). According to Stern, this is the common bond. This is what allows the group to understand that level of subjectivity that artists access through their permeable sieves, the preverbal qualitative gestalt. This is what enables the group to understand that artistic expression connected to group activity makes it special. This connects the group, as individuals sharing a group experience, to the need for art. This is what allows the arts to function as cultural selfobjects and to support, not just self-cohesion, but group-cohesion. The most meaningful aspects of culture capture this necessity.

Of course, art is a symbolic representation. However, Dissanayake (2000) argues that symbols and images themselves do not make art. The need to elaborate, to assign special significance, is intrinsic to our need for aesthetic experiences. Dissanayake explains:

> While it is true that only humans make images and that images are symbolic, an image (or symbol) need not be elaborated any more than a tool or word or movement need be elaborated. . . .

The remarkable fact about humans is not only that they began to make images or symbols but that they so frequently elaborated these images or symbols or used them to elaborate something else. (p. 146)

Through elaboration we take symbols and once again connect them to the rhythm and modes of amodal perception:

Even to modern adults, it is not only *symbolic* but *analogical* meanings in the arts that are affecting; we respond cross-modally and emotionally to the swoop and exuberance of a dance movement, the sense of hesitation or resignation and defeat in an actor's gesture, or the thick guttural innuendo in a jazz singer's voice, usually before recognizing or assigning symbolic "meaning" to the dance style or the spoken or sung words. (p. 147)

To accommodate our needs for mutuality, belonging, exploration, self-assertion, vitality, competence, meaningful ideals, we use elaboration to tie us to our fundamental emotional and psychological human existence. In contemplating Stern's and Dissanayake's work, I feel a profound respect for those artists who make use of symbolic language—poets, dramatists, writers, choreographers involved in dance-theater—who strive artistically to bridge these gaps, who, through talent and perseverance, evoke global amodal experiences through words.

Early modern choreographer Charles Weidman (Weidman, in Brown, Mindlin, & Woodford, 1998) captures the sense of the artist connecting, through her/himself, to the group, to contribute to the meaning of culture:

I have always been impatient with the "art pour l'artist." Clarity and understandability has remained the basis of my dance creations. Their intent, concerned with human values and the experience of our times, must be carried by the fullest emotional impact the artist can muster. Then, with the conception of the idea, the intelligibility of its message and the emotional intensity of presentation, the artist's primordial task is fulfilled and—however his artistic deliverance may be judged—his sincerity cannot be doubted. (p. 67)

ARTISTIC ANTICIPATION AND OPTIMAL OPERATIVE
PERVERSITY

Kohut (1977) believes that artists, as participants within the sense of group self and culture, because of their heightened sensitivities and vulnerabilities, because their experiences of self develop within prevalent child-rearing practices and the specificity of their historical era, reflect to society the most important psychological realities of their times at an accelerated rate. Kohut calls this the "hypothesis of artistic anticipation" and claims:

> The artist—the great artist, at any rate—is ahead of his time in focusing on the nuclear psychological problems of his era, in responding to the crucial psychological issue man is facing at a given time, in addressing himself to man's leading psychological task. (p. 285)

One aspect that permits the "great artist" to accomplish this feat is described by analyst Carl Rotenberg (1992) as "optimal operative perversity." Optimal refers to the "quality and degree of unusualness that also achieves an [artistic] integration" (p. 177). Operative refers to the technical skill of the artist to create an artistic whole. Perversity refers to the "artist's initiative . . . to call into question and reverse a previously held artistic structural assumption. . . . Art is ordered but within that structural consistency there is the expectable introduction of disorder, and perverse expression is an agent of this change" (p. 172). Clearly, perversity just for the sake of perversity is not enough to create significant and meaningful art. The artist's subjectivity must push her/his work in a dynamic and changing direction, in response to the medium, the art field, and culture. The work must reflect these multileveled subjective relations. Rotenberg asserts this important goal of optimal operative perversity:

> The artist engages in perverse expression because it is essential to the process of creativity. The artist's goal is to incorporate information that will transform or expand existing assumptions and structures by changing the rules. He achieves this goal within a context of evolving artistic knowledge that has its own traditions and does so in some form that is readily observable. In the course of this activity he creates problems to which he must respond. Hopefully, this series of initiatives and subsequent responses will result in an integrated aesthetic that expresses the artist's individual style. (p. 174)

Modern dance has always had its full of optimal operative perversity from its early inceptions through the present. Indeed, the premise of modern dance is based upon the belief, and dependent upon the existence, of such perversity. Without it Isadora Duncan would never have lifted her chest to the heavens; Martha Graham would never have contracted her pelvis; Charles Weidman would never have developed pantomimic dance dramas; Doris Humphrey would never have fallen and recovered; Merce Cunningham would never have thrown the I Ching; the postmodern choreographers would never have walked across the stage, or carried mattresses, or danced on rooftops; Laura Dean would never have spun; and Bill T. Jones would never have produced multimodal pageantry.

Martha Graham's optimal operative perversity can be seen not just to reflect her intrasubjective expressions, but clearly her intersubjective relation to her medium, and her metasubjective relation to culture—a culture that did not expect a woman to be an artist. Feminist scholars Deborah Johnson and Wendy Oliver (2001), in their book *Women Making Art*, illuminate Graham's muiltileveled subjective perversity:

> As early as 1926, she said her audience "came because I was such a curiosity—a woman who could do her own work.". . . They also came because that work was groundbreaking—especially in the ways in which it smashed expectations of the dance and woman's role in it, and thus contributed its own clear voice to the polarized cacophony around women's proper sphere. In contrast both to classical ballet and her teacher, St. Denis, Graham had little use for "feminine" grace and lyricism as enacted by the female dancer, or even as it appeared in traditional dance dress. Often designing her own costumes of stark lines and dark colors, the movement she choreographed was radically energized, angular, and staccato. (p. 5)

Through her subjective aesthetic endeavors Graham broke through tradition artistically and culturally and helped ensure a new revolution in dance.

Decades later in the 1960s Yvonne Rainer continued this role of optimal operative perversity. In her landmark work *Trio A* (1966), Rainer wanted to desexualize the female performer, to avoid the "male gaze." As with Graham, Rainer's subjective response is clearly multileveled and perverse. Oliver (2001) explains:

> Rainer's *Trio A* avoids the "seduction of the spectator" in many of the same ways that women camouflage themselves walking down city streets. . . . Her focus away from the audi-

ence, her task-like movement, her vertical, neutral body alignment, and her simple, everyday unisex clothing all lead the audience away from sexualizing the performer. . . .

Decades later, some feminists might be inclined to look back at *Trio A* and call it regressive. They could argue that it denied any sense of female sensuality, and in fact appears to be trying to deny natural expressivity. *Trio A* is hardly a piece that celebrates woman in any obvious way. However, in 1966, it was a feminist work precisely because it took the established norms for female social and performance behavior and turned them upside down. Instead of personal drama, sexuality, and audience connection, Rainer gave us movement for its own sake, asexuality, and audience distancing. . . . Rainer had created her own novel solution to the problem of the viewer's tendency to sexualize the performer. By repudiating the "male gaze," Rainer took control of the way audiences (read: men) viewed performers (read: women). (pp. 37-38)

Rainer's work, historically situated, revolutionary for her time, demonstrates optimal operative perversity. Her work effected numerous choreographers, significantly influencing the dance world, and consequently our culture.

Kohut (1973/1978), in particular, feels that modern artists depict the experiences of fragmentation so often encountered in our contemporary emotional lives. Demonstrating this psychological cultural phenomena, through optimal operative perversity, are "the musicians of atonal sound, the sculptors of disjointed form, the painters of disintegrated line and color, the poets of decomposed language—who in their work are demonstrating the breakup of the unresponded self and its artistic reassemblage" (p. 680).

In dance, a striking illustration is the work of choreographer Merce Cunningham. Before Cunningham began to choreograph he was a dancer in Martha Graham's company from 1939-1945. He was immersed in what had become the traditional modern dance of his times. Graham's work, which was originally perverse in its own percussive expressionism, clearly set out to communicate psychological tales and dramas. Cunningham's artistic direction was a perverse break from the traditions that surrounded him and his ideas continue to influence contemporary choreographers.

Wanting to free his mind from the conscious manipulation of movement, Cunningham began in the 1950s, and continues today, to use methods of chance, such as the I Ching, to organize movements and virtually all aspects of his choreography. He often sets up a performing "Event" that takes place in a large space, such as a gymnasium. The selection of dance material, the ordering of sections within a dance, the use of music, and the lighting design are all decided by chance operations. The performing space is decentralized and several pieces are performed simultaneously in the arena. Every aspect of the performance is fragmented and then reassembled. The audience is given the freedom to pay attention to whatever aspect of the performance draws her/him most significantly. Dance critic Allen Robertson (1980) states that the Event format reflects Cunningham's "genuine, deeply felt response to the multiplicity of our urban environment" (p. 11).

Today, in his eighties, Cunningham continues with perversity. Following his long-term interest in computers and choreography, Cunningham has collaborated with media-artists Paul Kaiser and Shelley Eshkar, creating *Hand-Drawn Spaces* (1997-1998). Here, the movement ideas were originally devised by Cunningham and executed by two of his dancers. But the movements were transfixed into a digital environment by connecting electrodes to the dancers that recorded the movements into a computer. Then Cunningham explored and played with the movements on the computer using chance methods. The choreography is set into virtual space. The resulting virtual human forms, depicted by lines and shadows, move across multiple enormous video screens creating a dance that involves audience members in our technological world kinesthetically. Are we as individuals in our modern world alienated by technology, or have we just not found significant ways to integrate experience with digital mediums? Cunningham is surely attempting to bridge the gap.

If Kohut is right regarding the anticipatory nature of great art, then artists like Graham, Rainer, and Cunningham have produced works that demonstrate the potential self-healing and self-expressive functions art may have for society at large. Through elaboration of meaningful significance these aesthetic forms give voice to important psychological realities, offering a selfobject function on the intra-, inter-, and metasubjective levels. This capacity of art helps ensure our biological, psychological, emotional, and spiritual existence. There are modern choreographers who express their belief that dance holds self-healing for society. Choreographer Mel Wong states:

> I do choreograph about things meaningful to me that relate to contemporary life. . . . Art gives hints about life and it functions in many ways. . . . I view art as a cleansing process both for the viewer and definitely for me as an artist. (Wong, in Kreemer, 1987, p. 74)

Choreographer and dance critic Gus Solomon, Jr., puts it thusly: "Art . . . illuminates reality by confronting it, exposing it, and re-examining it to help its audience gain insight into reality and thus deal more effectively with it" (Solomon, in Kreemer, 1987, p. 181).

Other choreographers describe an integration of self-expressive and self-healing functions of art for society. Betty Lind (1960) writes: "Although it is not . . . [the choreographer's] purpose in that he is not trying consciously to teach, the effect is that he enriches our vision, enlarges our awareness, and what may be most important, sets our own imaginations working" (p. 102). She describes this experience between the choreographer, the performer, and the audience thusly:

> The audience must participate actively and when every part of its being is set working and when the sparks fly back and forth between performer and audience, that is when the dance has achieved its reason for being, and a little bit of self-knowledge has been gained for all the participants—the creator, the interpreter, and the receptor. (p. 102)

Finally, choreographer Elizabeth Keen states it succinctly: "If someone choreographs a dance worth its salt, the quantity of good rises in the world" (Keen, in Dunning, 1978, p. 35).

Of course, if the art is anticipatory, understanding what it depicts culturally in the immediate may be difficult. A colleague of mine living in Los Angeles recently disclosed to me that it has become distressing for her to attend dance concerts. She is deeply disheartened by the amount of violence being depicted through the body. Choreographer Stephen Petronio's work dynamically exemplifies such use of anger and speed:

> In his hands, dance rhythm is . . . a cracking whip. . . . Because Petronio allies a slamming force to the busyness of his choreography, his dancers are frequently described as seeming on the verge of ripping apart from their centres. . . . [Petronio's work] shares characteristics with other choreography from his generation; in both the United States and Europe, for instance, aggression and speed are the predominant themes in the 1990s choreography. (Collins, 1999, pp. 189-190)

In 1990, the United States Congress passed a law requiring the National Endowment of the Arts to ensure standards of decency when offering grants. This law was upheld by the Supreme Court in 1998 as constitutional. Many choreographers, especially those dealing with issues concerning sexual orientation, reacted towards this influence from the political religious right. Petronio (Petronio, in Collins, 1999) is one of them and states: "The body is the last bastion of freedom. . . . My politics is the action of my body" (p. 190).

British choreographer Lloyd Newson's work with his company DV8 clearly demonstrates this impulse towards violence. Josephine Leask (1999) describes Newson's movement style, which Newson calls "physical theatre":

> Hurling the body onto another at speed, climbing up a body, falling or being thrown, often repeated until a state of real exhaustion and desperation is reached to evoke the nihilistic aspect of relationships in an unsympathetic society. . . . Each performance is so physically and mentally demanding for the dancers, who have to maintain authenticity and honesty throughout, that the works only have a limited performance life. (p. 174)

Both Newson and Petronio have introduced text to their work placing them within a very contemporary trend in dance called dance-theater. Quite possibly such an introduction of text, along in some cases with video footage, may be responsive to the multimedia, technological aspects of Western culture. Perhaps, the TV generation is standing up and taking its place in the art world.

Undoubtedly though, this more violent trend in dance is in response to feeling an unempathic, unresponsive political world that must not take control over personal private existence. In these works, the prevailing feeling is that movement has not been enough, abstraction not powerful enough, to communicate the intensity of what it means to live in the modern world. The personal is political and more direction is implied. In Tere O'Connor's piece *Hi Everybody* (2000), he repeatedly returns to the theme of the lack of universal health insurance in the wealthiest country in the world. How does someone express her/his personal response to this political reality explicitly without words? Can this be done just through amodal global perceptions, or does the need for direct verbal symbolic representation become a must? Does this diminish the power of the art or augment it to a level of greater integration?

Dissanayake (1988, 2000) asserts that originally the arts were to support group cohesion and, as part of ceremony, were multimodal. Such cross-modality demonstrates the original amodal perceptions used to create intimacy between parent and child. Song, dance, theater, visual displays joined together enhanced the power of the experience, to signify to others the seriousness of what was expressed. I present the possibility that some choreographers find a greater intensity in their power to communicate and express their compelling ideals through a multimodal presentation, enhanced now through technology. Additionally, because multimodal pageantry was originally geared towards group cohesion, possibly these choreographers are expressing a need for humanity to listen more closely to contemporary tragedies and to find greater cohesion and strength to respond.

Dance critic, Deborah Jowitt (1999) comments on the more violent trends in dance:

> Economic pressures, feelings of political helplessness, and the spread of AIDS may have had some influence in spawning themes of dependency, helplessness, anger. And, in response, a gritty physicality. . . . The lifts and supports are neither effortless nor attractive; they may be about a person who can hardly stand up trying to help another, about the terrible weight of a human body, about embraces that never quite work, about diving through the air and daring someone to catch you. (pp. 9-10)

Kohut (1987) reminds us that a healthy person does not express only the joys in life, but can poignantly express feelings of violence and even rage. The healthy individual is not overwhelmed by these emotions, but can dynamically choose when and how to elaborate them. Most likely, these recent trends in dance exemplify a contemporary healthy response to the pain and tragedy humanity must confront and integrate—the self-expressive and self-healing aspects of art undoubtedly with us.

I do not feel the toll that AIDS has taken on the arts, in general, can be overestimated. I believe modern dance's political awareness of the inherent violence in society has been intensified by the AIDS epidemic. The world of modern dance has unquestionably experienced the impact of this destabilizing contemporary reality. The list of choreographers and dancers who have died seems without end. The list of dances created about death seems without end. Choreographer Joe Goode (Open Meet the Artist Discussion, April 18, 2000, Santa Barbara, CA) keeps saying that he isn't going to make any more dances about death, but he does. And years after Arnie Zane's 1988 AIDS-related death, collaborator and lover Bill T. Jones still calls his company the Bill T. Jones/Arnie Zane Dance Company.

But Jones has taken his own perverse path in response. He has choreographed several pieces concerning loss and has sought to find redemption in his HIV-positive status. Not to be defeated by the possibility of an early demise, Jones (1995), in his moving autobiography *Last Night on Earth*, describes the creation of his dance, *Still/Here* (1994). As an African-American gay man, Jones has understood experiences of marginalization. He sought not to feel, or to be, ostracized because of AIDS, but to use his status and his art to bring about a greater sense of understanding and community. Through his art he sought to be expressive and healing for himself and others.

To build this sense of commonality, Jones conducted Survival Workshops in fourteen cities with individuals who had life-threatening illnesses. The emphasis was on multimodal self-discovery and community awareness. Together participants explored subjective and idiosyncratic movement gestures, visual artistic expressions, and verbal testimonies responding to who they were, in health and illness, and to, perhaps, discover their own value in hope. The movement vocabulary for *Still/Here* is derived from the survivors' bodily expressions, the text from their words. Gretchen Bender created video footage of the workshop participants to augment the dancing and narrative. Jones (1995) created multimodal based art to communicate about the effect of life-threatening illnesses on humanity, to explore questions such as: "How do I deal with fear, anger, and pain? How can I find the strength to love, plan, create? How can I defeat the perception that I am an abnormality, cut off and doomed?" (p. 251).

Still/Here, in general, was received with tremendous success. Interestingly, however, the blatant content of the piece did not sit well with all critics. Dance critic for *The New Yorker* Arlene Croce refused to see the piece, let alone review it, "on the grounds that as 'victim art' it begged her sympathy and therefore made itself impossible to be written about objectively" (Hutera, 1999, p. 126). Many disagree with Croce. But the debate highlights the current trends in modern dance away from abstraction towards an integration of movement and more literal narrative. Perhaps it also captures the intensity that occurs when artists attempt to bridge the gap between amodal expression and verbal symbolization, and the optimal operative perversity that might be required to accomplish this daunting feat.

What these directions in dance signify in terms of modern life continues to be open to debate. But it feels to me almost like a scream, trying to make sure one is heard. Choreographer Mark Dendy (Lecture: Art and the Politics of Sexuality, July 24, 2000, Santa Barbara, CA), who has made significant contributions to dance-theater, acknowledges the importance of choreographer Doris Humphrey's advice from the 1950s. Humphrey insisted that if a subject was too close, the choreographer should put the idea aside and respond to it later. But in response to watching so many of his friends die, Dendy felt compelled to respond choreographically, because "when it came to AIDS there was no time." With so many dying, and so many others waiting for their bodies to respond to their HIV-positive status, one couldn't wait. If one wanted to be heard, to be heard on behalf of others, the expression had to be poignant, immediate, and powerful. This was the compelling force for choreographer "Ishmael Houston Jones' performance piece using the carcass of a dead goat on stage to shock his audience with the actual smell of death in an attempt to confront them with the reality of AIDS as a sign of the times" (Osmuare, p. 26).

To want to be heard is to want to be empathically understood. At times in modern life, that can feel insurmountable. But to strive to be heard expresses hope, and with hope comes the possibilities for self-expression, empowerment, and healing. Choreographers strive to explore and assert what deeply touches them, on all subjective levels, through elaboration to connect guiding ideals to a meaningful existence—to be heard. Herein lies hope and beauty, even if the beauty of the elaboration is the poignancy experienced by the stench of a dead goat. Hagman (in press) describes this transcendent human quality:

> Beauty in its reparative and preservative function asserts love over aggression, life over death and harmony over disintegration. . . . For a civilization not to value beauty would mean that they are a people who cannot hope, and cannot assert life over the inevitable and ubiquitous forces of entropy and death. (pp. 38-39)

Sometimes I fear there is almost nothing more depressing than reading the newspaper. Perhaps there are no more horrors in the world today than 50 years ago, but now we have greater access to information. We can be inundated with facts that can be demoralizing if some sense of power, action, hope, and beauty, is not found. On July 11, 12, and 13, 2000, the *Los Angeles Times* ran articles on the front page on the 13th International AIDS Conference in Durban, South Africa. The news continues to be dismal. In the United States the male gay community was the first to be hit hard by the AIDS epidemic. Now an even wider population is struck. The highest rates in the United States are among minorities—African Americans and Latinos. In Africa the life expectancy in many countries is dropping to 30. Where 300 infants a year are born in the United States infected, 200 infants a day are born in South Africa infected. Randy Shilt's (2000) detailed and heartbreaking book *And the Band Played On: Politics, People, and the AIDS Epidemic* chronicles the lapse in response from the Reagan administration, and even the denial within the gay community, that enabled this plague to reach disastrous proportions. I cannot help but wonder if some of the recent trends in dance are telling us that culturally we must take individual responsibility for what humanity does to humanity, within our own communities, and worldwide.

Choreographer Joe Goode's moving and humorous multimodal dance-theater piece, *Deeply There* (1998) details stories through dance, text, and song of a neighborhood coming to grips with a dying friend, continuing to find hope in life. Goode describes his need to move beyond just movement as a vehicle to connect more directly to the world at large:

> Ultimately, I'm not making dances about dance, I'm making dances about life. . . . What's important to me is to ask the big questions: How do we live in the world? How do we feel compassion for one another? How do we understand how to get through the day?
>
> If I have to bring in the kitchen sink with running water and dirty dishes inside to get that message across, then I will do that. I'm not a purist. (Interview conducted by Starshine Roshell, *Santa Barbara News-Press*, April 14, 2000, SCENE, p. 4)

I attended a concert given by choreographer and performer Margie Gillis (May 11, 2000, Santa Barbara, CA). Gillis has personally felt the ravage of AIDS with the death of her brother, Christopher Gillis, who was a principal dancer in Paul Taylor's company. Margie Gillis's work can be edgy and dark. But, in addition, she performs a piece like *Slipstream* (1985). This brief dance, beautifully executed by Gillis, captures a sense not just of the motion of a slipstream, but of the qualitative and sensual experiences one might have of being in the motion of the slipstream. This simple piece, reminiscent of earlier times in modern dance, portrays the more amodal global realities of our preverbal worlds. As I try to describe my response to this dance, I am at a loss for words. The overwhelming experience of vitality affects washed over me as the air and power of a slipstream. The dance brought the audience spontaneously to their feet with a standing ovation in deep appreciation. Perhaps, no matter what other historical and psychological consequences we share, we will always yearn collectively for the confirmation of the basic rush of vitality affects and their connections to our subjectivities.

THE ARTIST, CULTURE, AND THE CREATIVITY OF EVERYDAY LIFE

The significance of understanding the creative endeavors of artists and their resulting processes of transformation extend far beyond them. At its core, it encompasses the way individuals, through finding creative and subjective meaning in their own lives, develop and transform psychologically. Through such self-development the ability to maturely respond to another increases; consequentially, the health of a society depends upon this capacity for self-growth.

Kohut (1973/1978, 1976/1978a, 1977) believes the great artists of our times reflect the fragmentation of our contemporary selves in everyday life. Dissanayake (1988), echoing Kohut's concern about the fragmentation of our modern lives, asserts that creative activity in everyday life serves a most vital function of delineating subjective and meaningful experience:

> Our world and our selves have fragmented to a degree unimaginable in earlier human history, and if there is to be any coherence at all in our lives, it is up to us to put it there. To this extent, we are all called upon to be artists—to shape, find significant aspects of, impose meaning upon, discern, or state what is special about our experience. Response to the mystery of life becomes a personal aesthetic gesture. (p. 190)

To accomplish this, individuals must engage their worlds with the exploration, assertion, and vitality necessary to give shape and form to the subjective meaning of their existences. Ultimately, their lives will be deeply enriched and more productive. The reciprocity with culture is invaluable. I believe this is paramount to understanding the subjective necessity and significance of culture, for the individual's cohesion, as well as the group's.

In the processes of the artist, we find the dynamics to engage the world with exploration, assertion, vitality, and reciprocity. The individual in everyday life finds, creates, and explores meaning by repeating these dynamics in the small details of one's existence. American philosopher John Dewey (1934) poignantly describes this artistic activity that transcends the realm of the artist: "The intelligent mechanic engaged in his job, interested in doing well and finding satisfaction in his handiwork, caring for his materials and tools with genuine affection, is artistically engaged" (p. 5). Such experiences are supportive of a cohesive sense of self, and consequentially, are supportive of a cohesive sense of group self. What is at stake here is the capacity for the individual to find a fulfilling, meaningful existence, expressive of guiding ideals, to sustain a healthful exchange with, and development of, society and culture. The partaking of culture and the ability to bring a creative and productive life to fruition brings a vital sense of lived experience, meaning, and competence to one's life, and the ability to share with others. Whether for the artist or the individual, creativity involves exploration and self-assertion, through a mulileveled subjective relationship that serves significant selfobject functions through the construction of an ideal form that embodies and expands self-delineation, self-cohesion, and self-development, and that is ultimately self-transformative. Through creativity we experience and nourish the dancing self within.

Chapter ▪ 5

Paul Taylor:
A Case Study

In this chapter I apply the insights of self psychology to modern choreographer Paul Taylor's (1988) illuminating autobiography, *Private Domain*. Taylor, as discussed in Chapter Two, danced with Merce Cunningham from 1953-1954, and was a principal dancer from 1955-1961 in Martha Graham's company. His choreographic career began in the 1950s as part of the avant-garde of that time. With a choreographic career now progressing almost 50 years, Taylor is a major icon in modern dance. Taylor's experiences help demonstrate the ideas of compensatory structures, archaic and mature healthy narcissism, transferences of creativity, the multileveled subjective creative process, the desperation of a fragmented sense of self, and suggest that a vital, subjective, and transcendent connection to creativity can be transformative.

Taylor's autobiography covers his early life, the first two decades of his company, his fall from grace as a performer addicted to amphetamines, and the greater contentment he finds in the exclusive role of choreographer. He characterizes his processes in writing his autobiography as "kind of like analysis" (Sommers, 1980/1981, p. 1). Analysis holds the potential for individuals to understand their own subjective truths. Journalist Eric Taub (1982) describes Taylor's autobiography exactly as "more truthful than factual" (p. 10). The truth revealed in *Private Domain* is Taylor's subjective and introspective view; his experiences are more significant than the facts.

Since the mid-1950s, the beginnings of Taylor's choreographic endeavors, Taylor has had an imaginary persona, Dr. George Tacet. At times, George Tacet is credited in concert programs for costumes and set designs that Taylor himself has created. Occasionally, as part of the "truthful" aspect of his autobiography, Taylor uses conversations with Tacet as a literary device to express and reveal very personal thoughts and feelings. The writing of one's story demands openness and vulnerability. Quite possibly Taylor uses the words of Tacet to distance himself from his own exposure. In this light, I feel it is particularly interesting that Taylor often engages in conversations with Tacet when Taylor is in need of emotional sustenance and soothing. These self-reflective conversations appear helpful to his creative life and reveal Taylor's capacity for self-soothing and self-empathy when under duress. Unfortunately, there are periods in Taylor's life when his sense of self seriously fragments. During those times Taylor's capacities for self-sustenance diminish and conversations with Tacet basically disappear from his story.

Tacet's presence in *Private Domain* reveals a core element of Taylor's life. Taylor is, undeniably, a creative individual. When he decides to write his autobiography, he does not use a ghost writer. Instead, and I feel quite tellingly, he enrolls in a creative writing class. By approaching the writing of his autobiography as a creative act, Taylor enters into an intersubjective relation to words, demonstrating his idiosyncratic presence by the specific nuances and coloring of his literary voice. This is particularly noticeable through Tacet's flamboyant expressions. In the end, the dominating force of *Private Domain* is Taylor's subjective life. The creative artist in him could not have written it any other way.

EARLY BEGINNINGS AND COMPENSATORY STRUCTURES

Taylor details his father's psychological abandonment of him when he was about three and his parents divorced. Even before, his relation with his father is unfulfilling. The marriage is not a happy one, and Taylor's three older stepsiblings, whose loving father had died, do not respond well to their stepfather's aloof and formal manner:

> My father had been unacceptable to his three stepchildren. To them he seemed an overly strict disciplinarian, peculiar and a typical absentminded professor. He insisted on having Mother

and her children address him as "Dr. Taylor," which they did, although thinking it a bit odd to be calling a physicist a doctor—not to mention the distancing effect that it had. The children, unable to transfer to him any of the love that they still held for their real father, considered him an intruder. My mother, too, soon regretted the marriage. (p. 5)

Taylor's father comes once a year to visit; he brings presents but no deep psychological nourishment for his son. "During the visits there was little communication between us. . . . When the visits were over, I felt relieved, then played surreptitiously with the gifts, always being careful to hide them away afterwards" (p. 6). Not only is his father not available as a functional selfobject for Taylor, but any sustenance that might have been there is hindered by his mother's and stepsiblings' dislike for the man. Taylor hides the gifts his father brings him. His needs for his father as an idealizable selfobject are severely hampered every way Taylor turns.

Taylor, obviously aware of the loss he experienced when young, first introduces Dr. Tacet as a comparison to the labored visits with his father. Exemplifying Taylor's intersubjective relation with language, his whimsical literary descriptions speak of the needs and desires of the child he once was. He gives Tacet a doctorate, not in physics, like his father, but, playfully, in phrenology (the study of the bumps on the head). In striking contrast to his father, who appears embarrassed by any idealization Taylor manages to have of him, Dr. Tacet welcomes idealization, perhaps to an extreme, from others or himself, no matter:

He sometimes materialized in the lobby, where he could be seen sitting in one of the art deco chairs and admiring a reflection that came across the room from a large rococo mirror. . . . [H]is elegant long trousers were made of the same navy blue serge as my short ones. If asked, he'd lift me up onto his bony knee, warn me not to interrupt, and become extremely talkative. Not even the song of a locust enchanted me the way his raspy voice did. His dissertations and grandiose airs were delightful, and it was a special treat to be permitted to finger the odd bumps on his head. I always eagerly anticipated these times with him, which unlike Dr. Taylor's visits, came often and were without embarrassment. (p. 10)

Mixed in with the obvious longing to idealize another, Taylor's description of Dr. Tacet reveals his desire for an experience of twinship; they both wear navy blue serge trousers. Twinship, along with idealization, is a repeated need of Taylor's throughout his tale.

As Taylor's childhood continues, he attempts to establish idealizing and twinship relations with father figures. The most apparent is Mr. Butts, who owns the camp/farm Taylor lives at for a while when he is around ten:

> I've been studying his manly movements from a distance, and timid about giving away strong admiration for him, I'm reluctant to speak. He doesn't know that I've adopted him as my father, or that I've been trying to copy the Western way he walks, and pulling at my nose daily so it will grow long like his, and pushing on my uppers so as to have the same buck teeth. (p. 14)

As with his father, Taylor does not speak much with Mr. Butts, but attempts to admire him from afar. Truth or fact, he demonstrates his desire for twinship by pulling at his nose and pushing on his uppers to look like him. But in remarkable contrast to his father, Mr. Butts accepts Taylor's idealization and his need for twinship. Together they do "manly" chores:

> Mr. Butts shows me how to herd his four cows into a milk shed by twisting their tails, de-dung and then milk them, how to drive and plow with a tractor, curry horses, and build electric fences. I also feed the chickens and do other chores. (p. 15)

Mr. Butts confirms Taylor's artistic talents, which, from childhood throughout adulthood, include painting: "When I ask, he lets me paint one of the camp station wagons with pictures of boys riding horses, cows, pigs, and each other" (p. 15). Mr. Butts' acceptance of Taylor's idealization and need for twinship reinforces Taylor's expressive talents and skills. I surmise Taylor's artistic tendencies, from early childhood, intensify in development as compensatory structures in an attempt to heal the fragmented structures left behind by his empty relation with his father. Therefore, confirmation of them by Mr. Butts is particularly significant. Additionally, Mr. Butts' acceptance of Taylor's idealization may help supply the roots for Taylor, himself, to experience his art-making as representing an ideal. Taylor's deep need for and gratitude to Mr. Butts for the bond between them becomes evident when Taylor contracts a dangerous case of scarlet fever: "I'm delirious, and deliriously happy. . . . Mr. Butts has leaned over and pressed his lips to my hot forehead. A symbol of affection, the kiss was one given at risk" (p. 16).

In contrast to his search for a paternal figure in his life, Taylor recognizes a far more rewarding relation with his mother, even though she is often absent because of long work hours. "I had . . . a mother whom I was wild about. Though more of a figure to love than an actual presence, she made me feel special" (p. 7). Here is a functioning selfobject that permits Taylor to experience "the gleam in the mother's eye" (Kohut, 1966/1978, p. 439) to reinforce his young and age-appropriate exhibitionistic grandiosity. This relationship provides the seeds from which his compensatory structures in self-expressive ambitions and talents evolve. By his mother's acceptance of his explorations and self-assertions, used to express his poetic abilities, she is, consequentially, supportive of his heightened need for compensatory structure:

> I was worried about her having to work so hard and, prematurely poetic at about age six, before going to bed every night, left verses for her to find tucked under her pillow. They were there to let her know that I loved and was proud of her. Dozens of them, lettered on small pieces of colored construction paper, were stuffed into a large envelope by her, tied with darning yarn and saved. (p. 7)

The child experiencing "the gleam in the mother's eye" also experiences that they are the "ideal in the object's gaze" (Hagman, in press, pp. 22-23). Quite possibly Taylor internalizes not just her support of his expressions, but her experiencing them with idealization, making them extra special. Additionally, for his mother, a woman working long hours during the Depression, widowed and divorced, the artistic displays of affection and love from her son were most probably reparative and soothing. If so, then Taylor's ability as an adult to be artistically productive, to experience his medium and his art as ideals may be partly derivative of his mother's capacity to acknowledge his early expressive and artistic offerings as deeply nourishing, and treasures to be saved.

Taylor does not describe many early experiences that lend themselves to the development of a sensual motivational system. However, he does remember times when his mother supplies soothing experiences reinforcing of a sensual/sexual motivational system. Such experiences most likely set into motion his own capacity for self-soothing: "Lulled by her rocker's rhythmic tick, and intoxicated by the scent of her sachet, I'd relax my grip from around her neck, drift off, and be carried to my bed" (p. 9). Taylor's capacities for self-soothing must originate with these early mutually rewarding interactions with his mother.

However, because Taylor's mother was often preoccupied with work, and he had no father, it is doubtful that the interactions necessary to enable Taylor truly to temper and transform his grandiose narcissistic strivings were present. His mother extends the basis for some primary structures in the pole of ambitions, and the kernel for additional compensatory structures to unfold, but not enough sustenance to establish fully Taylor's cohesion. Additionally, Taylor's stepsiblings, Sophie, Tom, and Bettie, are all significantly older than he, leaving him often by himself:

> Soph and Tom were away, Mammy nearly always at work, and only teen-age Bettie around. Naturally, she tended to be more involved with her own affairs. . . .
> A lot of time was spent amusing myself with made-up games and imaginary playmates. (pp. 6-7)

From the beginning, Taylor is playful, inventive, and resourceful, abilities that allow the youngster to entertain himself. Most especially, Taylor's solitude, his isolation, and his ability to be creative appear to have grown from his early childhood. But it is doubtful that his home situation allows these important self-structures to transform fully into more cohesive narcissistic configurations.

Consequently, even though his mother's presence supplies some stability for Taylor's developing sense of self, and there is reinforcement from experiences with Mr. Butts, the faulty mechanisms from his early life, especially the lack of a responsive relationship with his father, continue to take a toll on Taylor's development. His compensatory structures in self-expression and artistic skills are fragile. He displays narcissistic vulnerabilities that Kohut associates with a more fragmented experience of self: "Increasingly, I'm aware that I possess traits that make me somehow different from the others—a sensitivity to slights, an anger maybe. And I sense continued isolation" (p. 17). Here, perhaps, Taylor longs, not just for twinship and idealizable selfobjects, but for an adversarial selfobject to give greater cohesion to his self-assertions, to help heal his narcissistic wounds. In fact, during junior high, Taylor has a run in with the police and is sent for three years to Virginia Episcopal School, an all boys' prep school. These three years are the longest amount of time Taylor lives in any one location during his childhood.

In response to his vulnerabilities from the lack of early responsiveness from his father and the basic core of sustenance he derives from feeling special for his mother, I believe, Taylor attempts to develop cohesive compensatory structures in ambitions expressive of his artistic talents. This psychological development is not a move towards defensive structures, but an attempt to supplement and secure a dynamic and cohesively functioning sense of self through creative work. Indeed, at the beginning of the autobiography, Taylor declares important information about himself: "Vital statistic: insatiable itch to communicate to the world at large" (p. 4).

Taylor's need for self-expression and experiences of isolation are prevalent in his life from the time he is young and continue throughout the autobiography. As a preteen he recognizes that his desire to do art furthers his isolation. Taylor again uses the self-expressive image of Dr. Tacet to write about this isolation and his itch to communicate:

> Though I still enjoy drawing and painting, I'm getting the idea that they are an unlikely way to earn a living. . . . My general impression is that art of all kinds has a taint to it. Nice people worked for a living, and good boys played football. Everyone has been very definite about that. Even so, Old Tacet and I agree that football is ridiculous and work something to avoid. (p. 17)

Eventually, Taylor's interests take him to Syracuse University where he originally majors in art and acquires an athletic scholarship for swimming. Even though his family is concerned about his financial future as an artist, Taylor's mother once again functions as a confirming and mirroring selfobject for his basic ambitions. She reassures him: "I'm sure you'll make your Mammy proud" (p. 24). Within a year at college, Taylor, feeling art is too two-dimensional, has a mysterious artistic epiphany and switches his major to dance. Taylor, forgoing the voice of Tacet, directly acknowledges his longing to find a paternal figure in the world of dance: "I thought that somewhere along the way I might run across a real Dr. Tacet to train and guide me—someone who, if not a true father, might at least be a professional one?" (p. 26). Taylor's search is for an idealizable mentor, who, perhaps, just by sharing the common experience of dancing, might also extend twinship and support his self-expressions, compensatory structures, and artistic ideals.

BABE—A TRANSFERENCE OF CREATIVITY

Taylor does not find a true professional father to idealize. However, he befriends a deaf-mute, George "Babe" Wilson, who idealizes Taylor, and who functions as a transference of creativity based on twinship. Taylor compares George Wilson to George Tacet:

It's unremarkable that old friend Tacet and new friend Wilson
are both named George, but it seems too coincidental, almost
predestined, that the correct spelling of my pseudonym turns
out to mean "he is silent," and that George Wilson happens to
be a deaf-mute. (p. 61)

The first time Babe is involved in Taylor's work, Babe executes a set
design for *Little Circus* (1955) that Taylor himself devises. Conceived
by Taylor, executed by Babe, the program credits George Tacet with
his first set design. For a moment, the three have merged into one.

Communicating at first by written word, Babe describes a life
that speaks directly to, and beyond, Taylor's own continual sense of
isolation. Here is someone who certainly understands loneliness:

More pages are scrawled with other unusual, yet somehow
familiar, details of his solitary, pauperish life. The words rush
onto the pages as if bottled up since birth. I try to picture the
isolation endured by him but don't get far. Compared with
his, any lonesomeness that I've ever experienced is chicken
feed. (p. 62)

Obviously committed to this friendship, Taylor learns sign language
within a month or so. In this realm, as well, Taylor appears to experience a sustaining twinship: "It's inspirational that Babe speaks
with his hands, especially to us dancers, who can relate easily,
speaking as we do with our feet" (p. 104).

Part of Taylor's appreciation of Babe is the experience of a
silent presence, quietly functioning as a vital twinship selfobject,
supportive of Taylor's creative energies:

We often fall into long stretches of comfortable silence. My
mind is usually full of dance. . . . At these times he becomes
almost invisible, more of a presence than a fact, and being
with him is to enjoy company and solitude at the same time.
He gives my mind the luxury of space to move in. (p. 63)

Kohut's (1984) description of his patient's twinship with her "genie"
in the bottle is reminiscent of the peacefulness Taylor finds from
Babe:

Her self was sustained simply by the presence of someone she
knew was sufficiently like her to understand her and to be
understood by her. . . . [Her need] was for a silent presence.

> She would talk to the twin, but the twin did not have to
> respond to her. As a matter of fact, just being together with
> the twin in silent communion was often the most satisfactory
> state. (p. 196)

Because of the silence of both Babe and Tacet, Taylor feels
the freedom to create them as he wishes and needs:

> I'm fond of who I imagine him [George Wilson] to be.
> Admittedly, there are great gaps to him which have been filled
> in with whatever traits I've fancied. George was a cardboard
> cutout waiting to be colored. With a deaf-mute this has been
> easier than ever. Dr. Tacet was simple enough to imagine,
> although a little effort was needed to keep him consistent; but
> tangible George was a pushover, his basic framework already
> existing. Facts always fled from fantasy, and the realities of
> silent chums can be whatever one wants. I've made him fault-
> less—it would be foolish to allow George to ruin George. (p.
> 63)

In addition to extending twinship to Taylor, Babe idealizes
him. Through the acceptance of Babe's idealization Taylor extends to
Babe that which Taylor had originally yearned for himself—an idealizable guide. Taylor, consciously or unconsciously, understands
what Babe needs because of his own needs. By acting towards Babe
as Taylor has longed for another to act towards him, he quite possibly internalizes these experiences, supplying Taylor with some healing for his own wounds.

But the acceptance does not always come easily. Babe moves
into Taylor's combination dance studio and apartment initially as an
idealizing and silent presence—one that has not bothered to ask.
Because of his intense relation to the space that functions as his
"studio," Taylor momentarily rebels and has the police evict Babe.
Within a few days Taylor relents. The need for a silent presence
crosses over into the reality of relationship that carries with it
Taylor's acceptance of another's idealization. Whether fact or just
telling truth, Taylor writes that shortly after Babe has moved back
in, Taylor notices Babe's just "sitting there, solid but less stony than
when we'd met. And he's talking to himself with the fingers of one
hand, his dear, forceful letters spelling out 'Until death do us apart'"
(p. 65).

The acceptance of idealization must be sustaining enough to
counteract any flaws in Babe's twinship, for the soothing twinship
acquired from Babe holds far more difficulties than the self-soothing

that Taylor supplies himself through the illusionary Tacet. Babe is a real-life person and his individuality keeps interfering with the pure essence of a silent presence. For the young child, the small nonchronic empathic failures of the significant caregivers lead to optimal frustration and the development of more cohesive self-structures. Babe's individuality presents to Taylor nonchronic empathic failures; in contrast to Tacet, Babe is not constantly in tune with the silent soothing Taylor desires from him. Through his very human relation with Babe, Taylor most likely develops a stronger, more cohesive sense of self, and his capacities for mutuality expand.

Having moved into Taylor's studio, Babe loves to make improvements to it, a situation Taylor finds taxing. Additionally, because Babe is deaf he cannot hear how incessantly noisy he can be. For Taylor, where is silence when he needs it? But the sustenance gained from Babe holds. Perhaps most telling, Taylor entrusts Babe to take care of his studio space when on tour, even when Babe, eventually, has his own apartment. Taylor describes the stability he found in the relationship:

> Babe is still refusing to be the quiet victim of my imagination, and what I've tried to envision as a stone colossus to lean on is turning out to be just another noisy person. Furthermore, he sometimes leans on me. Though not what I had in mind, our symbiosis is more durable than my house-of-cards company. Dancers keep coming and going, but Babe's bulldog face and craggy chin remain. Unlike the dancers, we've learned a fairly consistent balancing act. (p. 191)

I feel Taylor's description of Babe possessing a bulldog face is quite revealing. Pets are often our silent partners and Babe makes sure that there is a parade of pets that cross through Taylor's studio. All of Babe's pets tragically are maimed or die. Babe places a stiff body in the freezer, waiting for the soft ground of summer to bury it. Taylor dedicates a whole chapter to Babe's pets. At the end, Taylor identifies with these ill-fated and silently loved creatures:

> If there is a conclusion to be drawn from Babe's beloved pets, you might easily surmise that they often carry with them a dark element of doom. Sure, we're all doomed, only some of us are more doomed than others. Since Babe loves me most, this gives me something to think about. (p. 193)

MARTHA GRAHAM—A TRANSFERENCE OF CREATIVITY

Even though Taylor does not find a real-life professional Tacet to guide him, he does find a real-life professional mother, Martha Graham. And, at that time in modern dance, if one is to have a mother, Martha Graham, the prominent cultural icon, is certainly the one to have. Even before he knows Graham well, before he is a member of her dance company, Taylor's familial comfort with Graham is obvious. When Taylor is a twenty-two-year-old student at the American Dance Festival he turns to Graham for advice. He feels confused about his sexual preferences and seeks her guidance:

> The only person I've met who seems worldly wise is Martha. . . .
> She's supposed to be an authority on caves and columns. . . .
> Trying to find the right words is harder than I expected. . . .
> Mercifully, she interrupts, says that she understands—that I
> have hot pants and don't know what street I'm on. (Not her
> actual words, but this is the gist.) Then she recommends mak-
> ing no choices of gender, to save that for later, just do nothing
> for the time being.
> It's a relief to learn that a person can just shelve his urges.
> I was worried that she might say that to Dance is to Live, and
> for me to go get laid, and call me sweetie pie or something.
> (pp. 36-37)

Taylor feels his relationship with his mother, her capacity to confirm his early exhibitionism and grandiosity, prepared him to be open to Martha and to life as part of her dance troupe: "When she took me into her fold, it seemed a perfectly natural occurrence. I sup-pose that my being the youngest child and my mother's Darlin' had given me a feeling of being special" (p. 330). Reflecting upon his time spent in Graham's dance company, Taylor writes: "It had been six wonderful, hideous, bewitching, boring, tickling, vivid years. Hardly a week has gone by since then that I haven't thought of her" (p. 121).

However, Taylor's appreciation of Graham comes with mixed feelings concerning Martha's use of men in her dances:

> Except for David [Wood], all of us are six feet or over; all move
> forcefully and archaically; all conform to the concept of a flat,
> two-dimensional figure that seems to be Martha's idea of a
> man. . . . We're usually stiff foils, or something large and
> naked for women to climb up on. A few of us would like to be
> more 3-D and think that less beefcake would be a good idea,
> but have been scared to say so. (p. 85)

But even with mixed emotions, his "admiration for this small, feisty woman who, for at least thirty-two years, has been lifting dance to new heights" (p. 84) is clear. Most importantly, her ability to be a reflecting mirror confirms his ambitions and compensatory structures: "Besides, her knowing eyes have seen something wonderful in me, and I'm determined to be worthy" (p. 84). As with his mother when he is young, Taylor finds in Graham her mirroring of his grandiosity, and her idealization of him as one who is "wonderful." He feels compelled to live up to her ideal of him. When Taylor is offered opportunities to join the companies of the "fathers" of dance, José Limón and George Balanchine, he turns them both down. Understandably, his heart is with Martha. Upon Graham's death in 1991, Taylor's public comment is revealing: "The tradition that's passed from one generation to another in modern dance—a real family—has helped me very much. . . . I'm her rightful son. She didn't leave me the studio, as she should have, but we are a family and I am her son" (*Dance Magazine*, July 1991, p. 45).

But his family relationship with Martha continues, at times, to prove difficult. Martha enjoys manipulating her dancers to orchestrate squabbles. Pablo, as she calls Taylor, is not exempt from her tricky endeavors. When on tour with her company in the late 1950s, Martha decides not to have Paul continue with the company when the tour is extended. After first firing him, she changes her mind and rehires him; however, Paul chooses to return to New York anyway, perhaps more guided now by his own personal strength. Yet once again, demonstrating his need and useful capacity for self-soothing, Taylor turns to Dr. Tacet to express his self-ruminations: "Things need to be sorted out, and it's times like this that old Tacet comes in handy" (p. 72). In Tacet's flamboyant style, the illusionary voice reinforces Taylor's ambitions and talents: "You have your own path to hew through the wilderness that is contemporary dance. Forget this old-style Graham folderol and form your own choreographic statements" (p. 73).

CHOREOGRAPHIC BEGINNINGS

At this point in time, 1957, Taylor begins work on his first full-evening concert. As he ventures into his creative processes, he acknowledges no significant transference of creativity on whom to depend. Babe is already in his life but Taylor makes no mention of him, perhaps indicative of Babe's silent presence. Prominent friends, such as artists Bob Rauschenberg and Jasper Johns, also are not mentioned. Instead, Taylor, as represented by conversations with Tacet, expresses stability within his own self-reflections. Taylor illuminates the capacity of an artist to gain sustenance from his own self-awareness; a true asset to have before risking the psychological stresses involved in creative engagement. Taylor's ability to do this is perhaps twofold—fueled by self-reliance grown from solitude and grounded by a confirmed sense of self supported by significant compensatory structures.

As Taylor enters the initial creative period, with precreative tensions, inspiration, and self-crisis, he permits Tacet, with his usual flair, to communicate to his readers his tale of uncertainty:

> The solution doesn't take long, however, as old Tacet supplies all the answers. He says that dance is as limitless as the universe, so full of possibilities and golden dreams that it can be anything that one cares to call it. "Hence, dear boy," he says, "simply decide what is irksome to you in other artists' work, eliminate it, and what is left over you can pilfer and pass off as your own."
> Considering Tacet's advice, I realize that when getting right down to it, there is little in others' work that doesn't irk me. (p. 76)

Through this conversation we see Taylor's building self-confidence to find his subjective and idiosyncratic aesthetic connection to movement, and to enter into an intersubjective dialogue with an "other"— the medium of dance. Importantly, Taylor finds possibilities within his intersubjective relation to dance, for the satisfaction of his strong needs for exploration, self-assertion, and expression. Additionally, Taylor indicates his idealization of dance in his descriptions of it as "limitless as the universe" and able to create "golden dreams." Dance and his creations are his ideals.

Taylor's subjective aesthetic desires draw him to change the rules, to explore his own optimal operative perversity:

> I decide to start over from scratch. Some kind of building blocks were needed, some clearly defined ABCs that could be ordered into a structure that would be antipersonality, unpsychological (no Greek goddesses), would achieve a specific effect (no Merce dice decisions), and would have a style free from the cobwebs of time (no ballet). So it is easy enough to know what not to do, and since it seems unlikely to find a solution in other people's work, I go out and look around in the streets. (p. 76).

Taylor turns to his medium—to movement. Significantly, his journey draws him to his surrounding culture. He expands his intersubjective relation with his medium into the metasubjective. His search taking him out to the streets of New York, he hones in on the abundant world of bodily activity that is all around him. What he sees excites him, indicative of the empowerment and selfobject function movement supplies him on all levels of subjectivity:

> They are standing, squatting, sitting everywhere like marvelous ants or bees, and their moves and stillnesses are ABCs that if given a proper format could define dance in a new way. All is there for the taking. . . . An array of riches surrounded me daily, and its timeless beauty needed to be pointed out and shared. (p. 76)

Taylor's exuberant idealization of the natural movements around him—their "timeless beauty"—propels him to explore posture and stillness. The selfobject function of movement sustains him to establish aesthetic resonance with his new vision and to break with the dance culture he knew so well. Through his kinesthetic explorations and assertions, reinforced by an experience of excited vitality, his intersubjective relation with his idealized medium expands as he pursues his sense of transcendent beauty. In so doing Taylor works diligently with his crew of three dancers to discover how to execute natural movements and postures without the stylized technique they have all learned as professional performers:

> Discovering how to hold still and yet remain active in a way that looks vital is the most difficult of all. The stillnesses are important and are to be on a par with the moves—as important as the negative space in paintings . . . silences in music. For dancers whose training has been in movement, this is like . . . a snail losing its pace. (pp. 77-78)

Taylor explores the sensuality and vitality affects of natural movement, highlighting not what the movement strictly is, but what it may aesthetically express. In so doing his appreciation of his dancers, the ways in which they, through their subjectivities, make the movements vital is obvious:

> When done right, there is much appeal to the tilting of Toby's shoulders as she stands with her weight on one leg, and the soft settling of Cynthia's arms as she folds them, and the way

that the pointy heel of Donya's shoe digs into the floor as she
lifts her toes—also, when the girls gaze downwards, the lovely
arching of their necks. (p. 77)

Toby, Cynthia, and Donya create the lived experiences of the movements, illustrating the intense dependency of the choreographer on
the dancer. In Taylor's use of language, such as "much appeal," "soft
settling," "lovely arching," he communicates his deep appreciation of
the dancers vital extensions of his creations. For the choreographer,
forever dependent upon the dancer to give life to her/his vision, forever accepting of the dancer's inevitable subjective enhancement of
this vision, the psychological sustenance gained or hindered through
this intersubjective relationship can never be overestimated.

What Taylor discovers through his intersubjective interactions with movement and the dancers is the qualitative aspect of
one's individual subjectivity, displayed by shape, space, time, and
energy, demonstrated through posture:

Undisguised, our individual traits are laid bare, and our
shapes, spacings, and timings are establishing definite emotional climates in all that we do. . . . I'd intended to present
posture pictorially and uncolored by emotional connotations,
but I'm now forced to accept that the piece contains not only
a collection of "facts" but the inescapable body language
inherent in all types of dance. (p. 78)

Taylor cannot deny the qualities of perception that inform our interactions with modalities. Through them he enters into an intersubjective experience with the medium of dance and discovers he also cannot deny the foundation of art—the expression of our subjectivities.

His intersubjective resonance leads Taylor to new discoveries,
but as the performance draws near he is uncertain that his work will
be successful. He has certainly been daring—a courageous stab at
optimal operative perversity—but he becomes aware that in his excitement of exploration he has forgotten the multileveled subjective relations between choreographer, audience, and culture. Immersed in his
experience of aesthetic resonance, Taylor appears uncertain of accomplishing an external ideal form that is self-expressive and communicative. Transmuting externalization does not appear to be forthcoming.

On October 20, 1957, Taylor's first full-length concert, enti-
tled "7 New Dances," is performed at the Kaufmann Concert Hall at
the 92nd Street YM-YWHA in Manhattan. Indicative of the seven
pieces in the concert is *Duet*. The curtain rises to find Taylor on
stage dressed in a suit; Toby Glanternik, dressed in an evening

gown, sits near him on the floor. After four minutes of attempted stillness the curtain comes down. Taylor claims what is quite possibly factual, that during his first full-length concert most of the audience walks out. Louis Horst, Martha Graham's musical director, dance composition teacher, and editor of the *Dance Observer*, reviews the concert. The now infamous critique consists of four inches of blank space with the initials L.H. at the bottom.

Taylor decides to take what he has learned, that posture and gesture are personally expressive, and apply this to more kinetic work. Even though his intersubjective relation to the medium of dance has been broadened, Taylor moves away from the style of piece presented in this concert. It seems unlikely that he found a truly transcendent selfobject function in the final form. His creative energies compel him to explore further. He dives "into new dances with a vengeance. I won't get mad, I'll get even" (p. 81). Even with the apparent failure of the concert, Taylor is aware that his courage to make an initial statement has not gone unnoticed; the provocative program has brought him notoriety. His subjective relationship with the field of dance has altered. Everyone now knows his name. "Martha shakes her gnarled finger and accuses me of being a 'naughty boy'" (p. 80). Martha transforms from a mirroring selfobject to an adversarial one, giving a new-found independence to Taylor to explore his self-assertions, and to connect more directly to an ideal form demonstrative of his talents.

THE STUDIO—A TRANSFERENCE OF CREATIVITY

Taylor, as do all choreographers, requires his "space" in which to create—his "studio." Taylor writes a brief but complete chapter that pays homage to his psychological relationship to the studio he occupies from 1955-1966. The intensity of Taylor's feelings towards his studio speaks of ritualistic transferences of creativity—transferences based on twinship and idealization—representing the aspects of Taylor's psychological structures that are most vulnerable. Entrusting the care of his studio to the "silent" Babe whenever he tours, Taylor's rituals include coping with whatever improvements Babe has made to his space in his absence. In tune with his acceptance of Babe's idealization and twinship, and his expanded capacity for mutuality, Taylor repeatedly goes along with Babe's additions, even though Taylor finds "a king-sized plaster Michelangelo David . . . and a nightmare table lamp with bulbous base that's been spat at with silver paint. . . . tasteless" (p. 132). The "humongous tire that . . . is to be painted white, filled with dirt from Central park, and planted with artificial flowers" (p. 162) doesn't thrill Taylor either. Yet Taylor lets it remain, supportive of Babe's own expressive needs. The tie between Babe and the studio is strung together for Taylor on some basic subjective level.

Illustrating an elemental aspect of this tie, Taylor's studio appears to represent a type of twinship with a silent presence:

> Our antiquated stomping ground, its blotchy skin of bricks and tin, its skeletal, subway-shaken beams, its lamebrain of a boiler in the basement, in fact its whole transitory soul—if it's to crumble and fall into Sixth Avenue, I never want to hear about it. That place is us. (p. 164)

Taylor gives his studio humanlike qualities, with skin, a skeleton, a lamebrain, and a soul. His proclamation that the studio "is us" seems to describe a psychological connection with a twinship selfobject. Within the "us" he automatically includes the presence of his dancers as part of his special space, demonstrating the significance they hold for extending the potential of twinship to Taylor during his creative processes. And yet, the "transitory soul" of the studio might also reflect that psychological vulnerability Taylor experiences as he enters his studio to work.

Additionally, Taylor describes his studio as an idealized place, where dreams overcome reality. Ultimately, in this special space, Taylor repeatedly risks taking leaps of faith that he will find his muse, create his ideals, and discover, through hard work, transcendence:

> The studio needs no changes, is already more than a place to dance in, is brighter than its own whiteness, bigger than its dimensions, more real than truth or reason. No studio can keep its mental health in conditions of complete reality. Let other dance studios be demented—ours will stay one of the sane ones that dream. On entering it, especially when its empty and quiet, you can see it for what it is—an illusionary place, a crenellated castle keep of smiles and sunbeams, a dream chamber, and this despite its aroma of perspiration and the sadness of baggy leotards. (pp. 163-164)

BETTIE DE JONG—A TRANSFERENCE OF CREATIVITY

Dancers leave baggy leotards and no dancer has been more influential to the Paul Taylor Dance Company than Bettie de Jong. Together, Bettie and Taylor danced in Martha's company, and it was there that Bettie asked to join Taylor's fledgling troupe. Bettie's association with the company, first as a dancer, and now as rehearsal mistress, has spanned almost half a century. Again, as with Babe and the studio, Bettie seems to have touched Taylor's need for solitude and the silent presence of an other—twinship:

> There have been times during our long dialogue when I've been able to free my mind from her sinuses and, inserting automatic "aw"s and "um"s, dream up some of my best dances. Probably, no one has ever had a muse like dear Bet. (p. 122)

The common bond of dancing seems to have tied them together. In the documentary *Paul Taylor: Dancemaker*, Bettie reveals that she and Taylor squabbled all the time, but when it came to dancing together, "nothing felt more natural." She felt his choreography reflected his reverence for women, and she trusted his choreographic expressions. She proclaims that dancing for Taylor was "terrific" and that if she had new legs she would do it again in an instant. Together they participated in their artistic ideals and brought out the best in each other as dancers and dance-maker.

Undoubtedly, their relationship has been a complicated one. In many ways it is the most obscure in *Private Domain*. Taylor asserts his undeniable love for her; he proclaims that had he married she would have been the only one for him. But for Taylor that was not an option. Perhaps from the experiences of dancing and touring together, they appear to possess a familial intimacy of acceptance of each other beyond words. During a rehearsal in 1965, Paul reflects back on a visit from Bettie in 1964 when he is home ill:

> Bet, after treating me to a detailed update on the weather, then offered to play any game of my choice. This was a generous gesture—she hates all types of games, and they hate her back. I picked the latest craze, Botticelli. After carefully reviewing its rules, we started to play. She, of course, insisted on adding her own rules and inserting her own nonwords. The game got hopelessly ensnarled, then soon died of strangulation. Undaunted, Bet—glowingly triumphant—reverted to the weather. I tried to respond with unhearing "um"s and "aw"s, but when she started hitting me with the whole week's forecast I wasn't able to stand one more humidity index. Unable to control my own saturation point, and there being no escape, I burst out, "Get out of here! You're driving me up the wall!"
> I regretted it the minute I said it. (I am a nice person.)

Unruffled, she went on sitting there, reaching out to lay her hand lightly on top of mine. I turned my palm to hers and we stayed several minutes like that, not looking at each other. Then our gazes met, asking unsaid things:

Paul, don't you care?

Sure, dear Bet. Haven't I mentioned that I love you? I shouldn't marry, but I love you hopelessly.

Nothing was out in the open, nothing resolved, nothing is changed. (pp. 231-232).

But in a sense Taylor and Bettie do share a family, both at the helm of his company. As in any parental alliance, they share their ideas of how the children are to be treated. In 1963, while on tour in Mexico, Bettie feels Taylor has been abrupt with the dancers, and her role in the company is obvious when she confronts him:

Later on, Bet gets me alone and says, "Paul, be careful. If you don't talk nicer to the dancers, we're [italics added] going to have a revolt on our hands." It's another of her bothersome remarks.

"They're just babies and have to be told what's right," I reply with a shrug. (p. 148)

Taylor, while on tour, places Bet's picture out, along with one of Babe and one of his mother, indicating her special place as a member of his family. And as family members often accept each other's foibles, Bettie, in *Dancemaker*, claims that as rehearsal mistress Taylor needs her because he knows she will forgive him if he yells at her.

Private Domain is dedicated to Babe, and dear Bet, and editor Bob. Taylor chooses to end his autobiography with whimsy and truth regarding the silent presence of those that instill him with sustenance—Tacet, Babe, his studio, and Bettie. He tells the reader he is in the studio with his dancers in 1974, choreographing his signature piece, *Esplanade*. Taylor announces to Babe that he can quit his regular job, because now he can be "our official studio supervisor" (p. 363). He announces to Bettie that she is "going to double as dancer and rehearsal mistress" and wants her to "answer some of those pesty letters that keep coming from misguided souls who're always asking Tacet to design their costumes" (p. 363). When he claims she protests, his response is indicative of their unique parental alliance: "Auntie Bet, dear old dear, let's not start with the excuses. Our scrapping might embarrass the new sprout" (p. 363). As Taylor embarked upon years of touring, there is no doubt that without Bettie de Jong's presence as dancer and companion, traveling around the world would have been even more difficult.

TOURING—ISOLATION AND DEATH IN BROOKLYN

For many years, the choreographer Paul Taylor and the dancer Paul Taylor are psychologically entwined. His body as a functional selfobject is primarily an experience of dancing. Reinforcing his compensatory structures, performing spiritually nourishes Taylor's expressive grandiosity and self-assertions through his talents, and ties him to his prevalent need to experience an ideal:

> Dancing was It. Dancing was what life was all about. If you wanted to be a dancer, you didn't just want it, you felt *chosen* to be one. . . . It's a religion, a monstrous itch, a huge and illogical church. In my case, even before learning to dance, I was positive I'd been ordained to it. (Didn't intend to be a choreographer. That came later and, even then, only served to scratch my itch. I made them to dance them.) . . . [O]nce the curtain lifts, there's security and power of a kind totally absent in everyday life. To perform is something that nothing in the whole world even faintly resembles. (pp. 330-331)

Dancing enables Taylor to experience the empowerment and joy that come from the efficacy pleasure discovered in creativity.

Beginning in 1960, the Paul Taylor Dance Company begins touring worldwide. The travels destine Taylor to years of dance performance. But the drain and isolation of touring overtakes Taylor—most especially, when his body, his instrument, begins to wind down, and, finally, fails him. Taylor's view, as he watches his body slip from near perfection to greater and greater accommodation, carries the quality of one looking down into a black pit.

While on tour in 1968, Taylor suffers an ankle injury that prevents him from dancing. He has company members cover his roles; secretly Taylor hopes they will flop. But they don't. His dances, his company, can exist without the dancer Paul Taylor. Taylor envies his dancers. His sense of self, normally buttressed by structures supported by dancing, is fragmenting:

> Taylor the dancer is gone, evaporated. . . . Watching them night after night and craving to be up there with them is firing up the stomach and building panic. . . . I've become a self-consuming cannibal. I dream of going to sleep and waking up dead. (p. 311)

Taylor's capacity for self-sustenance is based on self-soothing and compensatory structures from dancing. But when his direct connection to his body falters, his capacity for self-soothing vanishes. Tacet is no where in sight. Taylor longs for closeness, yet intimacy is not available to him. "I'll tell you that always in the past, for all of my life, there has been a good deal of emotional sparsity. There has been affection and kindness and sometimes warmth, but not so much emotional-type love" (p. 313). Taylor decides, if there can be no salvation in love, he will, at least, settle for lust. In desperation, Taylor leaves the company behind to fulfill their touring obligations, and heads for Liverpool. There, for a week, he embarks on a self-destructive binge of drugs, alcohol, sex, and potential death from an assault. In the end he has found no solace in his sexual exploits. "That cold kind of lovemaking was dishonest as well as dehumanizing. It rubbed the romantic side of me the wrong way, ran against a preference for fidelity which ran strong" (pp. 319-320).

In contrast, Taylor once again contemplates his relation to his dancers and his work that he shares with them. Here, he finds some comfort: "Clearly, the relationship between the dancers and me comes a lot closer to love. Even though we aren't all that passionate toward each other, at least the work we do together is an act of commitment, a symbol of love" (p. 320). He catches up to the company in London; in preparing to return home with them he expresses hope in finding greater sustenance from his dancers and the art that binds them:

> As far as romance goes, I can forget it. Probably the closest I'll ever come to making human contact will be when correcting the position of someone's hand in rehearsal. Well, anyway, the hands would be "family." Maybe that wouldn't be so bad. (p. 324)

Taylor's emotional struggles in relation to his dancers are ongoing. One, he is dependent upon them for his art, and his primary psychological mode has been based on solitude. Two, as a young child, with his stepsiblings so much older and no family companion near his own age, Taylor may find the "family" aspect of touring strains his psychological structures. Continually, his relationship with his dancers while touring seems to be plagued with stresses. Obviously, after Liverpool, Taylor strives to place a higher value on the selfobject function that they potentially can extend to him.

But touring continues to take a toll on Taylor's psychological cohesion. As his performing abilities diminish, the capacity of his body to serve a vital selfobject function dwindles. His compensatory structures are still dependent upon this important psychological sustenance. As these structures begin to disintegrate, his self-cohesion becomes more fragile. In a desperate attempt to vitalize his experiences

of self, Taylor develops an addiction to amphetamines. The speed but-
tresses his sense of grandiosity and power, momentarily filling in the
psychic hole left by his failing body. But the selfobject function of the
amphetamines supplies only temporary defensive structures:

> a pseudovitality . . . [that hides] low self-esteem and depres-
> sion—a deep sense of uncared-for worthlessness and rejec-
> tion, an incessant hunger for response, a yearning for reas-
> surance. All in all, the excited hypervitality . . . [is] an attempt
> to counteract through self-stimulation a feeling of inner dead-
> ness and depression. (Kohut, 1977, p. 5)

Addiction is compelling because it must be repeated again and again
to supplement the dread. At this point in his life, Taylor has a deep
psychic emptiness; no matter how hard he tries to fill the hole, it
continually drains empty.

As his body ages, his sense of isolation intensifies, and his
relationship to dancing becomes even more precarious. "I have seen
dance as being a home, in dreams a family castle; but lately it seems
to be more and more of a shrinking cell" (p. 198). In Taylor's chapter,
"Gray Rooms," he not only describes the dismal rooms of hotels, but
his deep loneliness they come to represent. "Frustrating sounds of
life and laughter came from the direction of elevators or lobbies.
Through the walls, inches away from the head of my beds came the
real or imagined moans of the heated romps of strangers" (p. 196).

In 1971, Taylor's mother becomes seriously ill. His Rock of
Gibraltar, the relation from which all compensatory structures originally grew, her body is now failing her. Taylor's significant selfobject
relation with his own body has become fragile. His psychological tie
with his mother is critical. Most likely, Taylor identifies with her tenuous physical condition. Again, his capacity for self-soothing is
severely diminished; Tacet is of no use to him.

Taylor, feeling desperately low, allows himself the dangerous
luxury of falling for one of his dancers. The affair ends horribly.
Additionally, he receives news that a sponsor in Texas is backing out.
Taylor, perhaps out of identification with his mother, and/or his
unconscious awareness that his own body is betraying him as a performer, attacks what is paramount in his life—his selfobject relation to
his body. Perhaps this is less threatening than to acknowledge directly
his fears of loss and betrayal. His sense of self fragmenting and disin-
tegrating, Taylor attempts suicide by cutting his wrist. Even though
Taylor has sufficiently sliced his wrist to pass out, he has not successfully cut deep enough to cause death. When he regains consciousness
there is nothing left for Taylor, the dancer, to do, but to bandage his
wrist, dress, and head to the theater for his next performance.

By 1974 Taylor has been addicted to amphetamines for six years. He needs sleeping pills to counteract the nighttime effects of the uppers. He has bleeding ulcers. Unbeknown to Taylor, he has contracted a deadly form of hepatitis. His company is to premiere *American Genesis* at the Brooklyn Academy of Music. Taylor not only sprains his ankle, but is confronted with the damage the years of dancing have caused. The doctor

> explains that my tendons have been pulling too hard on the ankle bones, causing them to splinter and giving their out-lines a feathered appearance. He warns me that there is some danger of the "feathers" piercing the flesh. . . . I . . . tell him that, no matter what, I've no intention of missing a perfor-mance. "Perform?" he responds. "I'm amazed you can stand up, much less dance. (pp. 339-340)

In the mounting stress, Taylor is aware that his self-soothing capaci-ties have dwindled. Regarding Tacet: "I'd fantasized a father or train-er or someone and had tried to think of him along these lines, but it wasn't quite working out anymore" (p. 338). Taylor takes thirteen amphetamines to prepare for his performance.

Taylor's dancers have, of course, noticed his diminished health. He overhears them discussing whether or not to intervene and attempt to convince him not to perform. Taylor fragments fur-ther, and with a streak of paranoia, accuses them of trying to gang up on him. They retreat from him as he hears one of them say: "'You see? When he's sick he's like an animal that'll bite anyone who comes near'" (p. 343).

During the disastrous evening, the one aspect of Taylor's life that pushes him forward is thoughts of his mother. He still needs to feel that he will make her proud, that he will still be her ideal, and that the love in the gleam of her eye is there for him. His strongest aspects of psychological health originate with her early confirmations of his youthful grandiosity. This connection for Taylor is strong enough that he believes, and perhaps is correct, that she continues to live, despite her illness, to fulfill his need for her:

> A heart attack during the past year has confined her to her bed. She'll be waiting in the nursing home and thinking of me—perhaps this very minute. She'll want to know how the performance went and be expecting her bedside phone to ring.
> Not long ago a wire saying that Mother was dying was handed to me at intermission during one of the West Coast dates. I finished the program, rushed to catch the first flight

out, and when I came into the intensive care ward . . . she
was able to see the desolation in my eyes, and she said,
"There, there, my darlin'. It's all right—I'm ready to go."
"Well, you may be, but I'm not ready for it," I replied.
Perhaps it was then that she decided to live a while longer.
And tonight, in a tilted-up bed with oxygen nearby and tiny
pills of digitalis handy in a small bag suspended from a string
around her frail neck, she's still prolonging her departure to
suit me. There isn't a doubt in my mind that the least I can
do is earn her continuing esteem. So far, my performance is
nothing to phone home about. I pop the fourteenth dexie of
the day, wash it down with Mylanta, slap two new globs of
blue makeup on my eyelids, and make some quick, broken
beelines to the stage for Act II. (pp. 346-347)

Act II does not fare well for Taylor, but Act III is fatally
flawed. Taylor swallows the blood spewing upward from his ulcers so
as not to sully the stage. He is repeatedly falling. The audience,
assuming Taylor is intentionally being comedic, begins to laugh.
Taylor feels without hope, without self, without others. "What I've
always held most dear now seems pathetically, hilariously insignifi-
cant, yet brilliantly foolish, and all communication through words,
dance, pictograms, through any means whatever, is no longer possible. Indeed, seems never to have existed" (p. 353). After dancing for
one-and-a-half hours, with only four minutes left to go, the amphetamines fail him and Taylor collapses on stage while performing:
"Body has lost all power of movement. . . . I'm locked at last, shack-
led, caged, am being sucked languidly down" (p. 353). Taylor, the
dancer, is fettered. Taylor's life as a performer ends; he calls it his
"death in Brooklyn" (p. 329).

REDEMPTION AND NEW CHOREOGRAPHIC BEGINNINGS

Salvation finds Taylor as he slowly accepts that his performing days
are forever gone. He kicks his addiction to amphetamines, and with
time and rest recovers from hepatitis. He reflects upon his relation to
dancing fueled by grandiosity—grandiosity that pushed him to success, but now needs to be tempered further: "There was only an
appetite for dancing, and an attitude that had to do with taking days
one at a time, and a naïve belief that there were no obstacles or rid-
dles that couldn't be solved by ignoring them" (p. 361). His grandiosity had run head-on into the limitations of his human body. The trials of Liverpool and collapsing on stage force Taylor to examine a
deeper meaning for his life:

They helped me win a renunciation of a charismatic view of self, and a redemptive view of my work, and showed me that a new sense of life could be made on the bodies of others. The downers helped me to discover the difference between a need and a calling, and to realize that ongoing changes of communicative style, continuing utilization of the faculties that have been given me, are what I'm made for, not impossible, over-the-rainbow consummations. (p. 361)

As Taylor's young grandiosity and narcissism temper and transform, the mature selfobject function of his work evolves.

Additionally, no longer viewing his choreography as a vehicle for his dancing, Taylor's relation to his dancers alters. He experiences them less as echoes of himself and more as subjective parts of the idealized medium with which he works:

I began to work within a movement vocabulary that was more easily transferable, thereby enabling the works to survive the cast changes that would inevitably occur; and when making up steps, I began to choreograph directly on the dancers' bodies. . . . [I]t seemed a good idea to take advantage of the dancers individualities by giving steps that they would naturally excel in, or if their range was to be given a chance to broaden, by presenting ones unnatural to them but more of a challenge. At that point both the dancers and the dances began to look better. (p. 359)

I highly suspect that this shift changes the intersubjective field between Taylor, as choreographer, and his dancers. The dancers' subjectivities are made use of, explored, and developed by him. A greater sense of mutual respect, presence, and reciprocity seems possible in the process. Taylor's sense of isolation seems to diminish. Speaking of what his dancers psychologically give him, Taylor writes: "Their individualities and strong sense of identity are the very things that bring me much pleasure in doing a job that otherwise would be a solitary one" (pp. 360-361).

In the end, Taylor finds greater fulfillment in the studio experience between himself, his work, and his dancers, reflecting a greater integration between his needs for assertion, idealization, and twinship. The creative process extends to Taylor a transcendent selfobject function where his "self is felt to be grand, the other ideal, and the companionship of the twin sublime" (Hagman, 2000a, p. 284). Taylor claims: "Today it's the dance making that brings excitement. The rehearsing in itself is everything and is its own reward. Even seeing the completed dances for the first time onstage isn't as thrilling as working in the studio" (p. 360).

Taylor's more archaic narcissistic grandiosity is tempered into a more transformed mature healthy narcissism. This permits him to return to new choreographic beginnings while maintaining a stronger and more cohesive sense of self. As a result, Taylor works with a greater connection between his motivations for exploration and assertion, and his subjectivity. Psychological risk is involved, but Taylor acknowledges the need for assertive vitality:

> Most [dances] begin as a swamp; all pose a danger of slippery footing. The only firm ground seems to be a certain craft that I've learned by trial and error, handy to fall back on—a roller to help squish the path dry. But craft is never the heart of the matter. No craft, however finely honed, can disguise a passionless base—that is, if the dance doesn't come from a particular and vivid place, my craft can't rescue it. (p. 360)

In order to explore this dynamic and vital assertion through dance, Taylor must trust his subjective sense of self. His deeply felt connection to isolation continues to guide him and command his respect:

> My earliest recognized pattern was a two-edged semaphore of solitude—a beautiful curse, and the one without which I doubt all other patterns would have grown. . . . I found that my lot was drawn from the early patterns of solitude. (p. 18)

Through his permeable sieve, his subjective reservoir, Taylor discovers greater self-delineation through his work:

> Strangely enough, the best places that new dances take me can usually be traced back to things in the past that have already left an imprint and are being revisited, continuations of paths or patterns that started in childhood, or maybe even much earlier, and which repeat themselves in different forms without me realizing it until later. (p. 360)

Self-healing and expressiveness seem to converge into a transcendent experience of transmuting externalization and transformation. His ambitions, ideals, talents, and skills form a continuum that brings him joy in creating: "Dances were no longer made out of necessity, or to prove anything . . . the strongest reason was that the act of making dances brought me happiness" (p. 359).

CONCLUSION

To suggest a conclusion when Taylor is still creating dances seems somewhat absurd. His autobiography, ending in 1976, leaves a quarter of a century of life and dance-making unaccounted for in *Private Domain*. Taylor is now 71, and certainly continues to choreograph and to reap the acclaim that comes to a great artist. But there are meaningful aspects of a creative life to be gleaned from Taylor's first 44 years.

Through the trials of his creative processes, Taylor manages to form some relations—with Babe, Martha Graham, his studio, Bettie de Jong, and dancers—that support his compensatory structures—his expressive talents. These transferences of creativity are of great importance to the maintenance of sense of self during creative activity. Additionally, Taylor appears to possess a specific faculty for self-soothing and reflection that in times of stress helps sustain him. This capacity probably grew out of his subjective relation to solitude. Taylor attempts to be self-sustaining when, in his isolation, other relations are not available, or he cannot psychologically partake of them.

Taylor, obviously, does not present himself as a man without foibles. But he does present himself as a man who strives. This is paramount to understanding the role of compensatory structures, in creativity and in life. They are not defensive maneuvers to hide a fragile sense of self. Instead they are structures whose very purpose is to bring forth the integrity of one's sense of self as cohesively as possible. Taylor's compensatory structures evolve out of his initial explorations and self-assertions, interacting with his talents and skills, lovingly confirmed and mirrored by his mother. Through these structures he attempts to assert a program of action that can fulfill his sense of self subjectively interacting with his world on multiple levels, creating significant selfobject functions through the construction of ideal forms that embody and expand his experiences of self-delineation, self-cohesion, and self-development, and that are ultimately self-transformative. Such activity holds the potential for Taylor to then experience more fully the idealization so thwarted by his early relations with his father. Dancing and choreographing become his ideals and provide transcendent selfobject functions.

Taylor never gives up hope of finding a vital bridge to his subjectivity; his continual respect for this process ultimately brings him to a place where his mental health and creative endeavors are more directly connected. In this realm, his young grandiosity that fuels his search is tempered into psychological structures more available for the adult Taylor to use constructively. Brought forth by a near-death experience and his continual connection to his creative work, Taylor's journey in these processes illustrates the basis of creativity as self-delineating and self-transformative. Such experiences of self fortify the essential meaning of one's existence, expressive of the dancing self within. Significantly, through Taylor's creative elaborations our culture has been immeasurably enriched.

Chapter ▪ 6

Creativity and Transformation:
The Heart of Education

Creativity supports and enhances the individual's ability to engage the world with exploration, self-assertion, vitality, and reciprocity, to discover, express, and elaborate meaning and competence, and to be transformed by these experiences. The partaking of such aesthetic endeavors is never passive, but requires, from creator and spectator, an active *engagement* of reciprocity between sense of self and other. Fundamentally, this engagement informs the coming-into-being of organization for all learning and creating. On a more complex level, engagement is the core of any multileveled subjective exchange. As we ascend into the 21st century these processes of engagement will be paramount to undertake the problems we will face, and to nourish our search for, and expression of, meaningful existence.

Artistic experiences, based upon engagement, reflect and expand our core ambitions, values, ideals, skills, and hopes. Through the inherent reciprocity between individuals and society, the arts ultimately reveal the heart and soul of a culture. When civilizations examine the accomplishments of the past, the judging stick is always the arts. How we create and value the arts speaks more profoundly of who we are than anything else, for it is the arts that leave the imprints of how we, as individuals and a society, engage meaning and significance in life and share a sense of humanity and ideals.

CREATIVE ENGAGEMENT

Engagement denotes that there must be an other; whether the other is an individual, an activity, an aspect of culture, or the artistic medium endowed with subjectivity, there must be someone or something that is encountered. Engagement must be engrossing and absorbing, and requires not just the experience of self, but the desire and will to interact with, and to be affected by, the other. *Engagement is always relational.*

Consequently, engagement is always subjective. Our subjectivity evolves from our early experiences of perception, of giving shape and form to our encounters with our world. Our intrapsychic ways of being are developed through engagement with qualitative global experiences of shape, time, and intensity, our modal perceptions through sight, touch, hearing, smell, and the people and things that are placed within our worlds. From the beginning of life to the end, experiences of vitality are based upon our need to explore and to assert, to influence others and to feel their effects upon us, to be nourished by functioning selfobjects, and to extend such sustenance to others. From here comes the energy, the force, to compel one to undertake meaningful engagement with an other, and to allow the potential for transformation through exchanges on the intra-, inter-, and metasubjective levels.

Psychologist Seymour Sarason (1990), in his book *The Challenge of Art to Psychology,* describes this interactive process between sense of self and other, fueled by engagement:

> Engagement is a constructive process: acting on and in turn being acted on, an ongoing transformation between "in there" and "out there," a willing pursuit powered by curiosity, interest, and the desire to master. It is knowledge acquired by action, not passive receptivity, knowledge about self and the world, and what that self can *effect.* (p. 130)

To articulate the value of this engagement in educational processes, Sarason portrays two different approaches to the teaching of crystal formation to Kindergartners. The first approach is to explain to the children what a crystal is, and then to allow the children to make them. Two objectives are met—first, the children can make crystals, and second, they can identify them. The second approach uses crystal making to demonstrate scientific exploration by mixing different elements together to create something new. Two objectives, again, are met—first, the children can make crystals, and second, they can identify them. However, because the emphasis is upon the children engaging materials to create something new and investigating the way different materials affect each other when boiled together, the purpose of the process is to excite children to the awe of scientific discovery through engagement. In this scenario, the children's encounter with an other is how their efforts create something new—crystals.

Consequently, and most importantly, Sarason reminds us that for the final step in exploring crystal formation, children can bring in any combination of things to be boiled together to see what can be created, to experience the exhilaration between process and emerging product through engagement. The children respond to the ways inanimate objects influence each other, creating something new through interaction. In an ideal educational world, children form a relationship of engagement to the way their actions affect the world and the ways objects around them have the potential to interact and create change.

In the end, the significant point that *everything we learn through engagement is relational* is emphasized. A date in history is only important because of its relation to lived events. The number eight only has significance because of its relation to other numbers, such as seven and nine. Words in a sentence only have the power to communicate because of their relations to other words and the overall structure and expressiveness of the paragraph. Patterns, and the relations that they represent, are all around us. By understanding the notion of engagement, children learn about the effect of one element to another, including their own capacities to explore, discover, and create. The basis of exploratory and assertive problem solving is found here. The significance is to subjectively engage such processes so that meaningful solutions and expressions are designed. Transformative education is founded upon this ideal.

OBJECTIVITY/TECHNIQUE/CRAFT AND SUBJECTIVITY/PRACTICE/PROCESS

Crystal making is, obviously, not the creation of great art. Nevertheless, it contains the basis of subjectively exploring the interaction and influence between different realities, which is simultaneously the basis of great art and the bedrock of a meaningful and transformative educational enterprise. Highlighted in the making of crystals is the contrast between an objective attitude that contains the *technique* necessary to discover facts and a subjective *process* that embodies the practice of engaging technique to illuminate the world around us and our meaningful connections to it. The technique of boiling different elements together to make crystals is quite direct. The subjective practice of using this technique to actually engage processes of exploration and assertion to create something new is an educational approach that transforms the individual to move past the obvious into a world of wonder and discovery—the exhilarating unknown of creative engagement.

Pedagogical methods always contain acknowledged and unacknowledged philosophical attitudes towards technique and practice. Conscientious teachers engage questions and debate intent and methodology to enhance the educational experience for all involved. Choreography teachers have entered into these philosophical concerns from the inception of modern dance. Indeed, the world of modern dance has often struggled with the understanding and teaching of choreographic processes from the dichotomy of objective facts and subjective processes.

In dance, objective technique is concerned with the principles of craft, which include such things as the mechanics of movement, the variations in space, time, and energy, and the presentation of dance on a stage. For instance, place a dancer upstage, far away from the audience, and the performer appears smaller. Simultaneously, place a dancer downstage, closer to the audience, and that performer appears larger. Additionally, spectators are more likely to pay attention to the dancer downstage, than to the dancer upstage. These spatial configurations are a simple example of technical stagecraft that every choreography student learns sometime or another.

These actions are endowed with subjectivity through the relationship that the choreographer establishes with them as she/he engages the creative process, through the practice of the art form. That is entirely different. Essentially, subjective involvement in this scenario responds to the very simple, yet all-important question: Why bother to place a dancer on the stage anywhere in the first place? The investment of sense of self, into and through the act, brings objective technique into a significant subjective relation with the practice of creative processes. An emphasis on the integration between technique and practice can be difficult to navigate and to teach. Technique is much easier to clearly convey.

HISTORICAL PERSPECTIVE ON THE TEACHING OF CHOREOGRAPHIC PROCESSES

To further illuminate the distinction between objectivity/technique/craft and subjectivity/practice/process and the pedagogical issues involved, I present a review of literature on the teaching of choreographic processes. This is not meant to be a comprehensive survey.

(For additional readings see Minton, 1997; Schrader, 1996; Smith-Autard, 1996; and Turner, 1971). To focus in on these distinctions, I have chosen writings that illustrate the contrast between technique and practice. Additionally, these important concerns and their effects upon the teaching of choreographic theory have been confronted, debated, mulled over, and influenced by two, at times intermingling, avenues of exploration: modern dance in higher education and modern dance in the professional art world. Within higher education, teachers concerned themselves not just with the developing artist, but with the student who wished to be enriched through artistic experiences. Dance was explored as an educational experience that enhanced the lives of all who participated, emphasizing the role of creativity in everyday life. Within the professional world of dance, emphasis was placed upon the growth of the artist.

Dance educator Margaret H'Doubler began teaching dance at the University of Wisconsin, Madison, in 1917, and there heralded in the first university major in dance in 1926. Her background was in physical education, biology, and philosophy. She attended Columbia University Teachers College for graduate studies in philosophy and was influenced by the progressive educational ideas of John Dewey. According to dance scholar Tom Hagood (2000), while in New York, H'Doubler observed the teaching methods of music instructor Alys Bentley. Bentley, demonstrating her elemental comprehension of the need for subjective engagement and learning through creative processes, allowed the children she taught to make up their own songs. Witnessing these very fundamental premises in action tremendously excited and deeply influenced H'Doubler. In the end, H'Doubler's rather varied background coalesced into a dynamic understanding of the need for an integration between objectivity and subjectivity, between technique and practice, between craft and process, for both teacher and student.

H'Doubler's emphasis on learning the scientific mechanics of movement, the principles of craft related to motion, was through the "kinesthetic sense, the subjective-sensory feedback received from proprioceptors (nerve endings)" (Hagood, 2000, p. 89). For H'Doubler, the kinesthetic sense was the bridge that connected the objective and the subjective; it was "the subject's appreciation of the objective experience" (p. 90). She understood that the objective needed subjective engagement to be relevant and meaningful. In self-psychological terms, H'Doubler (H'Doubler, in Hagood, 2000) acknowledged the potential for an individual to use a sensual motivational system to experience and to create a subjective and intersubjective relationship to the global experiences of space, time, and energy through motion:

We base our judgment of force and duration of movement upon these sensations, and these judgments are the basis for further general judgments of effort, resistance, and weight. Our sensations of space, as well as of time, are also associated with the movement sense. . . . This objective-subjective relation between the "knowing subject" and the "object known" forms the structure essential to a vital learning experience in any field, for the subjective phase of experience can act creatively only as it is interactive with the stimulating forces. (p. 90)

Through her teaching, H'Doubler's students somatically engaged the dynamics and potential of movement to undergo "a vital learning experience" based on an intersubjective relation between the objective mechanics of the body and subjective reality. H'Doubler set the stage for her students to experience the selfobject function of movement through sensory exploration and from this to develop greater self-awareness and the capacity for transformative self-development. She "believed that the function of dance in education was to enable students to discover themselves, physically, mentally, and creatively, through expressive human movement" (Hagood, 2000, p. 100). As a dance educator, H'Doubler integrated technique and practice into a meaningful correspondence for herself and her students. Besides her teaching, and the many educators she trained, her legacy is left through her works: *A Manual of Dancing* (1921), *The Dance and its Place in Education* (1925), and *Dance: A Creative Art Experience* (1940).

The professional world of dance also entered into pedagogical explorations of the relations between objectivity/technique/craft and subjectivity/practice/process, sometimes in agreement and sometimes in controversy. In 1949 and 1950, Martha Coleman interviewed Louis Horst and Alwin Nikolais, respectively, about the teaching of choreography. Their responses demonstrate the divide that at times has existed in teaching methods and the philosophical base for each.

Horst proclaims that form, based on an understanding of craft, is primary in dance and defines form as "the application of traditionally accepted rules" (Horst, in Coleman, 1949, p. 128). Strongly influenced by his musical background, these "rules" are derived from musical forms such as ABA patterns, and theme and variation. The form of the dance develops from objective and external "devices of manipulation" (p. 128) of these technical rules based on musical compositions. Horst considers the content, and one's subjective relation to it, secondary. Indeed, he says, "The technique of composition must concern itself much more with problems of structure than of content. . . . If an artist has command of form, he need not be concerned so greatly with content" (p. 128). Horst's approach is committed to an objective understanding of choreographic technique through "traditionally accepted rules" of craft, but there appears no true emphasis upon finding one's relationship to these rules. How does one engage these techniques into a significant and subjectively enriching process of choreographic practice?

Nikolais' interview illustrates the integration between process and craft, brought into a meaningful intersubjective experience. In contrast to Horst, he states that the idea for the dance is primary and develops "from the impress of the universe upon the artist and his perception of it" (Nikolais, in Coleman, 1950, p. 148). Such an exchange between artist and "universe" speaks directly to a multi-leveled subjective relation. Nikolais claims that the structure of the dance, "must serve to manifest the idea" (p. 148). Nikolais has an intuitive grasp of the difference between aesthetic emotions, connected directly to the medium and the form, and nonaesthetic emotions connected to the idea, or content. By integrating content and form into an aesthetic whole, Nikolais establishes the groundwork to create art that leads to transmuting externalization, and ultimately, self-development and self-transformation.

To accomplish this, Nikolais does not follow Horst's lead and advocate the use of prescribed musical forms. Although Nikolais acknowledges that, at times, a choreographic idea might naturally develop into an ABA or rondo, he clearly asserts that this is only good choreographic practice when through process a significant relation between the idea and such structures evolve: "Better to recognize these forms as necessities of an idea rather than validities held to be so because of their successful use in music" (p. 149). Instead, he advocates that "dance should strive for its own forms" (p. 149). To accomplish this, he encourages the use of exploratory improvisation. Nikolais implies a dynamic interaction between content and form with *content forming the form.* Thus, the use of form is no longer an objective manifestation of craft, but contains the core of a subjective and intersubjective relation between creator, content, medium, and form—the basis of dance-making as a mature selfobject experience.

Continuing to add to the stew of choreographic theory from the professional realm was Doris Humphrey during the late 1950s. Humphrey's (1959) landmark book, *The Art of Making Dances*, grew out of her desire to codify "a theory of craftsmanship . . . [and] compositional techniques" (p. 17). Her approach reflects her felt need for a definition of craft in a relatively nascent art form. She outlines four elements of choreography, "design, dynamics, rhythm and motivation" (p. 46), significantly placing motivation last. Her understanding of the core of art-making I feel is demonstrated by her identification of elements that illustrate the amodal global perceptions outlined by Daniel Stern: design = shape, dynamics = intensity, and rhythm = time. Additionally, her inclusion of motivation implies the need for subjectivity. Unfortunately, the pedagogical approach she advocates separates elements of craft from motivation to clearly delineate them; there is no integration. Humphrey's directions for teaching the concepts of space designs illuminate this methodology:

> To realize these ideas, the student is asked to bring in space designs for the single body. That is, he is to prepare several symmetricals and asymmetricals, both in oppositions and successions which do not move in space or time (except for the simplest transitions from one to the other) and are not motivated, but are merely exercises for the manipulation of line, in order to become familiar with the ideas of their organization. (p. 59)

Humphrey's statement has several philosophical implications. First, craft can be experienced objectively and is best, initially, taught objectively. Second, there is, consequently, a right and wrong way to explore an element of craft. Third, by studying objective choreographic craft, students grasp, on their own, the connections between craft and the making of meaningful art. Unfortunately, Humphrey's pedagogical approach contradicts her own philosophy: "A movement without a motivation is unthinkable" (p. 110).

Certainly, Humphrey's writings demonstrate her understanding that significant art needs more than objective technical craftsmanship: "Theory is no substitute for enthusiasm and desire. . . . In any case, it seems to me that a thorough knowledge of the craft, if it can be kept mostly in the subconscious, is invaluable in all circumstances" (p. 155). So the student learns the technique of craft objectively, then tucks this away to unconsciously inform her/his subjective processes of choreographic practice. But without an authentic engagement of subjective processes this leap of faith is, to say the least, difficult to accomplish. Humphrey's lack of educationally understanding the relation between technique and practice illustrates her belief that creativity cannot be taught, so don't bother. Her earnest desire to help choreographers develop does not contain a pedagogical approach that enhances the subjective connection to art-making. Humphrey writes:

> I like to think that choreographic theory and the study of it is a craft, and only that, for I do not claim that anyone can be taught to create [italics added], but only that talent or possibly

genius can be supported and informed by know-how, just as an architect, no matter how gifted, must understand the uses of steel, glass and stone. (p. 19)

Missing from Humphrey's thoughts is a compelling pedagogy connecting the subjective sense of self to an intersubjective relation to the medium to develop an authentic and vitalizing selfobject function for self and others. Without this art-making never nourishes the metasubjective.

The teaching and writings of Robert Ellis Dunn during the early 1960s, immediately following the publication of Humphrey's book, exemplify the revolt against craft-oriented pedagogy and the need for a more direct and fulfilling connection to the subjective practice of dance-making. In Dunn's classes, held at the Merce Cunningham studio, right and wrong became obsolete and process became paramount. The young choreographers and artists from other disciplines who engaged Dunn's workshops needed only be aware of their processes in forming their work. This engagement and awareness of processes was expanded through group discussions demonstrating teaching methods that directly enhanced subjective involvement. This relation to subjective process gave birth to the postmodern generation of dancers.

While Humphrey and Dunn were influencing the professional world, Dr. Alma Hawkins' influence on ideas of choreographic and pedagogical practice became known through her teachings at the University of California, Los Angeles, and her books, *Modern Dance in Higher Education* (1954/1982) and *Creating Through Dance* (1964). Her effect continued with her final book, *Moving From Within: A New Method for Dance Making* in 1991. As did Margaret H'Doubler, Hawkins attended Columbia University Teachers College, receiving her Doctorate of Education in 1949. Her writings concentrate on the exploration of teaching methods that promote the creative process. Specifically, Hawkins is concerned with the establishment of a constructive educational environment. Her books encourage teachers to provide a safe, structured, yet permissive atmosphere in class, to accept students' individual creative growth, to respect and encourage a supportive peer group, to help clarify choreographic principles when they become relevant, and to assist students in drawing their own aesthetic generalizations.

These two latter points demonstrate Hawkins' attempts to integrate process and craft in a meaningful, intersubjective relation in her classes. She advocates the introduction of choreographic principles when they become *relevant* to the student, and to help students, *themselves*, to draw aesthetic generalizations. Illustrating Hawkins' (1964) awareness of the effects of dichtomizing objectivity

and subjectivity, technique and practice, craft and process, and the
necessity for integration she writes: "As a craftsman the dancer may
construct a sequence of movements, but as an artist he creates an
organic entity" (p. 5). Most especially, Hawkins (1954/1982), in
sharp contrast to Humphrey's educational approach, believes that
"from the very beginning the student should experience dance as a
creative art" (p. 119).

Hawkins (1954/1982) comprehends the vital role of the
sense of self in creative engagement: "The creative process starts
with the self, and the self remains the controlling agent throughout
the process, which ends with the expression of the self" (p. 64). Most
importantly, Hawkins intuitively understands that the intersubjective relation between experiences of self and the medium brings
about a mature selfobject experience that delineates and enhances
self-cohesion, and is self-transformative:

> Creative expression through dance may also bring about a
> new response to self. As the student works to create or mold
> something that is his own, he must clarify his feelings and
> sort out and organize his ideas. Through this process he
> gains a new awareness of self and a feeling of integration. (pp.
> 92-93)

The divisions between objectivity/technique/craft and sub-
jectivity/practice/process continued on through the 1980s. In
Melissa Nunn's 1982 article, "A Method to the Madness," she deals
with a stressful situation understandable to many college teachers—
having students with strong backgrounds in ballet and jazz take her
modern dance choreography classes. Demonstrating the intermingling between the university and professional dance world, Nunn
acknowledges the strong influence of Louis Horst upon her. She
takes the educational stance "that the principles of good composition
remain the same, that it is only the style of their application which
changes" (p. 14). Following the technical orientation of teaching
craft, her solution is to teach "standard compositional formulae" (p.
13). Consequently, to demonstrate the concept of shape, she suggests that her students from ballet pick eight familiar shapes, four of
which must be on a high level in relation to the ground, four on a
middle level, devise eight count transitions, hold the first and last
shape for eight counts and all other shapes for four. The same basic
recipe is suggested for jazz and modern students.

In this scenario students are not inaugurated into modern
choreographic practice as a uniquely expressive and relational enterprise. Instead, students are encouraged to believe that good compositional practices remain constant throughout time and are not

dynamic in terms of an interchange between sense of self and environment. The significant relations between experiences of the intra-, inter-, and metasubjective are not enhanced. Without this multileveled subjective awareness, students do not comprehend that over time principles of composition do change. For example, with the continually sustained, repetitive, and mesmerizing spinning in some of Laura Dean's work, it is doubtful that Dean would agree with Doris Humphrey's (1959) assertion that "monotony is fatal; look for contrasts" (p. 159). *Creativity is constantly forming and reforming form.*

Avoiding the same pitfall as Nunn, Alice Trexler, in her 1981 article "Making and Dancing Improvisational Games," designs situations for her college students to experience play as the foundation of choreographic exploration. Through improvisational engagement students can encounter their qualitative and sensory experiences in direct interaction with the medium of movement. For Trexler, her role as teacher is to create an environment for her students to engage their own subjective processes, instead of handing out formulae. The articulation of modern dance as meaningful art-making is preserved. The future choreographer has the elemental tool of improvisational play to begin her/his own journey to discover and explore the subjective processes involved in the practice of dance-making.

Lynne Anne Blom and L. Tarin Chaplin, in their books, *The Intimate Act of Choreography* (1982) and *The Moment of Movement* (1988), further develop this insightful trend in dance education. For these teachers, the avenue to understanding choreography is also the use of improvisation. Through these processes students discover the relevance of choreographic concepts by direct manipulation of the medium of movement. Students gain access to the understanding of dance-making as an inner-directed activity by experiencing concepts through improvisation. Such exploration and assertion hold potential for the student to sensitively connect to her/his sensual motivational system and to experience the selfobject function of movement. From here students can actively and creatively engage their subjective processes through their idiosyncratic relations with motion. In this instance, choreographic practice is not taught as the objective technique of craft, but as a powerful and vital interchange between creator and the medium. The potential for significant reciprocity with culture begins.

Penelope Hanstein's 1986 doctoral dissertation, *On the Nature of the Art Making in Dance: An Artistic Process Skills Model for the Teaching of Choreography*, presents an important philosophical rethinking. Hanstein's concern is not with objective technique, but with the skills students need to engage the practice of choreographic process playfully, and consequently, to supply the foundation for their growth as artists:

Not only is choreography a highly personalized process it is also constantly evolving and changing with the passage of time. One only has to survey the history of twentieth century dance to become aware of the changing artistic attitudes that have shaped the major aesthetic shifts in the dance world. . . . One can look at the life's work of any mature artist and see an evolution that can only occur over a period of many years. . . . Therefore the young choreographer should emerge from a choreography program, not only with a thorough knowledge of the dance medium, but also with an array of artistic process skills so that he or she may continue to grow as an artist. This growth may lead to channeling these abilities in new directions, incorporating them with a new style, or abandoning them altogether in favor of more personally relevant methods of working. (pp. 9-11)

From Hanstein's perspective the most fundamental artistic process skills are the "thinking, perceiving, and forming" (p. 150) of qualitative experience. She emphasizes that in the creative process "thinking, perceiving, and forming are intermeshed, interdependent, and inextricably linked" (p. 150), providing the basis of many of the skills and activities involved in creative engagement. Hanstein's accentuation of qualitative experience corresponds to Daniel Stern's core position that our sense of subjective sense derives from our early experiences of qualities of perception that are the bedrock of our needs for learning and creativity. Additionally, her emphasis resonates with Dissanayake's assertion that our early experience of rhythms and modes sets the stage for later creative elaborations, and to Hagman's claim that the qualitative idealization of our intersubjective exchange with our mother's face informs our aesthetic way of being.

According to Hanstein, qualitative thinking "is concerned with a cycle of creative actions, resultant effects, assessment, and new actions" (pp. 150, 152). Perception requires

being open to encounters with the world and actively attending to, or perceiving the diverse qualities derived from those encounters. . . . Perception . . . refers to the diverse ways one may derive insight, intuition, or understanding about the world (or work-in-progress) through active attention to qualitative aspects. (p. 155)

The activity of subjectively engaging qualitative thinking and perceiving leads to the forming of qualitative experience into the artwork, enabling the "production of creative ideas and the ability to realize these ideas in a concrete form" (p. 155).

Hanstein applies these skills of qualitative thinking, perceiving, and forming to elemental activities found in choreographic practice and creativity, in general: idea-finding, problem-finding, idea-shaping/forming, idea-transforming, and solution-finding. This philosophical approach concentrates on the subjective engagement and navigation of creative processes. Hanstein characterizes idea-finding as "unbridled exploration . . . [when] the choreographer gradually moves from the known to the unknown, from the familiar to the unfamiliar" (pp. 161, 163). The choreographer utilizes "imaginative and free thinking with a conscious attempt to defer judgment" (p. 163). If the artist can maintain enough self-stability to encounter this unknown and risky territory the result is a greater sense of problem-finding and idea-shaping/forming. These experiences are illustrative of the initial phase of creativity of inspiration, potential self-crisis, and the need for exploratory assertion.

Once through this initial stage, Hanstein's description of idea-transforming acknowledges the aesthetic resonance of the second phase of creativity:

> The transforming of ideas can be broadly described as an exploration of the medium motivated by the qualitative dimensions of the idea. The medium and the idea participate in a conversation-like manner, the idea shaping the medium and the resultant effect impacting on the idea. (pp. 163-164)

According to Hanstein, the activities of "exploring and experimenting . . . [are necessary] to move beyond known movement vocabulary in search of movement that is a qualitative realization of . . . artistic conceptions" (p. 164).

For Hanstein the final stage is solution-finding. Here "the conversational process continues between idea and medium often revealing new ideas and problems. . . . [T]he choreographer edits and refines the work-in-progress with a view to creating a work that is an aesthetic coherent whole" (p. 164). The artist must define "artistic intentions with clarity and purpose" (p. 164). If the artist is successful, then she/he experiences transmuting externalization and the finished dance serves a mature selfobject function for creator and spectator, influencing all levels of subjective experience.

In striking contrast to the work of Humphrey, Hanstein's approach does not concentrate upon such things as design concepts per se, but upon the practice of qualitatively engaging design elements. Emphasizing this point for future teachers, Hanstein asserts:

Choreography is an experience that is rooted in the individual's ability to find and establish his or her own rules of aesthetic order. It is not important for a student to be able to identify and reproduce, for example, symmetrical and asymmetrical designs in movement. However, the ability to distinguish *qualities* [italics added] of balance and lack of balance, harmony and discord, or stability and lability, and to transform these qualities in an imaginative and relevant manner are vital to being able to establish one's aesthetic organization. Symmetrical and asymmetrical designs may be an element of that organization or order but only because they originated and emerged through an interaction of idea and medium. (pp. 164-165)

The process of engagement between student and the medium is relational. Hanstein uses improvisation and multidisciplinary exploration (drawing, writing) to aid students to discover and utilize their artistic process skills in a clearly intersubjective exchange. She encourages teachers to examine their methodologies to discover their own creative pedagogical practices to help students engage the skills and activities necessary to discover and explore their subjective rules of aesthetic order. Hanstein's philosophical approach to pedagogy assists her students to engage their talents, skills, and knowledge to creatively problem solve, to find significant and vital solutions that transform self-development through their artistic encounters.

Qualitative thinking, perceiving, and forming are not only necessary for the making of the artwork, but for the critical evaluation of the dance as a meaningful aesthetic product. Even before the dance is finished, these processes are mandatory for the important choreographic revisions that are imperative for the experiences of transformative aesthetic resonance and transmuting externalization. Through such critical evaluation the choreographer finds new dynamic information and clarification to bring to her/his artistic endeavors. As in analysis, the giving of verbal shape and form to experience can serve a vital selfobject function. Such sustenance supports a greater, and perhaps riskier, sense of self-awareness, self-reflection, and the subjective realities of others—the artistic medium and potential audience. The relation between sense of self and other is enhanced. Art-making and the partaking of art potentially become aesthetically enriching and transformative through multileveled subject exchanges.

Consequently, the teaching of choreographic practices needs to include a pedagogical awareness of the qualitative and subjective enterprise of engaging evaluation. In Larry Lavender's (1996) book *Dancers Talking Dance: Critical Evaluation in the Choreography*

Class, he outlines the basic skills needed for critical discourse to promote and enhance productive aesthetic evaluation. As in Hanstein's work, the emphasis is not on craft-oriented criteria, but on skills necessary for critical engagement of the work, of one's interaction with the qualities inherent in the dance, and of the educational processes of the group and teacher that support these intersubjective exchanges. In other words, Lavender is concerned with the skills necessary to engage the practice of critical evaluation subjectively, extending empowerment and transformation to the choreography student. For Lavender, these skills consist of the capacities for what he calls ORDER—observation, reflection, discussion, evaluation, and recommendations for revisions.

Observation, the foundation of his approach, is based upon experiential openness, coinciding with both Stern's and Kohut's belief that the core of aesthetic activity is the ability to be open to experience. Lavender claims: "Perceptual openness is a matter of active control: Critical viewers must make a point of opening their minds to an *experience* [italics added]" (p. 62). For Lavender, the purpose of observation is to pay attention to the aesthetic qualities of the dance, not passively but with active engagement. As for Stern, Dissanayake, and Hagman, Lavender asserts that the partaking of art is based upon qualitative perceptions.

During Reflection the final goal is the description and analysis of the visible features of the dance—the manifestations of the aesthetic qualities—that have been observed. This is not yet a critical evaluation of the dance. To promote the process of reflective description, Lavender introduces the activity of freewriting. "Focused freewriting is informal writing that helps students become conscious of the nature of their perceptual experience before hearing the responses of others. . . . The viewers' aim is to achieve a greater awareness of the sensuous features of the dance" (pp. 69, 71). Lavender encourages his students to become consciously aware of their sensual perceptions of the work, the foundation that must be an awareness of their own sensuality. I believe such a sensory connection is an absolute fundamental element of the dance-making process.

To move from description to analysis, Lavender has his students engage their perceptions of the relationships between the aesthetic qualities of the dance—to examine the dance as an intersubjective entity unto itself. According to Lavender: "In the reflective analysis stage, then, viewers move from the identification of the visible properties of the work to writing about the way they think these properties interacted with one another in the work" (p. 73). Here students are encouraged not only to view the medium as a subjective entity to be creatively engaged, but additionally to engage the cause and effect between the different elements of the medium—reminiscent of the Kindergartners engagement with crystal making.

For Lavender, the ultimate goal of such description and analysis "is a time for recording in words one's perceptions of the dance as it was *experienced* [italics added] during observation" (p. 74). To accomplish such a feat, one must become aware of one's subjective engagement with an other. Lavender believes reflective writing empowers students long after they leave his class: "Reflective writing gives student choreographers an opportunity both to anticipate and to observe their own learning process, enabling them to become more autonomous learners who are less reliant on the information and authority of others" (p. 76).

Discussion initially is the sharing of the reflective notes of description and analysis. The class then moves onto a discussion of interpretation. Lavender emphasizes two important aspects of interpretation: "One is that interpretation is a process through which the critic articulates his or her view of the meaning(s) of the work, and the other is that plausible interpretations are grounded in description and analysis of the work" (p. 82). Hence, students are encouraged to use their own descriptions and analysis to articulate their experiences of the work and to listen closely to the interpretations given by others. Lavender asserts:

> The interpretative stage of the critical discussion is both a continuation of the process of reflectively describing the work under review and a separate stage of criticism during which the viewers move toward making sense of the work. In formulating interpretative hypotheses about a dance's meaning and accepting or rejecting alternative interpretations, the viewers must continually make specific reference to the visible properties of the work. (p. 83)

Repeatedly, Lavender takes his students back to the visible properties of the work, which they have qualitatively experienced during observation. The end result is a specific move away from a craft-oriented approach to choreographic principles. For Lavender: "The aim of critical discussion is not to rank or evaluate whatever artistic rules or principles are evident in the dance, but to assess *how* artistic principles are operating in the work" (p. 86). In other words, Lavender encourages his students to examine the subjective relevance of the use of technique and craft. Additionally, the students look at how the choreographer has used the medium, and how elements of the medium impact upon each other. Bringing these components into discussion permit a student choreographer, who may not be conscious of her/his use of such principles, greater awareness of her/his choices and their dynamic influence upon the viewer. Here craft is clearly introduced within relevant interactions in the classroom, instead of in isolation, integrating technique and practice. Lavender asserts that the educational value for all students in these processes is

> the idea that substantive critical evaluation can play a valuable role in the creative process. Moreover, these discoveries help students to see that art-making is a process of revision through which the artist develops the work-in-progress by considering both what it is at any given moment and what it can become through further effort. (p. 87)

The emphasis is on an intersubjective encounter with the medium, the work, and the skills and activities to engage such processes, ultimately leading to experiences of transformative aesthetic resonance and transmuting externalization.

Imperative in understanding evaluation is the acknowledgement that aesthetic judgments are not facts. According to Lavender the purpose of such judgments is

> through description and analysis to persuade others to review the perceptual evidence—i.e., the work itself—and make the same assessment the viewer has made. Thus, judgments are negotiable in a way that factual claims are not. . . . To justify an aesthetic judgment of a dance and make it persuasive, one must clearly describe the precise manner in which the choreographer has structured and manipulated the materials of dance to bring about particular effects and create particular images. (pp. 92-93)

Once again, Lavender brings his students to an experiential intersubjective encounter with the medium and the work, to become more consciously aware and articulate regarding the aesthetic emotions they discover embedded within the dance.

The final aspect of revision begins in Lavender's classes as a form of play. His students brainstorm potential revisions that respond to the previous directions, trying to critically project possible outcomes of such suggestions. Lavender specifically emphasizes that such "critical projection" is not an attempt to objectively fix the dance, but to play with possibilities for expansion, to intersubjectively act even more directly with the medium and the evolving dance. Essentially, the whole class is asked to participate in aesthetic resonance with the work and to enter into a final stage of revision to produce experiences of transmuting externalization. Such discussions reinforce again that the creative process is recursive and that the

core skills involved in observation, reflection, discussion, and evaluation can lead a choreographer to a wider range of possible resonance
and revision. In the end, Lavender emphasizes the importance of
respecting the individual creator's subjective and intersubjective
encounter with the medium and the work, returning the initial qualitative impetuses for the dance to the choreographer. He reminds his
students that "ultimately, the qualitative character and organization
of a work can be revised only by the artist" (p. 103).

Lavender's respect for the individual's self-experience within
the group processes of the class resonates with analyst Irene
Harwood's (1998a) description of the role of the facilitator in group
therapy:

> Thus, it is a particularly important task of the group leader to
> safeguard and protect the individual members' emergent
> goals and expressions of the authentic self from pressures to
> comply to suggestions from individual members of the group-
> as-a-whole. Only when it is a group ideal that every member
> has a right to his or her own direction, can the individual not
> only hope to attain his or her own way, but find and define
> his or her own self. (p. 35)

Such a group ideal establishes a classroom culture that is respectful
of the idiosyncratic individual's process toward transformation.

Most importantly, Lavender's philosophy of pedagogy is to
help students discover their capacities to engage the choreographic
process and ultimately to be empowered. He asserts:

> They get better at making dances. Their understanding of
> how dances work and how they might work better is enriched,
> and this improves their dance-making skills. . . .
> Seen in this light, the ORDER approach to critical evalua-
> tion is an instrument of empowerment for student artists. Its
> use in choreography courses strengthens each student's cre-
> ative and critical voices, which are, in the final analysis, truly
> one voice within each individual. (p. 133)

Lavender's teaching methodology establishes relevant and subjective
connections between technique and practice. Consequently, the possibilities for sensory awareness, qualitative experience and perception, the intersubjective relation between sense of self and the medium, and the multileveled subjective relations within the classroom to
serve selfobject functions is intensified.

SELF PSYCHOLOGY AND THE TEACHING OF CHOREOGRAPHIC PRACTICES

Fundamentally, the mission of education is the development of individuals who can meaningfully engage the world with exploration, self-assertion, vitality, and reciprocity, for the enhancement and transformation of sense of self, group self, and the evolution of significant culture. Self psychology extends a valuable working vocabulary to explore, examine, and articulate the creative act as relational and to exemplify potential educational philosophies that develop and transform these experiences between sense of self and others. Pedagogy that engages and enriches our talents, skills, and knowledge, to actively and creatively problem solve can be examined more fully. As a result, technique and practice become integrated.

I use the vocabulary of self psychology to explore and address the following issues: the empathic and multileveled subjective educational environment; transferences of creativity, mentorship, and peership; the intersubjective phases of the creative process, the teaching of choreographic practices, and the metasubjective arena; self-awareness and self-reflections on the college-level choreography class; self-awareness and self-reflections on designing a multileveled subjective elementary lesson; and the implications for creativity, culture, and transformative education. Repeatedly, I return to the importance of creative engagement, self-awareness, and self-reflection. I hope to create bridges for others to cross over into their own expansions on pedagogical philosophy.

Indeed, for teachers to be authentically engaged and to find meaningful relations to their teaching practices, they must explore and assert who they are in the act. The teacher's sense of self is the springboard from which these practices evolve. Analyst D. W. Winnicott (1970/1986) captures this important impetus for the creative act: "Creativity is . . . the doing that arises out of being" (p. 39). Creatively engaged teaching derives its energy from the capacity to "be" in the act of "doing," to forge an integration between "being" and "doing." Within the creative teaching experience, the capacities for self-awareness and self-reflection are paramount. Dance educator Sue Stinson (1998) highlights: "What we teach is who we are" (p. 24).

THE EMPATHIC AND MULTILEVELED SUBJECTIVE EDUCATIONAL ENVIRONMENT

The foundation of the classroom environment is intersubjective. The environment is psychologically interactive; all participants bring their experiences of self to the arena. The relational is always more than just the individual components; indeed, the intersubjective field can feel like a breathing, living entity that has its own creative forces. Additionally, the metasubjective is always present; we incorporate our experiences of culture into our ways of being in the world. Sociological issues such as gender, race, economic class structures, political and sexual orientations, are all experienced through the intra-, inter-, and metasubjective. The permeability of these forces shape and transform us. The recognition of the powerful influences between sense of self, others, and culture is of the utmost importance.

Therefore, empathic awareness is the bedrock of a constructive milieu. We cannot be inside of others to feel their experiences; we create our understanding of others through imagination. This is the basis of empathy. Consequently, to be empathically aware of others, we must first be empathically aware of ourselves. The fuel for our imagination to understand others, with some degree of accuracy, must come from a self-empathic stance.

This is not always an easy task. We function in our lives consciously and, significantly, unconsciously. Our transferences and countertransferences are always prevalent and we are always interacting with the transferences and countertransferences of others. Hence, the teacher's availability and openness for self-awareness and self- reflection contains the most elemental ingredient for the evolution of a constructive classroom environment.

Self-awareness is, obviously, the prerequisite for self-reflection. Without self-awareness there is nothing upon which to reflect. Most importantly, the capacity for these psychological endeavors must be supported by experiences of a cohesive and *fluid* sense of self, open to development, evolution, and transformation. A person with a rigid sense of self does not actively engage authentic reciprocity with an other. From Kohut's perspective, such experiences of self are rigidly contained because of a psychic dependency upon archaic untransformed narcissism. Such a statement is not a criticism; the statement is a psychological observation. A teacher who experiences archaic narcissism and who judges her/himself harshly will not be able to move forward into a more vital and interactive realm. I am not at all suggesting that teachers need to be perfect in their psychological wholeness; I do not believe that such a person exists, and if she/he does, I am certainly not the example. What I am suggesting is that a primary attribute of a teacher needed to construct an empathic classroom milieu is a kind and self-loving attitude towards self-awareness that is conducive to a journey of self-reflection, self-development, and self-transformation.

My suspicion is that in my field, the teachers who are best at accomplishing this are individuals who most directly connect to a sensual motivational system, first through awareness, and second, through reflection. My belief stems from my assertion that the capacity to authentically relate through the art form of modern dance requires an entryway through sensation. Hence, a teacher capable of awareness and reflection in this vein derives a fluid sense of self-cohesion from the same initial spring that motivates her/his students to find subjective and meaningful selfobject functions in motion, the medium, the evolving and finished artwork, the anticipated audience, and the field of dance. Such a teacher is sensitive to movement/motion as a vital and invigorating selfobject function for cohesion, providing the foundation for an empathic understanding of the idiosyncratic selfobject functions of movement for each individual student. Certainly, an emphasis upon somatic experience and training can significantly support a teacher's self-investigation. From here, an interactive conversation with oneself, the elemental foundation for interactive conversations with others, can evolve. Such an emphasis is critical in the teaching of choreography.

Unfortunately, many students enter choreography class without the preparation to benefit most productively from their bodies as functioning selfobjects. For many, their training to develop their bodies as the instruments of dance has actually been contrary to this effect. In this arena, the traditional dance technique class, taken to develop the skillful execution of movement, has often been taught with an objectification of the body. Students strive to obtain an external image of the dancer's instrument. The elemental premise of such classes is that teaching and learning occur through imitation, not through the engagement of processes that lead to a vital sense of practice. There is no acknowledgement of a subjective and sensory connection to one's body. In this scenario, many dance students are highly critical of their bodies and accomplishments, and their abilities to derive sustenance from their bodily felt experiences are severely curtailed. Dance educator, Sue Stinson (1998) addresses these issues:

> Surely such feelings about the body are enhanced by a pedagogy in which the goal is an unattainable ideal and every attempt is met with corrections—indications of how one does not measure up—all the while dressed in clothing that reveals every flaw and looking in a mirror. In traditional dance classes the body often seems to be regarded as an enemy to be overcome or an object to be judged. (p. 29)

The moving away from one's body as object, towards the ownership of one's body as a container of subjective experiences, enables the evolution for the dancer to utilize her/his instrument, not just to execute technical craft, but as a vital element of a relation to the practices of process. Herein lies the groundwork for the nourishing selfobject function of motion and the core foundation for authentically expressive choreography that speaks meaningfully of one's sense of self in interaction with the world. Dancer and feminist writer Sherry Shapiro (1998) describes her transformation from experiencing her body as an objective tool, to the embodiment of her subjectivity, thus allowing for

> the possibility for the body to be understood as subject—that is, that which holds the memory of one's life, a body that defines one's racial identity, one's gender existence, one's historical and cultural grounding, indeed the very materiality of one's existence. . . .
> By resisting the objectification of the body I began to understand the body as a site for critical reflection in one's life. (pp. 9, 11)

The technical training of dancers often establishes a dance culture that hinders the creative growth of students. Larry Lavender (2000), in his article "Teaching Choreography after the End of Art," addresses these issues. Through his self-awareness and self-reflection as a teacher, he empathically examines what his students are experiencing and how they are evolving. Through their technical training Lavender believes something is lost:

> As we teach dance we teach, in a way, a systematic approach to effacing one's bodily self-identity. . . . [S]omething . . . seems to be erased; instead of moving more and more uniquely, or independently, dancers—as they "improve"—begin to move more and more like each other, and more and more like us. (p. 12)

As he pays attention to his students, he reflects upon how he, as a teacher of choreographic practices, might respond to help his students reconnect to a more authentic relation to motion—the selfobject function of movement deepened. He proposes the following assignment and pedagogical intent:

> Make a piece that gradually unveils you of your dance technique, exposing you as you are behind the mask of dance. My interest in this assignment is to help students to come to terms *in their bodies* with the difference between "dancing"

and "moving." I would like students to discover the movement
identities that I think they possess beneath the dancing identities they have constructed during the course of hundreds, if
not thousands, of technique classes. In conjunction with this
assignment I would discuss with students the difference
between an authentic and an aestheticized self—that is, the
difference, if there is one, between "performing" and "being."
(p. 12)

Lavender then proposes further interaction in the classroom to
explore and examine the significance of the assignment:

Thus the purpose of my "unveil yourself of your dance technique" assignment would be to problematize with and
through the students the nature of what has been transpiring
within and upon them during the course of their developmental narratives as dancers. Perhaps if they are helped to
become conscious of the terms of these narratives, they will
gain more power in shaping the next chapters. (pp. 12-13)

Through his own self-awareness and self-reflection, Lavender
seeks activities for his students that motivate his students' engagement of self-awareness and self-reflection. As a result, the potential
for them to utilize their explorations and assertions to create more
empowering and transformative choices is enhanced. Lavender
guides them through processes that increase the possibility of movement serving significant selfobject functions connected to their sensuality through an experience of "being." Perhaps nothing provides a
better basis for creativity in dance.

Dance educator Jill Green (2001) in her article "Somatic
Knowledge: The Body as Content and Methodology in Dance and Arts
Education," illustrates the importance of understanding such a sen-
sual motivational system through multileveled subjective experience:

One commonality among the literatures of social somatic theory is a general shift that moves outward from micro to macro
dimensions and from self to society. . . . Whether looking at
bodily experience from an inner perspective or more globally
through a social lens, our constructions of body are influenced by the interaction of our somas with the world. In this
sense, bodily knowledge may be seen as the ways we understand our selves and our environments through the body; it is
also the ways we make meaning of the world through our
bodily experiences. (pp. 2-3)

Green demonstrates the capacity for self-awareness and self-reflection when she emphasizes the need to examine bodily experience as
dynamically influenced by culture. Green encourages us to not

> make the mistake of delving into personal subjective ways of
> knowing the world without also looking at inner experience as
> a socio-cultural construction. . . . [B]odily experience is not
> neutral or value free; it is shaped by our backgrounds, experi-
> ences and socio-cultural habits. (p.10)

Dance educator Luke Kahlich (2001) expresses his concern
regarding the impact of culture on our bodily experiences of gender
in his article "Gender and Dance Education":

> Our inner life is tied to our physical beings. Movement
> springs from how we perceive and how we feel about our
> physical selves. Each culture is specific on what is accepted
> or preferred regarding the body, how it is treated and present-
> ed. . . . What is more personal than our bodies and inevitably
> gender identity and role? . . . [T]his inevitably impacts on a
> culture and ultimately its processes and forms of art and edu-
> cation. Since the body is central to dance and to gender, the
> inclusion of dance in education necessarily brings forward
> issues of gender into the educational process. . . . Are we real-
> ly sensitive to and tolerant of diversity in a manner that con-
> tributes positively to the student's experience and education
> in a general atmosphere of openness and support for his/her
> personal exploration, discovery, expression, and development
> of self? (p. 45)

Kahlich's attention to such issues contributes to his self-awareness
and self-reflection regarding his pedagogy:

> What can I do as a dance educator? Perhaps it is part of my
> role as educator to construct within my methodology new
> ways of perceiving students, providing stronger bridges, not
> only to content and principles of process, but a bridge to aid
> their development as human beings whatever gender or sexu-
> ality. . . . Dance is especially important and valuable in this
> because it is based on the instrument that holds the signs of
> gender; it is a personal resource that provides inspiration and
> ownership, and can be non-judgmental in providing choices
> and levels of expression and sharing. (p. 46)

Lavender, Green, and Kahlich use their self-awareness and self-reflections to empathically examine what their students may be experiencing subjectively, and what they in their educational practices can do to be responsive to their students. Through these endeavors I suggest they lay the foundation for an empathic and multileveled subjective educational environment. Within their pedagogical approaches they all emphasize body awareness. From the point of view of self psychology they present excellent examples of educators empathically relating to the seeds of creative expression for the choreographer—exploration and assertion of one's sensual motivational system to enhance the selfobject function of motion.

TRANSFERENCES OF CREATIVITY, MENTORSHIP, AND PEERSHIP

A capacity for openness, self-awareness, and self-reflection through a sensual motivational system contains the essential source for the choreography teacher to enter into an intersubjective arena with her/his students with empathy. From here other relations in the classroom situation evolve, such as mentorship and peership, providing important transferences of creativity. Students who experience their teachers as actively engaged in self-awareness and self-reflection in their creative, pedagogical, and life endeavors are more likely to feel psychologically safe subjectively experiencing self-awareness and self-reflection.

Such a situation sets the stage for the transferences of creativity described by Kohut, inclusive of mirroring, idealizing, twinship, and adversarial selfobject experiences. Mentorship and peership are psychologically grounded in transferences of creativity. In an empathic environment, these transferences evolve on their own, created to fit the intrapsychic needs of the individuals involved. First, the location, time, and rituals of the class serve vital psychological functions. Second, the relations established between participants extend support. Finally, these relations permit the journey of exposure, vulnerability, and openness that are necessary to risk creative engagement.

Some fortunate students have previously studied dance technique without an emphasis on objectification. They may be more attuned to partake of the selfobject transferences they discover in their choreography classes. Choreographer Dan Wagoner acknowledges his significant relationship to technique teacher Maggie Black. As a mentor, she appears to function as an idealized transference of creativity for him, having a soothing and calming effect:

Although her technical help has been invaluable, it is from
this spirit of creativeness that I've learned the most. And all of
her help has been given with a feeling of great positiveness—
that everything is possible if you'll just stand straight, get
your weight on both feet, and "lift your pelvis." (Wagoner, in
Kreemer 1987, p. 30)

In actuality, technique teachers who help dancers train with
a direct connection to finding one's center of gravity and initiating
movement subjectively may more easily incite powerful and constructive transferences of creativity. Dancers must open themselves
to bodily felt experiences to discover idiosyncratic movement patterns and a connected center. There are times I muse that the pelvis,
the center of gravity, when dynamically experienced by the dancer,
may function as the ultimate selfobject in modern dance. The support of a guiding and trusting presence as one ventures to discover
such somatic self-knowledge can feel imperative. Choreography and
technique teachers who understand such connections and orchestrate their classes to accommodate their students' discovering their
own sensual motivations through motion, create an atmosphere for
constructive transferences of creativity to evolve spontaneously.
      Such openness may be scary for both teachers and students.
Teacher Robert Ellis Dunn (1972) acknowledges the anxiety that students may feel when faced with the vulnerability of subjective openness. Such anxiety is easily experienced during the initial phase of
creativity when one's sense of self is most vulnerable to fragmentation. In discussing assignments he gives his students, his role in creating an atmosphere that functions as a supportive container for the
risks involved is evident:

The assignment must leave ample room for the personal
approach and inventiveness of the choreographer. We have
become so accustomed to would-be fixed standards, that I
usually meet a certain initial disbelief and anxiety stemming
from the fact that my assignments leave so much to personal
choice and invention. It seems somewhat difficult to grasp
that I am providing a challenge, and not a concealed and
coded recipe. Once this misunderstanding is past, productivity usually soars, and we have literally dozens of dances to
train our eyes and minds on in discussion. (p. 18)

I surmise that Dunn's capacity to respond constructively to
the anxieties of his students derives from his awareness of his own
and his students' psychological boundaries. Dunn understands that

the anxiety of a student belongs to the student and is not his. Consequently, Dunn, himself, is not overcome with anxiety, anxiety belonging to another's psychological state. Not overcome by another's affect state of anxiety, Dunn's own sense of self is available to respond to his individual students. He is empathic towards his students; he does not psychologically merge with their affects. In the educational situation, the awareness of and respect for psychological boundaries is imperative. Merger is not empathy. Lose oneself into the experience of the other and reciprocity cannot be felt. Constructive mentoring is based upon this capacity to differentiate between sense of self and other.

Teachers can feel overwhelmed by the psychological needs expressed by their students. At those times, teachers must respect their own feelings and needs and examine them to understand what conflicts or difficulties they face. Perhaps there is a momentary breach of psychic boundaries. Teachers may need to explore what transferences and countertransferences are affecting the relationships. Again, a self-trust in awareness and reflection must be the bedrock. Most especially, at these times teachers must determine what levels of optimal responsiveness, provisions, and optimal restraint are most conducive for empathic constructive relations to enhance that particular educational environment.

Teaching is a part of real life. *Teachers will have empathic failures in response to their students. Students will have empathic failures in response to their teachers. Empathic failures are a significant part of our psychological existence.* When nonchronically experienced within an empathic milieu, these failures provide the foundation for optimal frustration, restoration, and growth. Teachers need not be perfect, just empathically available. Again, there is no better place to begin than with self-empathy.

When the teacher/mentor functions well as a transference of creativity, the peer group can more effectively follow suit. Of course, when the teacher, because of chronic empathic failures, does not function as a constructive selfobject (remember even an adversarial selfobject must be empathic), the peer group may supply needed sustenance. However, under these stressful circumstances, the capacity for the classroom environment to provide an empathic milieu will be harmed and sustenance gained through peership limited. I feel this is particularly detrimental. Even though the teacher/mentor may supply mirroring, idealizable, twinship/peership, and adversarial selfobject functions for the students, the group's capacity to extend twinship/peership is naturally intensified. As students they automatically share a common ground. Of course, selfobject functions are supplied through many avenues, often unconsciously, and almost indescribably, within the intersubjective field. After all, selfobject needs are idiosyncratic, dependent upon the individual's unique psychic structures. However, the exploring of the medium through group improvisation, the showing of their works in progress, exploratory and responsive dialogues, and the rituals that develop in the class through interactive exchanges, are all key elements for supportive transferences of creativity to be experienced through peership. From here participants can experience a cohesive group self and a nourishing classroom culture can unfold.

Within the educational environ, mentorship, peership, and sustaining transferences of creativity are intertwined. Grounded on the bedrock of an empathic milieu, vital and sustaining psychological support systems, supplied by functioning selfobjects, evolve spontaneously and in response to the idiosyncratic psychic patterns of the participants. From here students and teachers risk the deeply enriching and transformative journey of the creative engagement of subjective teaching and choreographic practices.

THE INTERSUBJECTIVE PHASES OF THE CREATIVE PROCESS, THE TEACHING OF CHOREOGRAPHIC PRACTICES, AND THE METASUBJECTIVE ARENA

With the subjective processes of practice primary, the choreography teacher cannot depend upon a craft orientation to design a class. The immediate delving into idiosyncratic engagement comes to the forefront. The establishment of an empathic environment is necessary, but one does not create such an environment and then proceed to subjective exploration and assertion. In reality, it is through the practice of creatively and subjectively engaging the act of teaching and learning that the environment and the day to day living and breathing empathic intersubjective arena of the class evolve. Doing must be informed by a sense of subjective being for both teachers and students. Consequently, I do not prescribe specific activities and events for the teacher to do. Instead, I hope to elaborate on psychological experiences that support the instructor's ability to creatively be in the act of teaching and that build upon students' capacities to develop their choreographic styles and, as Hanstein put it, own rules of aesthetic order.

Accepting that the foundation of creativity requires subjective qualitative perception through exploration and assertion, then a choreography class needs to concentrate on the idiosyncratic qualitative experience. In dance this is through a sensual motivational system. Therefore, sensory awareness, exploration, and self-assertion are the starting points, perhaps most readily available through improvisation. Choreographer and dance educator Joan Woodbury (1956), having studied with the German choreographer and teacher Mary Wigman, reflects on the use of improvisation: "In improvisation classes every imaginable experience becomes danceable. . . . Improvisation is an experience of the moment . . . a free flow of unhampered ideas" (p. 117). Nearly any type of exploration is acceptable as long as it is open-ended so that each individual can discover personal relevance within the acts. The initial impetus must be on sensory awareness of the relation between sense of self and the medium. Through this sensory realm the student enters into an intersubjective dialogue between experiences of self and other. As a result, the spontaneous and relevant engagement of space, time, and energy unfolds.

Such a beginning is congruous to the beginning phase of creativity: pre-creative inspiration and self-crisis. The individual moves from the habitual to the new. Risk is always involved. The need for functioning selfobjects heightened. The student may experience the vulnerability of self-fragmentation. Always some degree of destabilizing is imperative to move beyond the predictable. But if this movement is not contained within tolerable psychological restraints, creativity cannot proceed.

Both Hanstein and Lavender suggest activities such as multidisciplinary exploration and free-writing. Leading to increased self-awareness and self-reflection, these activities are conducive to the courageous engagement of the intersubjective realm. Lavender and Hanstein wisely warn that initially judgment must be curtailed. Student dialogue can be helpful, but no evaluation is required. A constructive environment geared towards exploration and self-assertion can be established. Teacher Berenice Fisher (1984) insightfully writes about this process in response to observing a choreography class taught by legendary teacher, Robert Ellis Dunn:

> One of the most important tasks for the teacher, then, is to create the conditions of trust under which students are willing to explore the sources of their own expression, to delay criticism, judgment, and analysis until the vitality of those sources has been established. (p. 85)

With increased self-awareness and self-reflection, the intersubjective relation with the medium intensifies. The choreographer consciously and unconsciously gains self-knowledge through interaction with motion. The second phase of the creative process, exemplified by aesthetic resonance and frantic creative activity, encapsulates this vital and interactive process. Through exploratory assertion the choreographer enters into a subjective dialogue with the

medium and the evolving work. Such actions enhance self-awareness and reflection as more information regarding sense of self is
shared. Again, judgment must be constrained. However, at this time,
a sharing of works in progress leads to a greater articulation of the
qualitative aspects of the unfolding dances. The intersubjective
dialectic between creator and medium is further elaborated.

Through aesthetic resonance, the individual may experience
movement and the medium serving important selfobject functions.
As the process unfolds, however, the conjuncture between creator
and the evolving dance is dynamic and fluid. Fluctuations in self-
esteem may occur. The class participants need to function as supportive selfobjects, sensitive to the idiosyncratic nature of each individual. For example, in my work an element of gesture often appears.
Peers attuned to this idiosyncratic aesthetic of mine are better situated to respond empathically to my subjective and qualitative intersubjective dialogue. Such interactions are significantly different than
responding objectively to whether or not I am varying the temporal
components in the dance. To paraphrase analyst James Gorney
(1998), we all have fingerprints, but none of us have the same fingerprints. For the peer group and teacher to enter into aesthetic resonance with each other's processes, they must become sensitive to
the different qualitative aesthetic fingerprints of the participants.
This encourages a culture within the classroom conducive to individual transformation.

As works progress towards the final stage of the creative
process, quiet work and transmuting externalization, the teacher
and peer group need to continue to be sensitive to the individual's
needs. The ebb and flow between self-cohesion and fragmentation
can still exist. Young choreographers must come to grips with the
physical realities of what they have created, which may not be what
they at all originally envisioned. Lavender's advice on evaluation
should clearly be taken to heart. The group must participate playfully, empathically, in the revision processes, but with a deepening
respect for the idiosyncratic and subjective practices of the individuals involved. Self-knowledge is gained. Students' abilities to articulate their needs should also gain greater clarity.

Once a dance is completed, the cycle of self-awareness and
self-reflection needs to continue as the young choreographer, peer
group, and teacher digest what they have experienced. The process
of self-awareness and self-reflection, through exploratory assertion,
connects us to our aesthetic sense of beauty and the potential for
meaningful transcendence. This journey is a continual spiral with
each layer deepening the experience. Such depth propels subjective
experience into further interaction on a metasubjective level. Sense
of self is always grounded within a cultural milieu. For art to be most

enriching for creator and spectator, subjective and meaningful connections to the surrounding culture must become part of self-awareness and self-reflection, part of a subjective and intersubjective exchange. A healthy biological, psychological, emotional, and spiritual existence depends upon these vital interactions.

Lavender (2000) describes his effort to bring about a multi-leveled subjective connection for his students through self-awareness and self-reflection:

> I am trying to develop ways to help student choreographers
> first to become conscious of the aesthetic, social, political,
> economic, and psychological assumptions and values of
> Western aesthetic modernism, and then, *if they are so
> inclined*, to negotiate with and to critique these assumptions
> and values directly through their art. I am not suggesting that
> we should stop teaching the forms and devices of mod-
> ernism—what Horst called the "laws which are the basis on
> which any dance must be built." It is just that we can no
> longer teach them as laws—we must teach them as culturally
> and historically contingent ideas. (p. 11)

Through self-awareness and self-reflection in relation to the intra-, inter-, and metasubjective realms, students acquire a greater depth of integration of technique and practice. The idea that creativity is constantly forming and reforming form in dance-making is articulated through a subjective, cultural, and historical understanding.

SELF-AWARENESS AND SELF-REFLECTIONS—THE COLLEGE-LEVEL CHOREOGRAPHY CLASS

In the mid 1970s Sharon (Evans) Betts was my first choreography teacher. As was quite customary back then, our text was Doris Humphrey's (1959) *The Art of Making Dances*. At the time, I was perpetually in the initial stage of creativity—drenched in inspiration and self-crisis. I was desperately trying to hold onto cohesion, my self-fragmentation taking several forms. But most clearly, I could not manage to get to class on time; I was overwhelmed. Sharon clearly illustrates the point that it is not just what a teacher does but who they are while doing it that has the greatest impact. Sharon's assignments demonstrated Humphrey's craft-orientation to choreographic principles. But as a teacher, being who she is as a person, Sharon noted my actions and empathically looked at me. In a recent discussion, Sharon mentioned how clear it was back then that I loved dance. I was late not because I did not take her class seriously, but because I took it *so* seriously. Fragmenting, I was having trouble functioning.

Sharon did something quite simple. Empathically responding to my fear, she told me to come into class even if I was a few minutes late. I relaxed more. She let me know, in psychological terms, that my tardiness, a symptom of my fragmentation, did not need to spill over into everything; I could still participate, I could still strive, I could become more whole, I could be accepted, I could just *come in the door.* I might not be writing this book today had I not simply come in the door, feeling accepted and seen.

My university dance career progressed; I continued to study dance-making. Following the pedagogical trends of the day, I took a choreography class in which we diligently studied the concepts of space, time, and energy, but primarily from a craft-orientation. Again, Doris Humphrey's influence was obviously present. The poin: was to understand the concepts, but there was little emphasis upon subjectively engaging these concepts. Late in the academic year, my professor, Rich Burrows, gave us the assignment to find a painting and to create a dance study, a brief initial response to it. As might be expected, students brought in studies responding to the space, energy, and time components of the paintings. I had discovered a painting by Dürer of what appeared to be the hands of a religious man in prayer—just the hands, no face, no body. In hindsight, it does not surprise me, given my gestural choreographic propensity, that I chose a painting of hands. Looking at the painting, I felt awe, and created a dance study in response to my bodily felt experience of awe, especially expressed through my relation to my hands.

After my performance, the class was silent. The silence itself spoke that something different had occurred from our usual fare. Rich acknowledged that he felt the work was excellent. But there was no classroom discussion, because beyond the objective technical elements of craft that describe the three-dimensionality of the body in space, time, and energy, we had no vocabulary to discuss the practices of subjective process. We had no vocabulary to discuss our subjective artistic ideals and meaningful creative elaborations. We had no vocabulary to discuss the significance of dance-making in our lives.

With the vocabulary of self psychology, what might a fantasy classroom discussion consisted of following my performance? Several exploratory questions could have been addressed. What qualitative elements of the work were expressive? What ways were space, time, and energy used, or not used, to express qualitative experience? The subjective qualitative impetus for the work—the feeling of awe— could have been acknowledged. What are different idiosyncratic experiences of awe? I believe that within this type of dialogue my idiosyncratic gestural expression would have come into focus. Unfortunately, that did not happen in my life until years later. For the students and teacher observing, what within their own reservoirs of subjectivity was touched, or perhaps even more importantly, not touched?

Because this was only a beginning study, a more subjectively responsive environment might have helped intensify my involvement in the spiral of process and product in an intersubjective dialectic. This can be an exciting course, described well by choreographer Doug Varone (1997), when he said: "I love the art of choreographing. . . . I love the journey riding the rapids to get there." Such exhilaration between process and emerging product requires continual awareness and reflection, continual risk, and sustenance.

For the other students, engaging in dialogue would have enhanced their self-esteem and magnified their comprehension of the significance of meaningful engagement. Additionally, further conversation would have given form to the experiences of the individuals involved and the dynamics of the group. Such a verbal construct of experience is congruous to the ways understanding and explaining can serve a selfobject function in analysis. The shaping of experience, whether through movement or words, helps give coherence to subjective response. All participants would have benefited from this selfobject function. And finally, such a discussion would have highlighted that the idiosyncratic needs in the creative process fluctuate and need empathic attention to experiences of self and other. In other words, through a more subjectively responsive environment, all participants, including the teacher, might have experienced greater self-cohesion, self-delineation, self-development, and self-transformation, supported by a functioning group self.

Another very influential choreography teacher of mine was Carol Scothorn, when I was undertaking my Masters in Dance/Choreography at the University of California, Los Angeles. My assessment of Carol as such is not because of a wealth of interactions that deeply touched me, but because of the beginning and ending of our endeavors together, and how her way of being in the classroom affected the peer group.

Carol's initial strong impact upon me took place the first day we were showing dance studies in class. A student went up on stage to perform her work in progress. Before she began, Carol asked the all-important question: "What do you need from us today?" From the view of self psychology, Carol's question encompassed many significant concerns. Foremost, it acknowledged that the individual student had subjective needs, needs that could not be predicted by any previously established criteria. As a mentor, Carol expressed her interest in these needs and specifically, the relation of these needs to the creative engagement of that particular student at that particular moment in her choreographic processes. Carol operated from an elemental premise that the student entered into a subjective and intersubjective engagement with the medium with an attitude of self-awareness and reflection. She honestly asked the student for a response, and obviously expected one. However, most importantly, I feel something in Carol's way of being in the class communicated that her question was not a demand, but a show of empathic respect. I felt that had the student responded, "I don't know what I need today," that would have been perfectly acceptable to Carol.

Additionally, Carol automatically acknowledged the "us" in her question. She did not just ask the student what she needed from Carol, but from all participants. From the very beginning, the class was experienced as a supportive community, interactive and available, securing a cohesive and supportive group self. At times Carol was late to class due to departmental responsibilities as Chair. Never once did the class feel slighted by her tardiness. We trusted her. But never once did we wait for her, either, when we were showing our works. Whether Carol was present or not, the presence of the group self was felt and we began our showings on time. After all, we knew we could psychologically count on each other; this was our work and our class. Her presence was welcomed, but more importantly, her psychological presence as an available selfobject enabled us to function whether or not she was physically in the room with us. That great gift taught me more about mentorship and teaching than almost any other experience I have had.

Carol's capacity to create such an atmosphere allowed the unfolding of constructive selfobject experiences between class members. This resonates with analyst Irene Harwood's (1998b) reflections upon her capacity as a group leader to enable the group participants to function independently from her and empathically toward each other:

> As an analytically informed group therapist, I listen and do not offer anything when I feel that each individual is heard and interacted with empathically and that other members are also able to bring up their own points of view as well. When there is open, affective interchange in the intersubjective group dynamics, there is no need for the group conductor to intervene. (pp. 170-171)

A final and significant note on Carol's effect upon me: Near the end of our two-year program, Carol sat down with my class and talked openly about her experiences as a choreographer. Then, she gave us her personal response to an area of our work that we had not yet tapped and might progress to some day. In other words, Carol gave us her impressions of aspects of our subjective deep wells of affect that we had not reached into, that might bring about a deeper and more transformative relation to our choreographic practices. Because of the empathic environment that had been built, the strong peer group present, and Carol's expression of her own vulnerabilities, I believe that none of us experienced her comments as critical or judgmental.

Carol gave me feedback which to this day I have not yet followed. Carol mentioned that my movements always demonstrated a sense of refinement. She suggested that perhaps someday I might explore more "gross" movement. By this she explained she meant coarse, not delicate. For someone like me, very aware that I am petite in stature and build, this experientially feels like a great challenge. I can imagine what Carol meant in terms of sculpture and painting, but I find it difficult to translate this into motion. Even though I have not explored this aspect of myself choreographically, almost 20 years later I keep it tucked away in my brain to perhaps make use of someday.

One might ask why I would bother to consider Carol's comment when "gross" movement feels so foreign to me? The answer is that part of the exciting and exhilarating challenge of accessing deeper wells of affect is to move beyond the habitual to gain greater depth of self-knowledge. I believe my intersubjective dialogue with the medium would gain intensity. My capacity for self-development and self-transformation would be magnified. My ability to express internal ideals through elaboration, to experience a mutual exchange through the metasubjective arena, would be amplified.

Not only is my natural tendency towards movement refined, but sustained in energy, slow in time, and curvy in space. I spent years learning to move percussively, fast, and straight. Through this accomplishment my sense of my self developed and transformed to a more cohesive and expressive level. I now love moving percussively, fast, and straight, as well as sustained, slow, and curvy. My movement vocabulary is expanded; my capacity for elaborating my inner depths is heightened. My multileveled subjective relations are extended. I still don't execute "gross" movement; however, Carol's observation might have been so astute that it may take me 30 years of unconscious mulling to manifest a response. No wonder that after so many years, Carol still functions psychologically for me as a constructive and supportive mirroring and idealizable selfobject.

SELF-AWARENESS AND SELF-REFLECTIONS—DESIGNING A MULTILEVELED SUBJECTIVE ELEMENTARY LESSON

I have, for almost two decades, taught extensively as a Dancer-in-Residence in the Santa Barbara County Schools. In my work with children I try to help them experience dance-making as a meaningful, significant, and transformative act. I base my ideas on the same choreographic practices used by modern dancers, because I feel they contain the core components of creative engagement. (For examples on creatively teaching dance to children see Benzwie, 1988; Gilbert, 1992; Hoeft & Keystone, 1998; Keystone, 1999, 2000, 2001; and Purcell, 1994). Additionally, I try to use these experiences to enhance and build their self-esteem, to be sensitive to their selfobject needs, and to their educational practices, in general. Analyst Ernest Wolf (1989) describes the primary and influential need for experiences of self-cohesion and self-esteem in the learning process:

> Unless we make sure that the child's sense of self is secure, that it has a minimum of self-esteem, it will not learn well either. The child needs a steady supply of selfobject responsiveness, its "psychological oxygen," in order for its self to be cohesive and functioning well. A cohesive self is curious, eager to learn, and we think of such children as well motivated for learning. (p. 383)

Many wonderful and gracious classroom teachers have assisted me in my endeavors, openly sharing with me occurrences from their classrooms and their perceptions of specific needs and experiences of individual children. My respect for, and deep appreciation of, these men and women who educate our young with sensitivity and love cannot be expressed with enough force.

In the following, I present a monologue of a lesson design. For brevity, there is much I leave out. I make no references to the national or state standards for dance education. I make no references to the connections between academic subjects—physics, math, social studies, language development—and dance, nor do I explore the integration between dance and other art forms. In teaching, I use these interdisciplinary connections to emphasize to my students the important relational component of learning. Nor is my intent to suggest a recipe for others to follow. My intent is to demonstrate my efforts to engage my teaching with self-awareness and self-reflection, to offer an example of my explorations of the differences between technique and practice, and to emphasize the psychological realities involved for my students and myself on all levels of subjectivity.

Within these endeavors I try to create an atmosphere for a sense of ritual and culture within the classroom to evolve. First, I present aspects of my teaching that, in general, occur in all my lessons— greetings, beginnings of sensory awareness, and the warm-up. From there, I progress to elements of a specific plan for the exploration of the qualitative experiences of sustained and percussive energy.

GENERAL COMPONENTS

Greetings

During our first meeting, I explain to the children that I have a doctorate degree. I tell them this means I went to the university for a long time, studied something I really love, which is teaching dance, and then wrote a little book about it. My hope is that this communicates to the children that I take what we will do together seriously and that I experience my time with them as meaningful and special. I suggest that if they feel passionate about learning something, they, too, can earn a doctorate degree. I let them know that even though my full name is Dr. Carol Press, I prefer "Dr. Carol." My preference is two-fold: one, I like the whimsy of Dr. Carol, and two, I do not find the name Press aesthetically pleasing and see no reason to listen to it all day. Once I have introduced myself, my classes always begin with a verbal greeting from me to the children, such as "Good morning, girls and boys!" and a reciprocal greeting from them to me. I like this aspect of the class because I feel it gives the children and myself an opportunity to acknowledge our being together. The potential for experiences of twinship is established through this affirmation of our community/class and the participation in a beginning ritual. Additionally, I suspect this exchange establishes me as a potential mirroring and idealizable selfobject, and my students as such for me. Not only do my students mirror me, but I feel idealization towards their capacities to be open to experience.

Beginnings of Sensory Awareness

I then, on cue (i.e., snap my fingers, beat the drum, shake my shoulders), ask the children to experience their bodies as unfocused, ready to enjoy a vacation at the beach. Then, on cue, I ask them to experience their bodies as focused, with their eyes, ears, brain, and whole body ready to move in an instant. Through this I hope the children begin to tune in to their physical sensations. Initially, children often experience the ideas of unfocused and focused bodies existing only between two realities, total collapse and a rigidly and tightly held body. Neither a collapsed nor a tightly held body can easily move through space. In this exercise the children get to experience their bodies in relaxation—unfocused—and in a heightened state of awareness—focused. The beginnings of sensory awareness are confirmed. After these simple experiences, we proceed to the warm-up.

The Warm-Up

During a warm-up, dancers/children execute movements to prepare their muscles, joints, whole bodies, and minds to move fully, expressively, and without injury to the body. I have thought long and hard about my warm-up, because it is the most traditional aspect of my class. The children are all in individual spaces of their own, facing front towards me, and I lead the exercises. Taken out of context, the physical set-up is reminiscent of military troops, executing unison movement, instructed by an officer. Even though I do not believe that my sense of being with the children portrays a militaristic position, I have been tempted to change my warm-up because of its traditional stance. I do not want to teach in a particular fashion just because it is what my teachers did. I do not want to rely upon teaching techniques that do not engage an examination of subjective practice. However, my enjoyment in teaching the warm-up, and the children's apparent enjoyment, has indicated to me that I am involved in a subjective and confirming practice. Therefore, rather than switch to a less traditional warm-up, I have used self-awareness and self-reflection to examine why I conduct the warm-up in this fashion, and why it just seems to feel so good to all participants.

During my first two years of teaching, I planned out everything I would say in my classes. Even though a major part of my lesson plans always entailed improvisation for the children, I still knew exactly what I would be doing in the process. *Ironically, I was concentrating on my teaching technique, while encouraging the children to engage process.* Teaching was scary for me and I wanted to do a good job. Every classroom teacher I work with is asked to do a written evaluation of my teaching. Some years this has been as many as forty-five different teachers evaluating me, teachers who often had been teaching for years, teachers who were observing me teach their classes! I had not quite yet learned what an incredible ally these teachers could be in my bringing the best I could to my students.

After a couple of years, I had a large repertory of activities geared towards improvisation and creating art forms, responding to concepts in dance. Even though I was obviously attempting to encourage the creative engagement of my students, I felt something was missing. I was not creatively engaged in the act of teaching. I was not fully integrating technique and practice. So I decided to experiment. I decided to trust that I knew what I was doing; I certainly had an arsenal of previous lesson plans. Instead, I would concentrate on being with the children, using dance as the vehicle. I preplanned only one thing for my classes—the idea or concept that I would emphasize that day. I did not think through what I would do. I had to move and think on my feet.

In my classes I might be moving and thinking on my feet, but most of the time I am not dancing; instead, I am verbally leading and responding to improvisation from the children. The warm-up became my creative dance time. Without preplanning, I just began the warm-up with however I needed to move to feel present in my body at that particular moment. I believe the children enjoyed my sharing with them something I so obviously loved doing. Additionally, because it was special to me, I think they felt special to be asked to participate with me. Both the children and I had dancing time in class; I felt a greater sense of reciprocity evolved. My evaluations from classroom teachers improved.

Certain movement patterns for the warm-up kept spontaneously reappearing. These patterns not only responded to my body, but to the needs of the children. In my effort to be more present in the act of teaching, I became more spontaneously aware of others. The movement patterns incorporated emphasis on body directions (forward, backward, sideways), levels in relation to the ground (high, middle, low), differentiating body parts, varying large and small movements, and changes in energy/qualitative experience. My increased engagement of practice enabled me to respond more empathically to the children, concentrating on elements of technique they needed to engage their own practices more dynamically. I believe their intersubjective relation to the medium of motion was enhanced.

Over time, the movement patterns in the warm-up became more established and the children began to expect them. The warm-up was a ritual for sharing, for focusing in on our body awareness and expression, as individuals and a community. I felt that a sense of mutuality increased, and through this the children understood that I valued their dancing; I took their dancing as seriously as I took my own. When I teach children for several years, the warm-up builds to greater and greater challenges deriving from previous years' exposure. Teachers tell me that children practice combinations from the warm-up on the playground. Children tell me that they practice combinations on the sidewalks at their homes. Parents tell me of performances for them in their living rooms.

From the perspective of self psychology, many aspects are occurring. The children serve as mirroring and peership selfobjects for me, confirming my love of dancing—the passion that brought me to my occupation in the first place. I believe I serve as a mentoring and idealizable selfobject for the children, because my execution of the movements is more sophisticated then theirs. Additionally, I suspect the children experience mirroring and peership from each other and from me. As the children's sense of mastery and competency of the warm-up increases, the selfobject function of their movements is enhanced. We acknowledge our dancing space as special, separate from the other activities of their day. In this special, sacred place we come together as a community with ritual, defining a secure sense of group self. Ritual becomes part of our classroom culture. Subjectivity becomes multileveled. I believe these experiences add to the sense of cohesion necessary for creative engagement.

These psychological events certainly could be attained through less traditional warm-up activities. I have seen many teachers create warm-ups that are more directly interactive with the children, and I am always impressed. Even so, I am aware that in being myself in class, I am not motivated to follow suit. Most of my dance training has occurred within the university setting. Much of the objectification of the body in traditional technique classes has not been my experience, thanks to many superior and sensitive teachers. I always loved the warm-up aspect of class, the sense of ritual. In bringing who I am into the teaching arena, I share this love with my students. Significantly, however, I vary the number of repetitions for each movement from class to class. In this fashion, I continue to respond to my own bodily experience at that particular moment. Simultaneously, I can respond empathically to what my students, or at times even an individual student, may appear to need in terms of body awareness.

The challenge I give to myself deals with language. I continue to search for language that enhances the children's experience of preset movement through sensory awareness, encouraging them to feel their breath in the actions, to sense what the movement feels like to them. I continue to search for means to explain movements that increase the children's intersubjective sensual connections to the medium.

For example, a plié, the bending and straightening of the knees, may appear a very simple exercise. But with an emphasis on sensory awareness, a plié is a rich and complex movement that enhances one's sensual connections between one's center of gravity and the ground. To teach these experiences, I begin by balancing my drum mallet across the finger of a child. I ask the children why the stick does not fall. Eventually, they figure out that gravity is pulling down equally on both sides, both sides have equal weight. Therefore, the mallet is balanced. I ask them where the center of gravity is on the human body. Eventually, one of them identifies the belly button or the stomach as the center of gravity. We place our hands on our stomach muscles right below our navels, and suddenly we have found our center of gravity.

I choose a child in the room, and place her/his body standing on only one leg with one leg stretched out behind, one arm stretched out in front, the other stretched out to the side—an arabesque. The children watch as I place my hand on the child's center of gravity and gently push in to help her/him balance. I explain this is the same as putting one's finger on the center of gravity of the mallet. For the children observing and the child experiencing pressure from my hand, it becomes clear that to use one's center of gravity, the muscles contract in towards the spine. Then all the children push on their muscles to feel them go in; then they pull in their muscles instead of pushing on them. Through this contraction, they muscularly feel their center of gravity lift up away from the ground.

I bring in a ball. I ask a student to bounce it. I ask why it rebounds. Eventually the children get the idea that the ball "pushes" away from the ground. I have the child bounce the ball harder. The children make the obvious connection that the ball "pushes" away from the ground with greater force and goes higher. I explain to them that their bodies work the same way. Push more forcefully away from the ground to jump higher. Muscularly lift your center of gravity by pulling in and you jump even further. When executing a plié, lift your center gravity when bending, and simultaneously add a forceful push against the ground when straightening. One's balance improves and one's ability to jump higher intensifies. We then use this somatic knowledge to practice jumping. The true purpose of the plié—to strengthen the legs for balance and to prepare the body to soar through space—becomes obvious to the children through sensation. Their competence in jumping increases, as does their self-esteem. My nephew Dylan tells me he has dreams in which he lifts his center of gravity so high that he flies around the room. Somatically experiencing the power of their bodies to jump high can be very reinforcing to the age-appropriate grandiosity of children. Over time, this grandiosity is tempered and transformed through a greater sense of bodily mastery and competency.

A SPECIFIC LESSON—SUSTAINED AND PERCUSSIVE ENERGY

After the warm-up, I go in and out of moving with the children, depending upon how much impetus from me they seem to need.

Often I am just witnessing their explorations. I orchestrate improvisational experiences for the children, emphasizing sensory awareness. My aim is to help them subjectively explore and assert themselves through the medium, to establish their own intersubjective relations with motion. Within these activities I consciously attend to the phases of creativity, the consequential psychological needs that may prevail, and what cultural influences may be present.

To illustrate, I present the example of teaching the concepts of smooth/sustained and sharp/percussive energy. In this endeavor, I try to assist the children's sensory explorations and assertions of these qualitative experiences. (No doubt my choice here reflects the amount of effort I have put into my own explorations of these concepts.) Following the warm-up I have them feel their breathing pattern. I ask them to concentrate on breathing without stopping at the top or the bottom of the breath. Then together we begin to move our arms (my own gestural tendency surfacing) in response to our breathing without any stops. Then I suggest the opposite experience, stopping the breath sharply at the top and bottom of the motion. Then we move our arms as well in response. My purpose is to help the children connect to their sensory awareness of their breath and its potential effects upon their qualitative experiences of movement. By an emphasis on the sensual motivational system, I hope my students, through sensation, gain entry into their deeper wells of affect to actively engage their creative processes.

Following these breathing exercises I ask the students to sit down and close their eyes. To begin to explore sustained energy, the children pretend they have a big wad of creamy, uncrunchy peanut butter that they move around in their mouths. I give them a few moments to experience the sensations. Then they open their eyes and begin to put the experience into words. Collectively we end up with such descriptions as smooth, creamy, squishy, gooey, soft, sticky, thick, and so forth. Then the children stand and pretend their hands are like a giant mouth moving through this creamy, gooey, thick peanut butter. Then their arms are like the mouth; then their whole bodies are like the mouth as they feel themselves moving through the peanut butter. Through these sensory experiences, I introduce my students to the beginning phase of creativity, connecting to subjective inspiration through exploratory assertion.

Then our whole special dancing space is filled with this magical peanut butter for the children to move their whole bodies through. By extending the structured improvisation to find as much variety in their movements as possible—for example, varying directions, levels, and body parts—I introduce the children to the second phase of frantic creativity, original thought, and aesthetic resonance. Greater sensory exploration and assertion of their idiosyncratic responses is needed. All along I encourage them to feel the connections between their movements and their breathing.

Then we progress to the quality of sharp/percussive. I have the children close their eyes and feel an imaginary ball in their hands, how hard and bouncy it is. They stand and pretend they are surrounded by balls and to the beat of my drum, they jab at the balls sharply with different parts of their bodies. Of course, then the whole space is filled with balls that they must move through percussively, finding as much variance and aesthetic resonance as possible.

I acknowledge to the children my understanding that they may have difference preferences and ease in movement. Quite commonly, individuals find that they are better at moving smoothly or sharply. I query the children if they felt one source of movement energy easier for them to execute. I emphasize that this does not have to do with intelligence, but with the personal aesthetics that reflect who we are as people. We acknowledge our own individual sense of beauty. Additionally, we talk about cultural influences that may contribute to our aesthetic tendencies. For instance, many of the children I teach are of Mexican descent. Their ethnic dances often include percussive stomping with the upper half of the body contained. They make the connection that moving the upper half of the body percussively may feel unusual to many of them.

I share with them my own natural tendency towards sustained movement and the work it took me to learn to perform percussive movement with some mastery. We talk about the importance in language to learn different vocabulary words so that we can communicate more elaborately. The same is true in dance. Even though we have aesthetic preferences based upon our multileveled subjectivity, the excitement of moving beyond what comes most natural provides self-delineation and self-development. To communicate more expressively with others is self-transformative.

At this point I usually have the children informally perform improvisation for each other. I always emphasize to the children that when they perform they give a gift of who they are, that this is special and deserves respect from both themselves and others. In other words, I encourage the children to treat their actions with value. I divide the class, with half as audience and half as performers. After one group has performed the groups switch positions. I want the children to gain whatever sustenance they might need from being watched by their peers and me, their exploratory self-assertions observed and responded to by mirroring, idealizable, peership, and/or adversarial selfobjects. From these experiences I hope the children gain self-confidence to be aware of their own responses, and to reflect upon what they are doing by seeing the choices others are making. Through their experiences of self-awareness and self-reflection I believe children can become more self-empathic, and consequently, more empathic towards others. I want the differentiation that they may experience to help establish a respect for psychological boundaries. We all have fingerprints, but none of us have the exact same fingerprints. The respect for cultural differences is grounded in such experiences of cultural mutuality.

I wish the children to understand that I value what they do. Once again, to do this I enter into the intersubjective arena as a dancer, as I do in the warm-up. I tell them that I wish to thank them for sharing their performances, and to do this I share my own with them. I perform for them the same improvisational activities they have. I find what they do meaningful and important enough that I will do the same activity. I believe this extends the possibilities of my serving important selfobject functions for them, depending upon the psychological needs of the individual child. Additionally, my selfobject needs for mirroring and peership are met. We discuss what they have seen. After having danced and been seen, seeing each other and seeing me, and verbalizing responses, all the children improvise one more time. Their dancing at this time usually reflects a deepening of their intersubjective relations with the medium. I feel my ambitions and ideals as a teacher confirmed by the fact that it is highly unusual for me to see children just "copying" my performance—my self-cohesion reinforced by their apparent belief that indeed I do value *their* dancing.

Following these activities I want the children to once again enter into aesthetic resonance, now enhanced by the performing and witnessing activities. Out of this aesthetic resonance, I assist the children to find movements that are particularly pleasing to them, the movements they experience as most ideal, beautiful, and transcendent. The children then choose movements to construct an aesthetic whole. This is an engagement of the final stage of creativity, the creation of a dance that coincides with the individual's subjective responses and ideals. The ritual of performance takes place once again, our creations shared within the culture of our class community.

FINAL NOTES

I design the class to engage myself creatively and meaningfully in terms of my own ambitions, talents, skills, and ideals as a dancer. I strive to create ritual, a sense of community, and culture. Then I actively assist the children to become self-aware and reflective through their sensory awareness. I involve the students in a three-phase artistic process, playing with sensation and movement in the initial phase, exploring and asserting further their movement preferences in the second phase, and finally bringing forth a dance for the third phase. Interspersed, I have the children perform informally for each other whenever possible. These performances help construct experiences of ritual and culture. I perceive each class as offering children an opportunity to experience microstructured programs of action, activation of their experiences of self into their worlds, and extending selfobject support. I hope that I am encouraging exploration and self-assertion through sensory awareness that contributes to their subjectively engaging the practices of process, to make the greatest use of technical craft. When children leave my class to progress through the rest of their day, I hope they have gained a greater depth of self-cohesion to take with them. As a teacher this is paramount to me, because armed with a strong sense of a cohesive self, the children can more actively partake of creative engagement in all their educational endeavors.

I confess frankly that I do want the children I teach to love dance and consequently, to love me for teaching them. But I really want much more. I want the children to be in love with their own capacities to find the intrinsic joy that comes from exploration, self-assertion, and competence, to creatively engage their worlds with meaning on all levels of subjectivity, to feel fulfilled as productive members of a vital community and culture. I clearly feel idealization towards my students. I am touched by their openness, courage to risk creative engagement, and contributions to their community/class. I hope my class extends reciprocity, mutuality, and the potential to partake of the creativity of everyday life. In the end this supports their mental health, my own sense of self in my ambitions, talents, skills, and ideals as a dancer, teacher, and idiosyncratic individual, and hopefully, the health of the society within which we live.

CREATIVITY, CULTURE, TRANSFORMATIVE EDUCATION, AND THE DANCING SELF

What have we gained by examining creativity and transformative education from a self-psychological standpoint? Most importantly, our subjective reservoirs are the impetus for creative engagement. Our intrapsychic ways of being provide the threads for all creative evolution. However, this thread intermingles with our intersubjective relations, becoming strands woven together. Indeed, the development and elaboration of our intrapsychic expressions are always relational. We create relations with our environment, including artistic medium and the people and things inhabiting our worlds. Together, these strands bond to make materials that culturally reflect and expand our sense of self to be touched by the metasubjective. For our lives to feel meaningful, they must be textured, multileveled, with internal and external significance.

Ellen Dissanayake (2000) describes the contribution of the arts to this significant cultural journey:

> Describing in words, finding expressive movements, or creating visual images and forms for one's own loves, hates, fears, fantasies, and aspirations can become a way of articulating the inner world and then imagining extensions or alternatives to it. By enabling the searching out and expressing of one's own feelings and the exploration of others', the arts expand awareness of what it means to be human.
>
> The arts of the past contain the treasures of humankind. In many cases they are the only records we have of past cultures. Throughout human history the arts everywhere have addressed common needs of belonging, meaning, and competence; they have elaborated the things people care most about: their bodies, possessions, and surroundings, their human relationships, their relationship with the verities and immensities of nature. The arts not only teach us about individual cultures but also, through the universal elements they use and our own responses to the universal concerns they address, tell us of our common heritage. But this way of looking at arts must be taught. (pp. 198-199)

For individuals to find meaning in the intra-, inter-, and metasubjective realms, to creatively engage day to day existence, our educational enterprises must respect, expand, and value this way of life. Self-awareness, self-reflection, and empathic attunement must be emphasized. The broad understanding that learning and creative engagement are relational must be maintained. Education must reinforce ways of feeling, thinking, perceiving, and forming that not only identify challenges, but additionally examine the multitudes of possibilities for solutions. Our destiny as a species, our destiny in relation to the planet we live on, is intricately linked to our abilities to creatively problem solve and to be transformed in the process. We must reach beyond where we are to evolve in our humanity.

Dissanayake (2000) delineates the connections between art-making and such educational endeavors:

> Making artistic connections and seeing aesthetic relationships gives experience with solving complex problems and understanding systems in a variety of contexts. Through the arts, one learns that many problems (such as important life

decisions) have no clear-cut method for solution but that an
awareness and exploration of possibilities is the first step in
addressing them. . . . Through experience of the arts we discover the intrinsic satisfactions of complexity. We recognize
that the goal is not always to arrive at a destination but to
enjoy the journey, and that the journey can become a way of
life. . . . [L]et thoughts and sensations roam as the arts allow.
. . . Analogy and metaphor give practice in connecting the
unlike but similar, fostering and rewarding imagination and
"creativity," the ability to conceptualize and cultivate possibilities from thoughts and feelings that would not otherwise
emerge. (pp. 196-198)

These educational experiences are intersubjective. Teaching
is a creative and relational act. Who the teacher is subjectively is
even more important than what activities the teacher instructs others to do. The teacher's awareness and reflection of experiences of
self and others is paramount. In his article "An Intersubjective
Approach to Supervision," George Hagman (2000b) details the important difference between technique and practice in the analytic situation: "Analytic skills are employed not to act upon, but engage with
another person in a relationship" (p. 1). I propose the same fundamental premise for teaching. The technique and skills that we use as
teachers must inform our educational practices so we may empathically engage and respond to the idiosyncratic and dynamic individuals we serve. Technique must be in the service of practice. Only then
can we confirm our students' experiences of self. Only then are our
students psychologically situated to explore, assert, and creatively
problem solve. Only then, without the confines of concrete absolutes,
can our students creatively engage experiences of self and world, to
transform and evolve beyond where they began. The exhilaration of
process and emerging product are brought about by one's own explorations, assertions, and competencies. Subjectively enriching culture
can unfold.

I have used psychoanalysis as a metaphor to give shape and
form to these compelling and significant relations. These relations
are indefinable; they are experiential. Empathy, self-awareness, and
self-reflection form the foundation for our understanding of and partaking in these experiences. Hagman (2000b), describing the relation
between analytic supervisor and supervisee, accentuates this subjective realm:

The irreducible subjectivity of the therapeutic and supervisory
encounters demands that we apply our theory and technique
flexibly and in the service of the unique, complex and

unknowable reality of human relationships. . . . This is the dynamic heart of supervision. . . . Psychoanalytic theories and techniques are conceptual tools that allow us to give meaning to clinical experience so that we can talk together and perhaps agree about what works in clinical practice. They should not be mistaken for reality. (pp. 3-4)

The arts illuminate the foundation of these relations—self-experience. Hagman (2000a), in his article "The Creative Process," highlights art-making's significant role in demonstrating experiences of self: "Art does not simply capture how we feel; it articulates who we are, a living person with an inner life with its rhythms and connections, crises and breaks, complexity and richness" (p. 283). The capacity for these endeavors is embedded in our early qualitative experiences of global perception, demonstrated in rhythms and modes, indicative of our primal relations with others. As we experience, express, and elaborate on these fundamental experiences, mutuality and reciprocity expands. Culture forms and informs us. Dissanayake (2000) quotes Robert Hughes's obvious understanding of the multileveled subjective significance of mutuality and reciprocity for enriching our sense of humanity:

The arts are the field on which we place our own dreams, thoughts, and desires alongside those of others, so that solitudes can meet, to their joy sometimes, or to their surprise, and sometimes to their disgust. When you boil it all down, that is the social purpose of art: the creation of mutuality, the passage from feeling into shared meaning. (p. 204)

Mutuality is embedded in the capacities to explore and express our ideals, to elaborate our subjective sense of beauty, to transcend the ordinary and mundane to experience the meaning of life—to discover one's dynamic and compelling "dancing self." Mutuality, formed through creative engagement, begins with self-experience. To live life most meaningfully for self, others, and society, each person needs to reach within her/himself to find the dance of one's creative sense of being. Modern choreographer Donald McKayle describes such experience: "Dance is movement that lights the soul" (McKayle, in Hubbard, p. 18). Our acknowledgement and expression of creativity in our daily lives is paramount for enriching human relations.

In choreographer Mark Dendy's moving dance-theater piece *Dream Analysis* (1998), we see the visions of a man surrounded by people, but he is split and alone. His struggle and desire to find intimacy is elaborated with wit and poignancy. As spectator, I find the touching and simple line, "I'm going home to me," illustrates our needs to engage and explore the "dancing self." In the final scene, we see two "twin" figures of Nijinsky dancing near each other, come together, not merged just as one, but integrated in their dance. Self, other, action, competence, ideal, beauty, transcendence brought together for a compelling moment; the rift is healed.

Ellen Dissanayake (2000, pp. 193-194) in her book *ART and Intimacy*, describes the deeply moving effect the arts had in war stricken Sarajevo. In May 1992, after the breadline massacre, cellist Vedran Smailovic, while under sniper fire, sat down in the street and played the Albinoni adagio. Why was Vedran not hit by a sniper? Was this luck or perhaps the power of his music? Perhaps the sniper also needed a respite from the dehumanizing effects of war? Many say this artistic gesture marked the beginning of the resistance movement. The bombed Obala Theatre became a thoroughfare for individuals trying to avoid the snipers. Artists created works along this avenue of safety; after the war the United Nations helped bring this "Witness of Existence" exhibition to Europe and America. At a time when life was darkened under the perils of war the arts are believed to have been a lifeline for the people of Sarajevo, connecting them to a courageous and kinder sense of humanity.

The arts encompass our greatest hope that we will rise to our finest for ourselves and society. At a time when violence has risen in our schools, and there are global threats of terrorism, I believe that the arts extend avenues for students to find their sense of respect, courage, and the capacity to make choices that exemplify us at our most empathic and compassionate. Our educational systems need to encourage, develop, and support creative engagement in all that we undertake. The creativity of everyday life is not a luxury, but a life sustaining necessity.

Consequently, we must use creative engagement to inform our actions with high ideals. We must experience and expand our sense of humanity. We must be vital to share our best with others. We need to value and nourish creative and aesthetic endeavors. Our lives and our educational systems need to accentuate significant human experience. Our need to investigate greater possibilities for our shared existence is exigent. Our biological, psychological, and spiritual survival hangs in the balance. Paramount to these aspirations is the understanding that creativity involves exploration and self-assertion, through a multileveled subjective relationship that serves significant selfobject functions through the construction of an ideal form that embodies and expands self-delineation, self-cohesion, and self-development, and that is ultimately self-transformative. To nourish our being and our relations, each of us needs to experience, express, elaborate, and share with competence and meaning, the dancing self within.

Glossary

DANCE AND CREATIVITY

Aesthetic Emotions: Affects related to the artist's experience of the artistic medium and form.

Aesthetic Signatures: The specific artistic manifestations that occur as artists develop their collections of work, producing aesthetic consistencies that profoundly speak of their individual experiences of self.

Amodal Perception: Stern (1985) proposes that the infant, across all modalities, experiences life in terms of "shapes, intensities, and temporal patterns" (p. 51). These amodal qualitative experiences are congruous with the basic elements of exploration in modern dance—space, energy, and time. Amodal perception establishes our most basic enjoyment of aesthetic experience.

Artistic Anticipation: Kohut's (1977) hypothesis

> that the artist—the great artist, at any rate—is ahead of his time in focusing on the nuclear psychological problems of his era, in responding to the crucial psychological issue man is facing at a given time, in addressing himself to man's leading psychological task. (p. 285)

Beauty: The perception that an entity or experience illustrates an aesthetic ideal and a meaningful expression of subjective reality, transcendent of the mundane. Even though experienced by the individual, is influenced by and often shared with others and one's culture.

Contact Improvisation: A dance form where two or more dancers, continually touching without the use of their hands, improvise movement through the exchange of bodily weight and energy.

Content: Refers to anything that significantly engages an artist, connecting to her/his inner life, and is used as a motivational force in the creation of an art piece. May actually be an aspect of the medium itself.

Culture: The manifestations within a society that illustrate and reinforce subjective experiences of self and group self.

Energy (Effort or Force): Refers to the qualitative attitude towards movement's execution, such as sustained or percussive.

Form: The structure and coherence given a piece of art.

Improvisation: The spontaneous and playful exploration of movement.

Medium: The basic elements of an art form that an artist utilizes to create. For example, in dance the three-dimensionality of the body in relation to space, energy, and time, is a basic component of the medium.

Nonaesthetic Emotions: Affects related to the artist's experience of the motivating content of an artistic work.

Optimal Operative Perversity: Assertion put forth by Rotenberg (1992). Optimal refers to the "quality and degree of unusualness that also achieves an [artistic] integration" (p. 177). Operative refers to the technical skill of the artist to create an artistic whole. Perversity refers to the "artist's initiative . . . to call into question and reverse a previously held artistic structural assumption. . . . Art is ordered but within that structural consistency there is the expectable introduction of disorder, and perverse expression is an agent of this change" (p. 172).

Phases of Creativity—Hagman:
Inspiration and Self-Crisis: First phase when the relation between artist and artwork to be created is obscure and the capacity for self-object functioning limited. The artist may feel inspired but filled with self-crisis simultaneously.
Aesthetic Resonance: Second phase when the artist feels a dynamic conjuncture with the emerging artwork and there is a reciprocal relation between evolving object and artist.

Transmuting Externalization: Third phase when the artist reflects upon what has been created to refine it into an ideal image. Consequently, the artwork, demonstrating the artist's subjective meaningful expression of beauty, has the capacity to extend a mature and transcendent selfobject function through intersubjective relating. The creator may even feel transcendent of the vulnerability of mortality. The ultimate result of transmuting externalization is self-development and self-transformation. One's dynamic exchange with culture expands.

Phases of Creativity—Kohut:
Precreative Time: First phase of the creative process when one's "narcissistic energies . . . remain in uncommitted suspension, waiting to be absorbed by the creative activity" (Kohut, 1976/1978a, p. 817).

Time of Frantic Creativity and Original Thought: Second phase when there is an outpouring of narcissistic energy towards the evolving artwork

Time of Quiet Work: Third phase when the external object has enough coherence that the artist can finish her/his subjective and ideal molding of it.

Rhythm and Modes: Ellen Dissanayake (2000) notes, "rhythm has to with an unfolding in time, the patterned course of an experience; modes are qualities of that experience" (p. 6). Our creative endeavors, expressive of these subjective experiences of rhythm and modes from early childhood, secure our sense of reciprocity.

Self-Transformation: An evolution within one's intrapsychic idiosyncratic patterns of experience.

Somatics: A field of study and a mode of technical training used in modern dance that emphasizes and values the direct sensory connection to one's body as the most elemental tool of learning to dance.

Space: Refers not just to an area for dancing, but to the fact that the body exists in space and therefore has shape and design.

Time: Refers to patterns of duration, pulse, and rhythms of movement.

Transferences of Creativity: Kohut's description of the transferences that individuals, while engaged in creative activity, seek out in order to fulfill their intensified needs for selfobject experience and to maintain experiences of self-cohesion. The ability to locate transferences of creativity is an important aspect of healthy creative engagement.

Vitality: To experience a dynamic connection between sense of self and one's actions in the world.

Vitality Affects: Stern (1985) describes these as "elusive qualities captured by dynamic, kinetic terms, such as 'surging,' 'fading away,' 'fleeting,' 'explosive,' 'crescendo,' 'decrescendo,' 'bursting,' 'drawn out,' and so on" (p. 54), which, at times, have the sensation of a "rush" (p. 56). They ultimately express a way of feeling as opposed to a specific content of feeling.

PSYCHOANALYTIC

Archaic Selfobject: Kohut's term for a psychological support system such as mirroring, idealizable, twinship, or adversarial that is experienced by young children as part of themselves. Such experiences are age-appropriate.

Adversarial Selfobject: Wolf's (1985) term for a psychological support system that enhances self-experience "by providing the experience of being a center of initiative through permitting nondestructive oppositional self-assertiveness" (p. 185).

Analysand: The patient undergoing analysis.

Bipolar Self: Kohut's theoretical understanding of self-experience developed around a three-part image—a pole of ambitions, a pole of ideals, and one's talents and skills as the tension arc between the two poles.

Compensatory Structures of the Self: According to Kohut, components of self-structure that intensify in development to counteract faulty development. Their purpose is to bring forth the integrity of self-experience as cohesively as possible.

Countertransference: A transference that is a direct reaction to the transference of another.

Cultural Selfobject: Kohut's term for psychological support systems that enhance experiences of cohesion and heal fragmentation for the group self. These are experienced by the individual, resonating with needs for mirroring, idealizing, twinship/peership, and adversarial relations. Examples are the leader who instills a society with a sense of direction and purpose, a religious icon that provides a sense of security and peace, great art that reminds individuals that they share a sense of humanity with others, and a past historical figure who confirms to a society what they feel adverse to occurring in their own historical times.

Defensive Structures of the Self: Psychic mechanisms used to conceal a defect or deficit in self-structures and cannot be used to bring forth the integrity of self-experience cohesively.

Developmental Line of Empathy: Kohut's description of the progression of empathic needs from archaic (early) development to mature configurations. Informs empathic response that appropriately fits the individual's developmental level. The young infant may need a direct touch, while the older child may just need a smile from the distance. In analysis, the understanding phase supplies direct empathic confirmation of what the analysand is feeling. In the explaining phase, the analyst extends interpretations of how and why the analysand came to experience what she/he feels. This interpretation is based upon empathic immersion by the analyst into the psychological life of the patient, mixed with theory, to offer the patient a higher form of empathic understanding.

Developmental Line of Narcissism: Kohut's description of the progression of narcissism from archaic (early) development to transformed mature healthy narcissism.

Disintegration Anxiety: Anxiety experienced when self-cohesion fragments to such an extent that one fears for one's psychological existence. May be felt most acutely when in an environment void of empathy and filled with indifference.

Disorders of the Self: A psychological disorder caused by a defect or deficit in self-structures resulting in a chronic experience of lack of self-cohesion and hampering constructive and nourishing relations with others.

Domain of Core-Relatedness: Stern's (1985) assertion that between 2-6 months the infant develops a sense of a physical self and is believed to understand that "mother" is separate physically. The infant's sense of self and mother are of "core entities of physical presence, action, affect, and continuity" (p. 27).

Domain of Emergent-Relatedness: Stern's (1985) assertion that between 0-2 months of age the infant begins to create organization out of its myriad of impressions and interactions. Significantly, Stern believes the infant not only becomes aware through organization but is also aware of the process of "organization-coming-into-being" (p. 47). This capacity to experience process as well as product is the foundation for all learning and creativity.

Domain of Intersubjective Relatedness: Stern's (1985) assertion that between 7-9 months the infant develops a sense of a subjective self. The infant becomes aware that separate physical beings have separate minds with "feelings, motives, intentions—that lie behind the physical happenings in the domain of core-relatedness" (p. 27).

Domain of Verbal Relatedness: Stern's assertion that between 15-18 months the infant develops a sense of a verbal self that allows the conveyance of personal meanings and experience through the symbols of language. The infant begins to have a personal history, and to develop the important capacities for self-reflection and empathy.

Empathy: The capacity to imagine oneself into the inner life of another with some degree of accuracy. Empathy, describing the basic mode of observation, defines the field of psychoanalysis. Additionally, our empathic imaginations are used to inform our actions for good or ill. Most importantly, empathy is the fundamental psychological element necessary for a responsive environment to foster psychological and emotional growth.

Exploratory-Assertive Motivational System: Lichtenberg's delineation of a specific motivational system concerned with exploration and assertion, discovery and action, that promotes a sense of competence, and the pleasure of efficacy.

Group Self: Kohut's notion that all basic psychological realities, components, and needs of the individual are understood to exist for the group, or society, as well, just on a much larger scale.

Idealizable Selfobject: Kohut's term for a psychological support system that resonates with our subjective sense of idealization and that confirms our sense of ideals and values.

Intersubjective: Experiences of relationships.

Intrasubjective: Experiences of self.

Mature Selfobject: Psychological support system that no longer is experienced as an archaic selfobject and part of one's self-experience, but as part of a dynamic and self-affirming relationship with an awareness of and reciprocity with an other.

Metasubjective: Experiences of culture.

Mirroring Selfobject: Kohut's term for a psychological support system that responds to and confirms our sense of healthy ambition and self-expression. Mirroring does not necessarily mean to duplicate what another does, but to extend psychological sustenance through confirmation of one's subjectivity.

Motivational Systems: Lichtenberg's delineation of a branch of self psychology that perceives our self-experience and the construction of self-structures in response to five basic needs: "the need to fulfill physiological requirements, the need for attachment and affiliation, the need for assertion and exploration, the need to react aversively through antagonism and/or withdrawal, and the need for sensual and sexual satisfaction" (Lichtenberg, 1988, p. 60).

Narcissism—Freudian Perspective: Defines the psychic energy of one who is selfishly concerned with oneself. Freud incorporates this view of narcissism into his ideas of the human psyche, mechanistically based on biological drives. These drives to satiate hunger and sexual desire are fueled by our libido, our sexual/psychic energy. Freud sees narcissism operating on a continuum from narcissistically cathected (invested) libido—sexual energy preoccupied with one's self—to object love—sexual energy cathected upon another. Here "object" denotes another person, such as when we speak of the "object of our affection."

Narcissism—Kohutian Perspective: The awareness and maintenance of sense of self.

Nuclear Self: Kohut's view of the self first experienced and developed during childhood.

Optimal Frustration: Kohut's description of the natural frustrations that occur in life and in relationships. If experienced within an empathic environment promotes the development of self-structures.

Optimal Responsiveness: From Bacal's (1985) view

> the responsivity of the analyst that is therapeutically most relevant at any particular moment in the context of a particular patient and his illness. Empathy or vicarious introspection is the process by which the therapist comes to understand the patient by tuning in to his inner world. Optimal responsiveness, on the other hand, refers to the therapist's acts of communicating his understanding to his patient. (p. 202)

Optimal Restraint: From the Shanes' (1996) view "a response within the therapeutic dyad that is neither in excess of what is needed or desired by the patient, nor so withholding or so unspontaneous that it serves to derail the process" (p. 43).

Peership Selfobject: Psychological support system that supplies a more mature form of twinship.

Permeable Sieve: Kohut (1987) uses the visual metaphor of a sieve to describe psychological structure: "Psychological structure is gradually acquired through various experiential interactions with the environment, so that layer after layer of a yet sieve-like substance is built up. . . . Structure is a sieve in depth" (p. 160). He claims that artists have permeable sieves that enable them to access their deeper wells of affect.

Primary Narcissism: Freudian view of the experience of the newborn infant merged with her/his surroundings and incapable of differentiating between experiences of self and other.

Primary Structures of the Self: The basic components of the self that develop in response to an empathic environment.

Program of Action: From Kohut's view, a blueprint of agency that allows one to feel one's actions resonate with, and enhance, one's sense of one's ambitions, ideals and talents.

Provision: A specific action that a therapist takes beyond empathic immersion and interpretation.

RIG: Stern's (1985) idea on the acquisition of structure as

> representations of interactions that have been generalized. . . .
> It is important to remember that RIGs are flexible structures
> that average several actual instances and form a prototype to
> represent them all. A RIG is something that has never happened before exactly that way, yet it takes into account nothing that did not actually happen once.
>   The experience of being with a self-regulating other [selfobject] gradually forms RIGs. (p. 110)

Secondary Narcissism: Freudian description of the narcissistic withdrawal of energy from others by adults. Parallels the primary narcissism of infants. In adults, is most likely to occur when we are pain. We have trouble paying attention to others when we have a toothache.

Self-Cohesion: A self-experience of feeling whole and self-confident.

Self-Fragmentation: A self-experience of feeling unwhole usually accompanied by a drop in self-esteem. In severe cases, leads to intense anxiety and/or depression.

Self—Kohut's Perspective: Because self is only known through subjective experience and its manifestations, Kohut's (Kohut & Wolf, 1978/1986) definition of self is one of experiencing patterns and actions:

> The patterns of ambitions, skills and [idealized] goals; the tensions between them; the programme of action that they create; and the activities that strive towards the realization of this programme are all experienced as continuous in space and time—they are the self, an independent centre of initiative, an independent recipient of impressions. (p. 178)

Self—Stern's Perspective: "Of self" means "an invariant pattern of awareness . . . a form of organization" (Stern, 1985, p. 7). Sense of self develops through four domains of experience: emergent, core, intersubjective, and verbal.

Selfobjects: Kohut's term for psychological support systems that function in our lives to sustain our intrapsychic experiences of self-cohesion. Even though in many instances selfobjects are other people, they can also be animals, things, places, ideas, or activities that serve to confirm and enhance who we are.

Self-Structures: Our subjective ordering of experience into recognizable patterns, conscious and unconscious, which persist over time and are experienced by us as our "self." They are, in essence, our intrapsychic ways of being.

Sensual/Sexual Motivational System: Lichtenberg's delineation of a specific motivational system concerned with sensuality and/or sexuality. Sensuality may play a significant role in the subjective motivation of a modern dance choreographer.

Subjectivity: Our intrapsychic ways of being that influence our experiences of self in and with our world.

Transference: Originally meant the crossing of information from the unconscious barrier into the preconscious realm (Siegel, 1996). From this Freudian perspective, slips of the tongue are transferences. Over time transference has taken on a different meaning. Transference is the way we create, the way we empower another, with what we psychologically need to find in the other. These transferences are based upon our past and the way our self-structures have developed through interactions with others.

Transformations of Narcissism: Kohut delineates five manifestations of transformed mature narcissism—creativity, empathy, the acceptance of our own impermanence, humor, and wisdom.

Transmuting Internalization: The process through which Kohut believes structure building occurs in response to optimal frustration. Whatever psychological needs were being met through the selfobject experience are internalized by the individual as part of one's own self-structure.

Twinship Selfobject: Kohut's term for a psychological support system that confirms our sense of essential sameness.

References

Acocella, J. (1993). *Mark Morris*. New York: Farrar Straus Giroux.

Albright, A. C. (1997). *Choreographing difference: The body and identity in contemporary dance*. Middletown, CT: Wesleyan University Press.

Albright, A. C. (1999). Steve Paxton. In M. Bremser (Ed.), *Fifty contemporary choreographers* (pp. 184-188). London: Routledge.

Alexander, F. M. (1971). *The resurrection of the body*. New York: Dell.

Banes, S. (1987). *Terpsichore in sneakers: Post-modern dance*. Middletown, CT: Wesleyan University Press.

Bacal, H. A. (1985). Optimal responsiveness and the therapeutic process. In A. Goldberg (Ed.), *Progress in self psychology* (Vol. 1, pp. 202-227). New York: The Guilford Press.

Bartenieff, I. (1996). *Body movement: Coping with the environment*. New York: Gordon and Breach.

Beaumont, C. (1981). *Michel Fokine and his ballets*. New York: Dance Horizons.

Beebe, B., & Lachmann, F. M. (1988). Mother-infant mutual influence and precursors of psychic structure. In A. Goldberg (Ed.), *Frontiers in self psychology: Progress in self psychology* (Vol. 3, pp. 3-25). Hillsdale, NJ: The Analytic Press.

Benzwie, T. (1988). *A moving experience: Dance for lovers of children and the child within*. Tucson, AZ: Zephyr Press.

Blom, L. A., & Chaplin, L. T. (1982). *The intimate act of choreography.* Pittsburgh: University of Pittsburgh Press.

Blom, L. A., & Chaplin, L. T. (1988). *The moment of movement: Dance improvisation.* Pittsburgh: University of Pittsburgh Press.

Brothers, D., & Lewinberg, E. (1999). The therapeutic partnership: A developmental view of self-psychological treatment as bilateral healing. In A. Goldberg (Ed.), *Pluralism in self psychology: Progress in self psychology* (Vol. 15, pp. 259-284). Hillsdale, NJ: The Analytic Press.

Brown, J. M., Mindlin, N., & Woodford, C. H. (Eds.). (1998). *The vision of modern dance* (2nd ed). Hightstown, NJ: Princeton Book Company.

Buirski, P., & Haglund, P. (1999). The selfobject function of interpretation. In A. Goldberg (Ed.), *Pluralism in self psychology: Progress in self psychology* (Vol 15, pp. 31-49). Hillsdale, NJ: The Analytic Press.

Coe, R. (1985). *Dance in America.* New York: E. P. Dutton.

Cohen, S. J. (1962, August). Avant-garde choreography: Part III. *Dance Magazine,* pp. 45, 54-56.

Cohen, S. J. (Ed.). (1972). *Doris Humphrey: An artist first.* Middletown, CT: Wesleyan University Press.

Coleman, M. (1949, November). On the teaching of choreography: Interview with Louis Horst. *Dance Observer,* pp. 128-130.

Coleman, M. (1950, December). On the teaching of choreography: Interview with Alwin Nikolais. *Dance Observer,* pp. 148-150.

Collins, N. D. (1999). Stephen Petronio. In M. Bremser (Ed.), *Fifty contemporary choreographers* (pp. 189-192). London: Routledge.

Dendy, M. Lecture: Art and the politics of sexuality. July 24, 2000, Santa Barbara, CA.

Dendy, M. (2000, July 25). Open rehearsal. Santa Barbara, CA.

Dewey, J. (1934). *Art as experience.* New York: Capricorn Books.

Dissanayake, E. (1988). *What is ART for?* Seattle: University of Washington Press.

Dissanayake, E. (2000). *ART and intimacy: How the arts began.* Seattle: University of Washington Press.

Duncan, I. (1903-1927/1981). *Isadora speaks* (F. Rosemont, Ed.). San Francisco: City Lights Books.

Dunn, R. (1972). Composition/1. Can choreography be taught? (Apologies to Louis Horst). *Ballet Review,* 4(2), 2-18.

Dunning, J. (1978, February 19). Modernists—Why do they choreograph? *The New York Times,* pp. 16, 35.

Erdman, J. (1948, April). Young dancers state their views: As told to Joseph Campbell. *Dance Observer,* pp. 40-41.

Feldenkrais, M. (1975). *Awareness through movement.* New York: Harper & Row.

Fisch, J. (1999). Summation of discussions. In A. Goldberg. (Ed.), *Pluralism in self psychology: Progress in self psychology* (Vol. 15, pp. 241-243). Hillsdale, NJ: The Analytic Press.

Fisher, B. (1984, January). Master teacher Robert Ellis Dunn: Cultivating creative impulse. *Dance Magazine*, pp. 84-87.

Fortin, S. (1998). Somatics: A tool for empowering modern dance teachers. In S. B. Shapiro (Ed.), *Dance, power, and difference: Critical and feminist perspectives on dance education* (pp. 49-71). Champaign, IL: Human Kinetics.

Freud, S. (1908/1957). Creative writers and day-dreaming. In J. Strachey (Ed. and Trans.), *The standard edition of the complete psychological works of Sigmund Freud* (Vol. 9, pp. 143-153). London: Hogarth Press.

Freud, S. (1914/1953). The Moses of Michelangelo. In J. Strachey (Ed. and Trans.), *The standard edition of the complete psychological works of Sigmund Freud* (Vol. 13, pp. 211-236). London: Hogarth Press.

Freud, S. (1914/1957). On narcissism: An introduction. In J. Strachey (Ed. and Trans.), *The standard edition of the complete psychological works of Sigmund Freud* (Vol. 14, pp. 69-102). London: Hogarth Press.

Freud, S. (1930/1961). Civilization and its discontents. In J. Strachey (Ed. and Trans.), *The standard edition of the complete psychological works of Sigmund Freud* (Vol. 21, pp. 59-145). London: Hogarth Press.

Genter, S. (1999). Anne Teresa de Keersmaeker. In M. Bremser (Ed.), *Fifty contemporary choreographers* (pp. 84-88). London: Routledge.

Gilbert, A. G. (1992). *Creative dance for all ages.* Reston, VA: The American Alliance for Health, Physical Education, Recreation and Dance.

Goode, J. (2000, April 14). Interview conducted by Starshine Roshell, *Santa Barbara News-Press*, SCENE, p. 4.

Goode, J. (2000, April 18). Open discussion with the artist. Santa Barbara, CA.

Gorney, J. E. (1998). Twinship, vitality, pleasure. In A. Goldberg (Ed.), *The world of self psychology: Progress in self psychology* (Vol. 14, pp. 85-106). Hillsdale, NJ: The Analytic Press.

Gottschild, B. D. (1998). *Digging the Africanist presence in American performance: Dance and other contexts.* Westport, CT: Praeger.

Green, J. (2001, April). *Somatic knowledge: The body as content and methodology in dance and arts education.* Paper presented at the Annual Conference of the National Dance Education Organization, Minneapolis, MN.

Greskovic, R. (1999). Pilobolus. In M. Bremser (Ed.), *Fifty contemporary choreographers* (pp. 192-196). London: Routledge.

Hagman, G. (1997). Mature selfobject experience. In A. Goldberg (Ed.), *Conversations in self psychology: Progress in self psychology* (Vol. 14, pp. 85-107). Hillsdale, NJ: The Analytic Press.

Hagman, G. (2000a). The creative process. In A. Goldberg (Ed.), *How responsive should we be? Progress in self psychology* (Vol. 16, pp. 277-297). Hillsdale, NJ: The Analytic Press.

Hagman, G. (2000b, Spring). *An intersubjective approach to supervision.* Paper presented at the National Psychological Association for Psychoanalysis, New York, NY.

Hagman, G. (2001, November). *A new aesthetics for psychoanalysis.* Paper presented at the Annual Conference of the Psychology of the Self, San Francisco, CA.

Hagman, G. (in press). The sense of beauty. *International Journal of Psychoanalysis.*

Hagood, T. K. (2000). *A history of dance in American higher education: Dance and the American university.* Lewiston, NY: The Edwin Mellen Press.

Halprin, A. (1955). Intuition and improvisation in dance. *Impulse,* pp. 10-12.

Hanstein, P. (1986). On the nature of art making in dance: An artistic process skills model for the teaching of choreography (Doctoral dissertation, Ohio State University). *Dissertation Abstracts International, 47,* 3640A-3641A.

Harwood, I. N. H. (1998a). Advances in group psychotherapy and self psychology: An intersubjective approach. In I. N. H. Harwood & M. Pines (Eds.), *Self experiences in group: Intersubjective and self psychological pathways to human understanding* (pp. 30-46). London: Jessica Kingsley.

Harwood, I. N. H. (1998b). Examining early childhood multiple cross-cultural extended selfobject and traumatic experiences and creating optimum treatment environments. In I. N. H. Harwood & M. Pines (Eds.), *Self experiences in group: Intersubjective and self psychological pathways to human understanding* (pp. 109-122). London: Jessica Kingsley.

Hawkins, A. (1954/1982). *Modern dance in higher education.* New York: Congress on Research in Dance.

Hawkins, A. (1964). *Creating through dance.* Englewood Cliffs, NJ: Prentice Hall.

Hawkins, A. (1991). *Moving from within: A new method for dance making.* Chicago: A Cappella Books.

H'Doubler, M. (1921). *A manual for dancing.* Madison, WI: Tracy and Kilgour.

H'Doubler, M. (1925). *The dance and its place in education.* New York: Harcourt, Brace and Company.

H'Doubler, M. (1940). *Dance: A creative art experience*. New York: Appleton-Century Crofts.

Hoeft, P., & Keystone, L. (1998). *Soaring into creative spaces: An integrated arts program*. Reno, NV: Lanie Keystone, Foster Educational Systems.

Horst, L. (1937/1972). *Pre-classic dance forms*. New York: Dance Horizons.

Horst, L. (1939, November). Modern forms: Introduction. *Dance Observer*, p. 285.

Horst, L. (1954). Louis Horst considers the question. *Impulse*, pp. 1-6.

Hubbard, K. W. (n.d.). Donald McKayle: Dance is movement that lights the soul. In G. E. Myers (Ed.), *African American genius in modern dance* (pp. 16-18). American Dance Festival.

Humphrey, D. (1959). *The art of making dances*. New York: Grove Press.

Hutera, D. (1999). Bill T. Jones. In M. Bremser (Ed.), *Fifty contemporary choreographers* (pp. 123-128). London: Routledge.

Jackson, G. (1964, April). "Naked in its native beauty;" Some aspects of a startling trend in contemporary dance. *Dance Magazine*, pp. 32-37.

Johnson, D., & Oliver, W. (2001). Introduction. In D. Johnson & W. Oliver (Eds.), *Women making art: Women in the visual, literary, and performing arts since 1960* (pp. 1-22). New York: Peter Lang.

Jones, B. T. (1995). *Last night on earth*. New York: Pantheon Books.

Jowitt, D. (1999). Introduction. In M. Bremser (Ed.), *Fifty contemporary choreographers* (pp. 1-12). London: Routledge.

Kahlich, L. (2001). Gender and dance education. *Journal of Dance Education, 1*(2), 45-47.

Kane, A. (1999). Richard Alston. In M. Bremser (Ed.), *Fifty contemporary choreographers* (pp. 13-18). London: Routledge.

Kendall, E. (1979). *Where she danced: The birth of American art-dance*. Berkeley: University of California Press.

Keystone, L. (1999). *Chance-a-dance: Creating dances in the classroom*. Reno, NV: Lanie Keystone, Foster Educational Systems.

Keystone, L. (2000). *ArtForm: Creating 16,000 integrated arts lessons across the curriculum*. Reno, NV: Lanie Keystone, Foster Educational Systems.

Keystone, L. (2001). *Focus fun for the classroom*. Reno, NV: Lanie Keystone, Foster Educational Systems.

Kligerman, C. (1980). Art and the self of the artist. In A. Goldberg (Ed.), *Advances in self psychology* (pp. 383-396). New York: International Universities Press.

Klosty, J. (Ed.). (1975). *Merce Cunningham*. New York: Dutton.

Kohut, H. (1971). *The analysis of the self: A systematic approach to the psychoanalytic treatment of narcissistic personality disorders.* New York: International Universities Press.

Kohut, H. (1977). *The restoration of the self.* New York: International Universities Press.

Kohut, H. (1959/1978). Introspection, empathy, and psychoanalysis: An examination of the relationship between mode of observation and theory. In P. H. Ornstein (Ed.), *The search for the self: Selected writings of Heinz Kohut: 1950-1978* (Vol. 1-2, pp. 205-232). New York: International Universities Press.

Kohut, H. (1960/1978). Childhood experience and creative imagination—Contribution to panel on the psychology of imagination. In P. H. Ornstein (Ed.), *The search for the self: Selected writings of Heinz Kohut: 1950-1978* (Vol. 1-2, pp. 271-274). New York: International Universities Press.

Kohut, H. (1964/1978). Some problems of a metapsychological formulation of fantasy: Chairman's concluding remarks to the symposium on fantasy. In P. H. Ornstein (Ed.), *The search for the self: Selected writings of Heinz Kohut: 1950-1978* (Vol. 1-2, pp. 379-386). New York: International Universities Press.

Kohut, H. (1966/1978). Forms and transformations of narcissism. In P. H. Ornstein (Ed.), *The search for the self: Selected writings of Heinz Kohut: 1950-1978* (Vol. 1-2, pp. 427-460). New York: International Universities Press.

Kohut, H. (1968/1978). The psychoanalytic treatment of narcissistic personality disorders: Outline of a systematic approach. In P. H. Ornstein (Ed.), *The search for the self: Selected writings of Heinz Kohut: 1950-1978* (Vol. 1-2, pp. 477-509). New York: International Universities Press.

Kohut, H. (1971/1978). Thoughts on narcissism and narcissistic rage. In P. H. Ornstein (Ed.), *The search for the self: Selected writings of Heinz Kohut: 1950-1978* (Vol. 1-2, pp. 615-658). New York: International Universities Press.

Kohut, H. (1972/1978). Discussion of "On the adolescent process as a transformation of the self" by Ernest S. Wolf, John E. Gedo, and David M. Terman. In P. H. Ornstein (Ed.), *The search for the self: Selected writings of Heinz Kohut: 1950-1978* (Vol. 1-2, pp. 659-662). New York: International Universities Press.

Kohut, H. (1973/1978). The future of psychoanalysis. In P. H. Ornstein (Ed.), *The search for the self: Selected writings of Heinz Kohut: 1950-1978* (Vol. 1-2, pp. 663-684). New York: International Universities Press.

Kohut, H. (1975/1978). The self in history. In P. H. Ornstein (Ed.), *The search for the self: Selected writings of Heinz Kohut: 1950-1978* (Vol. 1-2, pp. 771-782). New York: International Universities Press.

Kohut, H. (1976/1978a). Creativeness, charisma, group psychology: Reflections on the self-analysis of Freud. In P. H. Ornstein (Ed.), *The search for the self: Selected writings of Heinz Kohut: 1950-1978* (Vol. 1-2, pp. 793-844). New York: International Universities Press.

Kohut, H. (1976/1978b). Preface to Der falsche Weg zum Selbst, Studien zur Drogenkarriere by Jurgen vom Scheidt. In P. H. Ornstein (Ed.), *The search for the self: Selected writings of Heinz Kohut: 1950-1978* (Vol. 1-2, pp. 845-850). New York: International Universities Press.

Kohut, H. (1980). Summarizing reflections. In A. Goldberg (Ed.), *Advances in self psychology* (pp. 473-554). New York: International Universities Press.

Kohut, H. (1984). *How does analysis cure?* (A. Goldberg & P. E. Stepansky, Eds.). Chicago: University of Chicago Press.

Kohut, H. (1987). *The Kohut seminars on self psychology and psychotherapy with adolescents and young adults* (M. Elson, Ed.). New York: Norton.

Kohut, H. (1981/1991). On empathy. In P. H. Ornstein (Ed.), *The search for the self: Selected writings of Heinz Kohut: 1978-1981* (Vol. 3-4, pp. 525-535). New York: International Universities Press.

Kohut, H., & Wolf, E. S. (1978/1986). The disorders of the self and their treatment: An outline. In A. P. Morrison (Ed.), *Essential papers on narcissism* (pp. 175-196). New York: New York University.

Kreemer, C. (Ed.). (1987). *Further steps: Fifteen choreographers on modern dance.* New York: Harper & Row.

Krugman, R. (1951, June-July). Walter Terry's "Open interviews;" 6. Martha Graham. *Dance Observer,* p. 89.

Laban, R. (1948/1963). *Modern educational dance.* London: Macdonald & Evans.

Laban, R. (1950/1960). *The mastery of movement on the stage.* London: Macdonald & Evans.

Lavender, L. (1996). *Dancers talking dance: Critical evaluation in the choreography class.* Champaign, IL: Human Kinetics.

Lavender, L. (2000, April). *Teaching choreography after the end of art.* Paper presented at the National Dance Educators Organization Conference, Salt Lake City, UT.

Leask, J. (1999). Lloyd Newson. In M. Bremser (Ed.), *Fifty contemporary choreographers* (pp. 173-176). London: Routledge.

Leib, P. (1990). The origins of ambition. In A. Goldberg (Ed.), *The realities of transference: Progress in self psychology* (Vol. 6, pp. 113-127). Hillsdale, NJ: The Analytic Press.

Levin, J. D. (1992). *Theories of the self.* Washington, DC: Taylor & Francis.

Lichtenberg, J. (1988). Infant research and self psychology. In A. Goldberg (Ed.), *Frontiers in self psychology: Progress in self psychology* (Vol. 3, pp. 59-64). Hillsdale, NJ: The Analytic Press.

Lichtenberg, J. (1989). *Psychoanalysis and motivation.* Hillsdale, NJ: The Analytic Press.

Lichtenberg, J., Lachmann, F., & Fosshage, J. L. (1992). *Self and motivational systems: Toward a theory of psychoanalytic technique.* Hillsdale, NJ: The Analytic Press.

Lichtenberg, J., Lachmann, F., & Fosshage, J. L. (1996). *The clinical exchange: Techniques derived from self and motivational systems.* Hillsdale, NJ: The Analytic Press.

Lind, B. (1960, August-September). The creative process. *Dance Observer*, pp. 101-102.

Livet, A. (Ed.). (1978). *Contemporary dance.* New York: Abbeville Press.

Louis, M. (1980). *Inside dance: Essays by Murray Louis.* New York: St. Martin's.

Matheson, K. (1999). Laura Dean. In M. Bremser (Ed.), *Fifty contemporary choreographers* (pp. 88-93). London: Routledge.

McDonagh, D. (1990). *The rise and fall and rise of modern dance.* Chicago: A Cappella Books.

Minton, S.C. (1997). *Choreography: A basic approach using improvisation* (2nd ed.). Champaign, IL: Human Kinetics.

Muslin, H. L. (1991). Hamlet: The self of despair. In A. Goldberg (Ed.), *The evolution of self psychology: Progress in self psychology* (Vol. 7, pp. 201-218). Hillsdale, NJ: The Analytic Press.

Myers, G. E. (Ed.). (n.d.). *African American genius in modern dance.* American Dance Festival.

Noverre, J. G. (1760/1968). *Letters on dancing and ballets* (C. Beaumont, Trans.). New York: Dance Horizon.

Nunn, M. (1982). A method to the madness: A basic system of dance composition. *Dance Teacher Now, 4*(4), 12-14.

O'Connor, T. (2000, July 13). Open discussion with the artist. Santa Barbara, CA.

Oliver, W. (2001). Disappearing act: Yvonne Rainer, Trio A, and the feminist dilemma (1966). In D. Johnson & W. Oliver (Eds.), *Women making art: Women in the visual, literary, and performing arts since 1960* (pp. 23-41). New York: Peter Lang.

Osumare, H. (n.d.). The new moderns: The paradox of eclecticism and singularity. In G. E. Myers (Ed.), *African American genius in modern dance* (pp. 26-29). American Dance Festival.

Perron, W. (2001, March). Twyla Tharp: Still pushing the boundaries. *Dance Magazine*, pp. 44-49, 102-103.

Purcell, T.M. (1994). *Teaching children dance: Becoming a master teacher.* Champaign, IL: Human Kinetics.

Rainer, Y. (1965). Some retrospective notes on a dance for 10 people and 12 mattresses called "Parts of Some Sextets," performed at the Wadsworth Atheneum, Hartford, Connecticut, and Judson Memorial Church, New York, in March 1965. *Tulane Drama Review, 1*(2), 168.

Robertson, A. (1980). Metaphor for life. *Ballet News, 1*(8), 10-15.

Rotenberg, C. (1988). Selfobject theory and the artistic process. In A. Goldberg (Ed.), *Learning from Kohut: Progress in self psychology* (Vol. 4, pp. 193-213). Hillsdale, NJ: The Analytic Press.

Rotenberg, C. (1992). Optimal operative perversity: A contribution to the theory of creativity. In A. Goldberg (Ed.), *New therapeutic visions: Progress in self psychology* (Vol. 8, pp. 167-187). Hillsdale, NJ: The Analytic Press.

Ruitenbeek, H. (Ed.). (1965). *The creative imagination: Psychoanalysis and the genius of inspiration.* Chicago: Quadrangle Books.

Saltonstall, E. (1988). *Kinetic awareness: Discovering your bodymind.* New York: Kinetic Awareness Center.

Sarason, S. (1990). *The challenge of art to psychology.* New Haven, CT: Yale University Press.

Satin, L. (2000/01). The legs of the theorist. *Dance Research Journal, 32*(2), 120-123.

Scheuer, W. (Executive Producer), Kupfer, J. (Producer), Diamond, M. (Producer/Director). (1998). *Paul Taylor: Dancemaker* [Film]. A Four Oaks Production.

Schrader, C.A. (1996). *A sense of dance: Exploring your movement potential.* Champaign, IL: Human Kinetics.

Segal, L. (2001, June 23). Adventures in postmodernism. *Los Angeles Times,* pp. F1, F16.

Shane, M. (1997, November). *Self psychologists consider boundaries: Developmental systems self psychology.* Paper presented at the 20th Annual International Conference on the Psychology of the Self, Chicago, IL.

Shane, M., & Shane, E. (1996). Self psychology in search of the optimal: A consideration of optimal responsiveness; optimal provision; optima gratification; and optimal restraint in the clinical situation. In A. Goldberg (Ed.), *Basic ideas reconsidered: Progress in self psychology* (Vol. 12, pp. 37-54). Hillsdale, NJ: The Analytic Press.

Shapiro, S. B. (Ed.). (1998). *Dance, power, and difference: Critical and feminist perspectives on dance education.* Champaign, IL: Human Kinetics.

Siegel, A. (1996). *Heinz Kohut and the psychology of the self.* London: Routledge.

Siegel, A. (1999). The optimal conversation: A concern about current trends within self psychology. In A. Goldberg (Ed.), *Pluralism in self psychology: Progress in self psychology* (Vol. 15, pp. 51-80). Hillsdale, NJ: The Analytic Press.

Smith, A. (1985, January). Autobiography and the avant-garde. *Dance Magazine*, pp. 50-53.

Smith-Autard, J. M. (1996). *Dance composition* (3rd ed). London: A & C Black.

Sommers, P. (1980/1981, December/January). Talking to Paul Taylor. *Washington Dance View*, p. 1.

Sorell, W. (1963, April). Martha Graham speaks . . . . *Dance Observer*, pp. 53-55.

Stern, D. (1985). *The interpersonal world of the infant: A view from psychoanalysis and developmental psychology.* New York: Basic Books.

Stinson, S. W. (1998). Seeking a feminist pedagogy for children's dance. In S. B. Shapiro (Ed.), *Dance, power, and difference: Critical and feminist perspectives on dance education* (pp. 23-47). Champaign, IL: Human Kinetics.

Stolorow, R. D. (1975/1986). Toward a functional definition of narcissism. In A. P. Morrison (Ed.), *Essential papers on narcissism* (pp. 197-208). New York: New York University.

Stolorow, R. D. (1998). Foreword. In I. N. H. Harwood & M. Pines (Eds.), *Self experiences in group: Intersubjective and self psychological pathways to human understanding.* London: Jessica Kingsley Publishers.

Strozier, C. (1985). Glimpses of a life: Heinz Kohut (1913-1981). In A. Goldberg (Ed.), *Progress in self psychology* (Vol. 1, pp. 3-12). New York: The Guilford Press.

Taub, E. (1982, April). Paul Taylor discusses his works. *Ballet News*, p. 10.

Taylor, P. (1988). *Private domain.* New York: Alfred Knopf.

Teicholz, J.G. (2000). The analyst's empathy, subjectivity, and authenticity: Affect as the common denominator. In A. Goldberg (Ed.), *How responsive should we be? Progress in self psychology* (Vol. 16, pp. 33-53). Hillsdale, NJ: The Analytic Press.

Terman, D. M. (1988). Optimum frustration: Structuralization and the therapeutic process. In A. Goldberg (Ed.), *Learning from Kohut: Progress in self psychology* (Vol. 4, pp. 113-125). Hillsdale, NJ: The Analytic Press.

Thornton, S. (1971). *Laban's theory of movement: A new perspective.* Boston: Plays, Inc.

Trexler, A. (1981). Making and dancing improvisational games. *Contact Quarterly, 6*(3/4), 13-15.

Tuch, R. H. (1995). On the capacity to be creative: A psychoanalytic exploration of writer's block. In A. Goldberg (Ed.), *The impact of new ideas: Progress in self psychology* (Vol. 11, pp. 243-257). Hillsdale, NJ: The Analytic Press.

Turner, M. J. (1971). *Approaches to nonliteral choreography.* Pittsburgh: University of Pittsburgh Press.

Varone, D. (1997, July 22). Open rehearsal and lecture, University of California, Santa Barbara.

Webster's New World Dictionary of the American Language. (1966). Cleveland: The World Publishing Company.

Winnicott, D. W. (1970/1986). Living creatively. In C. Winnicott, R. Shepherd, & M. Davis (Eds.), *Home is where we start from: Essays by a psychoanalyst* (pp. 39-54). New York: Norton.

Winnicott, D. W. (1971/1986). The concept of a healthy individual. In C. Winnicott, R. Shepherd, & M. Davis (Eds.), *Home is where we start from: Essays by a psychoanalyst* (pp. 21-38). New York: Norton.

Winter, R. (1955). Form in relation to art. *Impulse,* pp. 2-4.

Wolf, E. S. (1988). *Treating the self: Elements of clinical self psychology.* New York: Guilford.

Wolf, E. S. (1989). The psychoanalytic self psychologist looks at learning. In K. Field, B. J. Cohler, & G. Wool (Eds.), *Learning and education: Psychoanalytic perspectives* (pp. 377-393). Madison, CT: International Universities Press.

Woodbury, J. (1956, October). Mary Wigman at seventy. *Dance Observer,* pp. 117-118.

Author Index

229

Subject Index

231

Carol Press is a dancer, choreographer, writer, and teacher. She earned her doctorate of education from Columbia University Teachers College in interdisciplinary studies between dance education and clinical psychology. Her master's of arts in dance/choreography is from the University of California, Los Angeles. She is published in the *Journal for the Psychoanalysis of Culture and Society*, *Journal of Dance Education*, *Studies in Psychoanalytic Theory*, *Focus on Dance XII: Dance in Higher Education*, and *Design for Arts in Education*. She is a dance artist-in-residence for the Santa Barbara County Schools in California. She conducts workshops for teachers and college students on creativity and dance education and has worked for the National Dance Education Organization. Most importantly, she loves to dance.